Where Life and Death Hold Hands

WILLIAM ALLISTER

Stoddart

First published in 1989 by
Stoddart Publishing Co. Limited
34 Lesmill Road
Toronto, Canada
M3B 2T6

CANADIAN CATALOGUING IN PUBLICATION DATA

Allister, William, 1919-
Where life and death hold hands

ISBN 0-7737-2268-8

1. Allister, William, 1919-   . 2. World War, 1939-1945 - Prisoners and prisons,
Japanese. 3. World War, 1939 - 1945 - Personal narratives, Canadian.
4. Prisoners of war - Canada - Biography. 5. Prisoners of war - Japan -
Biography. I. Title.

D805.J3A58 1989   940.54'72'520924   C89-093437-1

Printed and bound in the United States of America

COVER ILLUSTRATION: Peter Grau
DESIGN: Brant Cowie/ArtPlus Limited

To those who didn't return

"Build on waste and desolation
Your green towers of affirmation."
E.MERRILL ROOT

Acknowledgments

THANKS TO MY WIFE MONA, whose watchful eye and unerring judgment helped pilot this ship through many rocky shoals and bring it safely to port; to Bob Warren, whose thoughtful insights added value to the work; to Jeanette Leduc, who wrestled with my fractured street Japanese; and to Walter Jenkins, Tony Grimston, Lionel Speller, Jack Rose, Lucien Brunet, Tom Marsh, Denise Bukowski, Sandra Tooze and Donna Barnes, among others.

Prologue

A S OUR TAXI NOSED its way through heavy Tokyo traffic, I stared out in disbelief at the profusion of soaring steel and glass, the multilevel railways, the fashionable, affluent crowds, the jam-packed stores. The last time I'd seen this great city it was a wasteland. Flat. Leveled. Driven across Tokyo to Sumidagawa, our last prison camp, in the spring of 1945, we saw it all: a stricken landscape, charred rubble as far as the eye could see, breathing stillness and death, a phantasmagoric surface of hell in whose presence one could only feel awe. There we became nightly spectators watching this great funeral pyre being cooked and recooked by U.S. B-29 bombers.

And now: these flashy crowds engulfed in the roar of motors, horns, traffic, exhaust — did they remember? Did they know? Hell, no, how could memory live here? It was all gone, a gigantic erasure. This explosive energy, this Present was the only game in town.

My thoughts and emotions churned as we sailed through the streets. Actually, twice as many died here as at Hiroshima. But that was ordinary old-fashioned bombing. Just bombing and killing and dying and dying and killing and bombing. Dull stuff, forgotten. And I? Floating through this great labyrinth of steel and concrete, a thing of no substance, a returning ghost who didn't belong here. Nor did the ghosts of these others, the dead in their thousands, hovering everywhere. I could feel them, hear them, see them among the racing pedestrians.

Yes, the human brain erases. That's as it should be. The mind, as I found in prison camp, is structured to survive — to make the Present all. If it didn't, the world would stop.

Then what in the world was I doing here, returning in 1983 to a country that held so many nightmare associations? Fellow ex-POWs thought me balmy. Dredging up all that? And we had come, my wife and I, not for a few days or weeks but for months. It was not a decision lightly taken. I had my reasons, mad they might be, but strong enough to bring me back across the Pacific.

I had to resolve the love-hate affair I had had going with Japan for decades. It was time. As an artist I have always been fascinated by its wealth of aesthetic marvels. I was romantically enslaved by its films, festivals, costumes, images, traditions, literature, art and history. For years, the Japanese influence had floated through my work like a shadowy presence.

But life in this land had hardly been pleasant. It had, in fact, been downright horrible. Starvation, beatings, illness, insults, psychological wounds. Hostility and anger ran deep in my blood. What greater paradox could there be than this reverent love and unholy revulsion?

But to root out any trauma one must get to the source, dig it up, confront it. And here I was, ready — ready? — to submit to this dangerous exorcism. I must return, not only to Japan but to the scene of the crime, Camp 3D, in Kawasaki. Back to the shipyards of Nippon Kokan where we had been brought as slave labor in 1943.

To their credit (and my surprise), the Japanese didn't try to sweep me under the carpet. Because of guilt, penitential remorse, whatever, I was given the VIP treatment. Nothing hidden, they even made it a media event. The man who gave the order, I later learned, was a survivor of Hiroshima, adding a new dimension to it all.

A special limousine came to collect us at our Tokyo hotel and drove us in state to Yokohama. We rolled into the shipyards toward a welcoming committee of top brass. A sort of triumphal re-entry. Slightly different from my entries on this very spot forty years ago.

And suddenly there it was — God, the same damn entrance, same tracks, unaltered! There it stood, bridging the road, that portal to hell that swallowed us up each day and spat out our remains at sundown. I broke away and made for the entrance, deaf and blind to anything else, dropping down into a sort of catatonic blackout, carried back across a time barrier to this spot, hearing the scratchy company song blaring out the corny notes so deeply embedded in my brain. I started humming the tune — I was back among a long line of dusty scarecrows. My 1983 persona had vanished. I was *san hiaku ni-ju go* — number 325. Our prison numbers were written in Japanese calligraphy on large white patches, front and back, and repeated on a ribbon dangling from the back of our hats. We were marching, four abreast, in our weird work clothes, a pair of grimy, baggy pants and a jacket that had to last the entire war. I felt and saw the morning crowds of workers all around us, streaming through the gates in their threadbare clothes, on foot, on bikes, the grungy reform-school kids jogging by in a cloud of dust, their bugler trotting and tooting alongside. How often we had come trudging over these very tracks toward another exhausting, interminable, gut-hungry day. Sweating in the unrelenting summer sun or shivering through the bleak winter days with all our worldly clothing on our backs and nothing inside to heat us . . . . Stealing over to a riveter's tiny brazier to catch a glimmer of warmth as he heated his bolts . . . . Sneaking into garbage cans, diving for discolored butts, chewing savagely on a much-trodden orange peel . . . .

At last I turned away and stared, dazed, at my wife, standing among the others. What the hell was she doing here? And all these immaculate officials — waiting for *me?* Their guest? The despised *furyo*, lowest of the low? I tried to shake myself free of visions as I faced this firing squad of managers, reporters, interpreters, camera crews, smiling, bowing, eager to please. What were my wishes? What did I want to see? I felt like the pilot in *Shogun*, arriving in Japan a prisoner marked for death (as we were in 1944) and ending up an honored guest in the halls of the mighty.

And this exalted treatment was accorded us not only here but throughout our stay, from the highest to the lowest, in homes, shops or the streets of Kyoto, where we lived during our visit. It began to act on my spirit as a healing balm against the demons that plagued me. Weeks passed. As we lingered in the magical gardens and ancient temples, allowing the fascination of this land, its people, its haunting beauty to weave its hypnotic spell, there came a gradual easing of tensions, a growing serenity, a new plane of peace.

One day we were in an enchanting temple watching the ceremony of a Heian princess being dressed in twelve-layer robes. And there it came — a flash of knowing, a lifting, a gleam of "enlightenment." I saw my bitterness, my hostility, my wounds, like her body, being gently covered in layer upon layer of exquisitely colored and embroidered robes, transforming me into a new being. I felt a new, broader vision take over.

But reaching this point took time, a slow, painful, gradual process. The days were full. The nights were heavy with memory and confusion. Many were the times I lay awake traveling back over the years, reliving nightmare moments. This nation of artists (everything they touched seemed artistic) — were they the enemy I had known? They couldn't be. These temples and priests that breathed infinite peace and contemplation: how could they be reconciled to war? That gentle shopkeeper, oozing kindness from every pore — was he a fake? Could he ever be transformed into a shrieking guard in the Bataan death march? Was there a special appetite here for horror? .

Our visit was dredging it all up again. I lay on my *tatami* floor mat reviewing my strange life and the bizarre series of events that had brought me to this land. Before Japan, there were the long prison months in Hong Kong. Before that, the battle, those chaotic eighteen days of concentrated lunacy when the Angel of Darkness came dancing around me, close to the brink, poking at me playfully. And before that, Canadians rampaging over peace-time Hong Kong, those hysterical three weeks of wild drinking, whoring, fighting and laughing.

And where did it all begin? In a godawful mud-hole in 1941 . . . .

Chapter One

I SUPPOSE MY FATE WAS sealed that memorable night when my buddy Hank Greenberg appeared at my bunk, eyes blinking like a signal lamp, mouth grinning, twitching, fear and delight and suppressed excitement chasing over his face.

"How'd you like to be on embarkation leave in twenty-four hours?"

"Very funny," I said coolly, as my heart did a high jump.

To grasp the full impact of such a suggestion, one had to know life at Debert, a camp in the middle of nowhere, a thousand miles from home, a place where hundreds of identical gray huts, humped and soggy under interminable rain, sat mired to their haunches in mud. Not a tree in sight, just a great sea of grayness and sameness rolling on and on into more of itself. One began to doubt the existence of an outer world. Boredom must have been invented here. If this soporific miasma of gloom was what war was about, I wanted no part of it. But there was no way out. These vast mud fields were a sort of glue that held everyone stuck down: gray, amorphous creatures we were — mud-blobs, hopelessly, drearily stuck.

Nothing to do but train by day and drink by night. We in 4th Division Signals, were doomed to spend at least a year here, possibly two, with no chance of an overseas draft till fully trained. And that, to a twenty-one-year-old fire-eater, was an eternity. We were training to be first-class signals operators. As an operator I was a disaster. Even third class was pretty remote for me since you had to send fifteen words per minute in Morse code. First class did twenty-five to forty. My top speed was a lightning eight.

Every night Hank and I sloshed two miles through the blackout to the nearest tavern, where we killed the dull hours guzzling beer. We talked, comparing our different backgrounds, his on the prairie, mine in show biz. I was drawn to his purity — in taste and spirit, in his transparent response to a happy life before his early death. He played hockey on his small hometown team, and baseball, and the violin — all described with the same contagious zest. He reminded me of a tree, rooted deep in prairie soil, solid on his flat feet, never tilting with the changing winds. With my mercurial moods, I needed that badly.

Hank was stocky, with a soft square face, full lips parted to ease his sinusy breathing, wide brown eyes under long lashes that blinked continuously at the world in unflagging wonder. A good audience, he ate up my stories of big-city life in New York. We drank till we were bleary-eyed and, thankfully, couldn't remember who or where we were. Then we would stagger back to camp through the darkness, yodeling the songs of Deanna Durbin, whom we both planned to marry. We would grope through the mud and drizzle, trying to find our hut in the blackout — impossible for me. I always clung to this prairie gopher with the instinct of a homing pigeon who, drunk or no, never failed. I admired and never understood this talent.

And now, suddenly, embarkation leave? Good God — how? when? where? It would need a miracle!

Hank began to babble incoherently and I caught phrases that set me afire: *secret mission . . . all hush-hush . . . overseas . . . special unit . . . destination unknown . . . volunteers . . . Category A.* It all sounded too wonderful to be true — this was Errol Flynn stuff. Of course I knew that war was a terrible, murderous exercise, a canker on the face of history and all that, but that was an abstraction somehow that did and didn't include me. There was that other side, the unspoken side, the dream compote never mentioned: of glory and crazy freedoms, of breathless escapades à la Gunga Din, laughing in the face of death . . . with all the horrible stuff landing on the other guy — just happy endings for you. You were the Doug Fairbanks, Jr., passing through the inferno unscathed, handsome, romantic, devil-may-care . . . taking a Nazi machine-gun nest single-handed . . . carrying a buddy through a hail of bullets . . . meeting *her* while on leave, or in a hospital with your white head bandage (angled jauntily over one eye) against a fetching tan, leaning on her shoulder as she helped your Hemingway limp . . . . This ersatz Hollywood nurturing was the shadowy stuff locked away in a golden chamber of the psyche marked "Strictly Personal" — stuff you didn't even examine too closely yourself. But here it was — *happening* — a secret mission!

I'm not sure which idea fired me up more, the secret mission or leaving Debert. Whichever, I was ready to crawl a mile over broken glass for a chance.

And so it began. Off into a darkened hut for swift medical tests by candlelight. Low voices, deliciously hush-hush, mounting excitement, then — *I failed the eye test.* Sh-sh-i-i-it! A once-in-a-lifetime chance slipping through my fingers! What to do?

Desperation bred inspiration. I remembered McCletchie, my old history teacher at Baron Byng High School in Montreal, reading to us from his World War I diary — how he couldn't get overseas because of bad eyes and memorized the eye chart and conned his way over. Yeah, that was *it!* And it worked: Satan shining a golden light. Brilliant! Amazing the lengths a man will go to in doing himself in. Then *clang* went the door behind me, and *I was in* . . . . The rest was a breeze. One blithe hop, skip and jump and I was into the fiery furnace.

Incredibly, I was rolling home by train within a day. It was on this trip that I met Blacky Verreault, a linesman in the Signal Corps. This was the man who was to be my buddy in the long years of prison camp. I think we were instantly drawn to each other as extreme opposites often are. A man of powerful build and dark complexion, he sat puffing at a pipe full of his beloved Alouette tobacco. While I was always a voluble clown, he was sparse of speech, though his humor did have richness and charm. I could sense a powerful presence and a hint of the classic swashbuckling heroism he was to reveal in the coming battle.

But where were we going? No one knew. Nor did we know anything of the real picture, the real insanity raging around us. The mad scramble was to grab anyone, *fast* — men greener than ourselves, men who hadn't fired a rifle. Better not to know that the whole slapdash foul-up was being tossed together in two weeks. That Tojo, the military fire-eater, had just taken power in Japan and we being sent to Hong Kong to throw the fear of God into him . . . that Churchill had said there wasn't a hope in hell of holding Hong Kong in a fight . . . that three divisions of seasoned Japanese troops were poised thirty miles from Hong Kong . . . that our two battalions were so badly prepared they were labeled "not recommended for operations" . . . that Army Intelligence (contradiction in terms) knew it all and sent us anyway . . . that the whole schemozzle, called "an act of stupidity and folly," was being likened to the Charge of the Light Brigade.

The reliable word came through at last: China. China? But . . . who the hell wanted that? Certainly not me. After all, I'd signed up to "fight fascism." Hitler was rampaging over Europe, bent on gobbling up the world, and must be stopped. Now *that* was a worthy cause, not this. I was laying my life on the line, after all. And guarding some faraway corner of the Empire was not what this war was about. "The hell with this," I told Hank. I was getting off.

He was shattered. "Jeez! We signed up together — that was the whole idea! What kind of a pal are you?"

The classic conflict: principle versus loyalty. "Well . . . " I sighed uncertainly. "Okay. Stop moaning. I'll go to China."

Famous last words. Spelling out the rest of my life.

And then there was that stopover at Winnipeg, with Hank's mother and a grinning kid brother waiting. And the way, somehow, she *knew*. We didn't but she did. Hell, we were off on a grand adventure, couldn't she see? She was weeping heavily, ominously, too much. Ah, war mothers. Always the biggest casualties. (I'd lied to mine, saying I was off to B.C.)

I offered Hank's mother comfort, embracing her, explaining, as she wept and nodded, that I'd take good care of him, keep him out of trouble. Trust me. Yes . . . .

We rolled across the prairies, past the Rockies, the soaring peaks, the bottomless gorges and the whole thing: the shattering changes, the newness, the idea of *China*, was just too much for Hank. At intervals his mad falsetto giggle exploded in the air: *"Hee-ee-ee-eeee! China!"* An eruption, bubbling up out of his depths. Our collective voice . . . .

Our ship was the S.S. *Awatea*. And we were off across the Pacific, with everything beginning to unravel. Our vehicles were late and left behind, our secrecy exploded by German radio announcing departure, destination, numbers. Marvelous. German subs in the Pacific and one slow, lonely little gunboat, the *Prince Robert*, to guard us. Better and better. We found ourselves crammed into the bowels of the boat, several flights below deck with single ladders as sole access to the hold above. And two-thirds of the boat was graciously cordoned off "For Officers Only" to keep out the low life. Inedible food. Flaring resentments. A mutiny quelled. We slept in hammocks over our mess tables — two pairs of sweaty feet on either side of my face. I lived on bread and jam.

We zigzagged across the Pacific to avoid subs. Farther south the heat grew unbearable and we lined up to collect a glass of tepid beer poured into a mess tin. Showers, with useless salt water, were bypassed, with body stinks rising a few decibels each day.

Brigade Headquarters, made up of assorted units — Signals, Postal, Ordinance, MPs, etc. — was a mixed bag from all parts of the country. I soon adopted Wally Normand and Bob Demant, two madcap dispatch riders from Montreal, whose clowning antics dovetailed nicely with my own. We entertained one another. Wally, twenty-one, short, stocky, abrasive, an amateur drummer, had rhythm to his fingertips. He would regale us with rapturous musical talk of swing bands and musicians — Krupa, Berrigan, Shaw, Goodman, James — bursting into song at the least provocation. Demant was a broad-shouldered, full-chested youngster of the same age, whose dainty Ronald Coleman mustache and rosy upturned nose gave him a more mature look. His gentle, easygoing manner made a good counterpoint to Wally's cocker spaniel personality. When he wasn't seasick, he was a born raconteur, taken to delightful flights of comic fantasy. Theirs was the most dangerous of jobs, riding dispatches on motorbikes between units, and it suited their temperament. Demant's death was to become, for me, a tragic symbol; he was youth in all its joyous life force, destroyed by cynical stupidity. Thanks to a vivid imagination, he nursed secret fears of capture and torture, which he masked in comic invention. Again and again he would paint pictures of himself, speeding along on his motorbike: "Out from behind some bushes jump a buncha serious-looking li'l men. Me, I jam my dispatch into my mouth — chomp, chomp, hurry, hurry, swallow — 'Hell-o, little men! Does it look like rain?' "

This fantasy was repeated with variations accompanied by contagious giggles to obscure the ogres that haunted him. "I don't mind getting killed," he admitted in a sober moment, "but I couldn't take torture. That bugs me. And sure as shit, that's how it'll be with me." I shared his misgivings on torture, unaware that this too was in the cards for me.

To fill the days, I taught them some of the comic routines from my happy-go-lucky days playing the Borscht Belt, a string of summer resorts in the Catskill Mountains where young comics learned their trade at the expense of long-suffering patrons. It was here that Danny Kaye, whom I resembled, learned to dance and prance like Harry Ritz, grand master of them all, a man who could walk thirty ways. I made his schtick part of the daily scene aboard the *Awatea*.

The crossing brought my introduction to Captain Matthews, our signals officer, who was to play a curious and important role in my life. He had us on deck every day doing PT to keep in shape. A tall, pudgy man, his face seemed to spell out the word *sag*, from the pouches under his eyes to his drooping jowls. He was partial to boys, it seemed, and when he lined us up for inspection, he zeroed in on my slightly effeminate baby face. At that age, twenty-two, I looked sixteen, my face having always been my misfortune. So when our good captain stroked my cheek and told me I needed a lesson in shaving and had better come to his cabin, I groaned. Here we go again. After parade, I followed him down to his stateroom, where I saw how the other half lived. The contrast was obscene. I thought of hammocks crammed together over our eating tables, the stench of vomit, feet, heavy sweat, the airless heat and foul food, as he proceeded to lather me up and get his jollies — *patta, patta, stroke, stroke* — but going no further. Harmless . . . and pathetic. I mean, I had no cavil with any offbeat sexual impulse so long as it passed me by. When he finished the shave I thanked him for his services, promised to keep in touch since I might be needing a haircut soon and left.

And this, I thought, is what I'm going overseas with. My bloody luck.

Part of our Sigs duty was our shift on the bridge, two men at a time. At night, on a blacked-out ship, it was a stirring and powerful experience. After the stifling heat of the hold, it was a blessed relief to pick our way over the crowded bodies sleeping on deck and climb up to the isolation of the bridge. Still half asleep we would catch the warm tropical breeze on our sweating brows and listen to the gentle susurrus of the ship's prow dipping and skimming through the quiet luminous waters. It had a soft dreamlike sense of unreality. Occasional phosphorescent fish would come looping out of the water. Sea and sky were shrouded in darkness. Stars followed silently, watchfully. This was Conrad's holy mystery and magic, and it set my imagination adrift. The entire galaxy seemed to form a vast amphitheater overhead, providing a celestial audience gathered to pass judgment on this tiny upstart toy of a boat charging ahead so defiantly on its brazen mission. To what destiny were the fates leading us, so silently, so inevitably? What were we to see and feel? What did the darkness promise: adventure? love? death? danger? The stars listened to me filling the skies with questions and smiled down enigmatically. Mercifully?

Our job was to exchange signals with the *Prince Robert* by lamp. The lamp could send at only four to six words per minute — my speed. But it was frightening to find that the *Prince Robert*, our mighty protector, couldn't even keep up with us and often fell twelve miles behind. How in God's name could it ever prevent a sub picking us off? The sleeping troops knew nothing of this.

Ah . . . and then Hawaii. The romantic associations! The teenage fantasies come alive! Bing Crosby crooning "Sweet Leilani, heavenly flower" . . . and "the moon of Manakoora fills the night with magic Polynesian charm" — how the heart soared! It was a time when our richest emotional yearnings — lust for adventure, love unexpressed, fear of the unknown — found their only expression in Hollywood corn. True, this was no Jean Cristophe evoking musical greats. But the intensity of feeling, if incoherent, was equally profound. Dorothy Lamour, icon of love, shimmered in the air. And there they were, the dancers, their twisting pelvises aiming at us, their undulating hula hips waving hypnotically as the troops roared, hooted, whistled, ranted and tossed gifts from the ship's deck. No touching, of course. We were Ulysses imprisoned by the ship's rail, maddened by the song of the Sirens . . . .

We took on supplies, then set sail in the sunset. And what a magical sunset — all there in full regalia! Crimson purpling clouds stretching like charging steeds across the vast horizon, arrested in mid-flight over the enchanted mauve-tinted islands! So many pop songs found new substance, dazing our minds, flooding our hearts.

We sang of love, of Treasure Island, of silvery shores, convinced that all the Hollywood tinsel had turned to gold.

The days grew hotter. We guzzled warm beer, sweated and cursed as conversation faded and spirits dulled. But the wonders were still before us — and the horrors. At last, after three long weeks, this interminable voyage, the sailing and sweating and waiting, the gambling and drinking and hoping and dreaming, did draw to a close.

The island of Hong Kong came into view. It was the beginning.

Chapter Two

WE ENTERED HONG KONG HARBOR on a bright tropical morning, November 1941. The air was throbbing with the explosive intensity of the excitement. The wonderful rib-sailed junks — sampans — right out of *National Geographic*! Kowloon! . . . exotic curling rooftops! . . . my first Asian city . . . .

"At-ten-HUP!" Two regiments lined the decks for roll call with uniforms scrubbed, buttons shined, boots gleaming, rifles oiled. Sergeants barked, officers buzzed, the sun was blinding.

"S-SNA-AT-HUP!" The at-ease call signaled the end of roll call.

We crowded the rails to gape down at an amazing frenetic world of packed sampans squirming below, a thrashing snake pit gone berserk — twisting, poling, struggling to reach the foreign giant — to catch the rich spoils sailing down from our garbage cans.

"Jeez!" Hank gasped. "Look! They wanna *eat* it!" A mash of rotten meat and grease and vomit and filth.

"Must be nuts!"

"Buncha goddam vultures!"

And the *stink* — the noxious blast of living rot rising to His Majesty's decks . . . .

We slithered down the gangplank, shouldering heavy packs, bags, rifles. A giant bearded Sikh stood at the bottom, rising like a towering apparition, all gleaming brass and crimson, a soaring turban to crown his supernal majesty — beautiful!

"A cop! Wow!"

Serene. Remote as a star. Perfect! Guarding the gateway to the fabulous Orient.

"Pile your kits here! Fall in!"

"No carrying! Heaven!" We were in a welter of jostling bodies, Royal Rifles of Canada, Winnipeg Grenadiers, red-tabbed high brass. Harassed sergeants snarled, ordered, cursed. I caught a glimpse of sun-browned British units lined up for parade and a

scattering of officials in movie-like white suits and safari hats —
the real thing — Hank's transparent face was a mirror of the
collective delight.

We marched away from the harbor with the band blaring a
bright marching tune. The stink of the harbor was supplanted by a
new stench as we turned down Nathan Road. It was suffocating,
alien, sickly. The reek of it seemed to penetrate my fresh denim and
clog my pores. But even that was forgotten as we marched into the
very thick of this teeming city. Vivid colors, bizarre sounds,
startling images attacked the senses on every side.

"Hey! See *that?*"

Grotesque beggars on street corners, legs, arms eaten away . . .
ragged women, children covered in filth . . . festering sores opened
like raw wounds.

Heads whirled, mouths agape. *"Sacré Vierge!"* Blacky gasped.
"Look!" A woman with bulging pregnant guts straining under the
load of a pole on her shoulder, heavy wood at each end and led by
a husband who carried nothing but authority. Look! Rickshaws,
right out of Hollywood! Rickshaw coolies running, sweating,
pulling a white man. There, a tiny tot, dwarfed, emaciated,
carrying a tinier tot on her back. Shrieking, wailing music, hawkers
crying . . . meat in shop fronts black with flies. Flies, flies, flies
everywhere like a plague swarming over torn stumps of human
flesh, over faces, over walls, flies that seemed to rule and cover
heaven and earth!

On we marched through this roiling caldron. I stared into this
face and that, for a light, a glimmer of welcome. I saw only human
masks carved in grimaces of hunger and suffering. They stared at
the powerful rifles, the shiny new boots, the healthy muscles under
the smart new uniforms, and turned silently away.

A little boy darted through our ranks to cross the street and a
British MP's boot sent him sprawling.

"That's the only language the yellow bastards understand!"

Chest out — chin in — clump, clump, clump!

> *With a tow-row-row-row-row!*
> *For the British Grenadiers!*

On we marched, through a mad, revolving fantasy, gawking,
gasping, pointing. Old mandarins in robes . . . Hindus in loincloths

. . . . Hey! A movie section! Harold Lloyd? Rin Tin Tin? It's the bloody Dark Ages! Ritz Brothers — *in Chinese?* White men in sun helmets riding rickshaws like Gable in *China Seas.*

"Dr. Livingstone, I presume!" Demant hooted.

"Shut up 'n keep in step! C'rrec' cher slopes! Laift! Laift!"

I floated through it all on a magic carpet, flying back through time, spinning through the markets of fabled Samarkand, swimming through a downpour of signs and colors, drunk with sights and sounds. I was Aladdin, I was Marco Polo, I was a swashbuckling adventurer awash in euphoria, I was powerful, invincible, bursting with limitless desires, all of them possible, as we sailed blithely on and on . . . *clump, clump, clump* . . . .

Marching . . . . We were as strange to this place as it was to us. A new, alien wind. Salted in the sprays of Newfoundland coasts, blown across great plains and mountains, from forest, poolroom, wheat field, jail, from millionaire estate and city slum. On we came, pure, untouched, blissfully unaware that in a few short weeks we'd be crawling down this same Nathan Road, what was left of us, noses down, tails dragging, backs bent, wounded, weak, shoved and kicked along like beaten dogs . . . .

Sham Shui Po Barracks, white and shimmering in the heat. A Kiplingesque film set with its broad avenues stretching out toward the distant mountains. Brigade HQ was privileged to be quartered in the Jubilee Building at the harbor's edge, with rooms and balconies overlooking large parade grounds. Where the good life began. Where we tasted the fruits of Empire. Where servants, at the lordly salary of twenty-eight cents a week, did your laundry, shaved you as you slept and brought you tea in bed. Where guilt and luxury became enmeshed in a giddy sense of disbelief.

Exploring the grounds, we stopped to buy photos of Hong Kong — sampans, junks, beggars. They'd eat this up at home . . . . We never paused to wonder how coolies could rate such expensive cameras. But they could, being Japanese Intelligence officers, taking random shots under our noses — manpower, equipment, locations, setting us up for the kill.

We wandered over to the fence at the city's edge where waves of the city's human flotsam surged against the barbed wire — the sick, the crippled, the dying, the shrunken children, their pleas rising shrilly as we approached.

"Hello *cumsha* one cent!" A chant, a mass chant we would grow to know: the plea for alms, *cumsha*. Even Demant looked sober. Hank tossed some coins over the fence and the group exploded in a shrieking whirlpool as barbed wire ripped into flesh and pus sores. We couldn't dream how soon we'd be reversing roles at this same fence when a passing vendor would toss a biscuit over the fence and watch us dive for it, crazed with hunger, fighting each other, clawing . . . the same frenzied scramble . . . the same horror.

Passes at last! Two ration-weary, sex-starved regiments were poised to come roaring over the colony like wild flood waters. An estimated ninety-thousand prostitutes waiting.

Off down to the gate we scurried, bubbling in anticipation. Wally truckin' on down as he walked, singing: "I can't get started with you . . . . " Hank sang: "I love to whistle . . . . " Demant chirped: "Shit, shave, shine, shower, shampoo! Looka me ladies, I'm beeoodeeful and ready for love — bring on your ninety thousand!"

The restaurants were filling up, tills clanging. We sank our predatory teeth into thick, juicy steaks in fierce ecstasy, in disbelief. The Canucks were doin' the town! MPs braced themselves for a heavy night, prostitutes were out in force, beer came pouring down thirsty gullets and volleys of uninhibited bellowing, hooting, yelling, echoed over the roofs of the colony. We moved over to the dance hall (Gonorrhea Racetrack) for dancing, drinking, clowning, guffawing. Where to next? Red-light Wanchai, maybe, offering up VD and pussy galore to the brave, the drunk and the stupid . . . .

Staggering through the dark streets, Demant's weak bowels demanded sudden action. We hunted wildly for a toilet and found nothing. We dashed into what looked like a hotel, rushed down a long corridor where we saw a light. We burst into a room filled with triple bunks full of reclining opium smokers stoned out of their skulls.

"Where's the men's room! Men's room!" Demant moaned desperately.

They gazed at him sleepily. We dragged him away. At last we found a toilet — a hole in the floor of a reeking, dingy, lightless cell. Hank drunkenly insisted on inspecting it first, holding back Demant, who was about to load his pants.

"Will you get outta my way?!!" Demant yelled.

"It's not clean enough," Hank pronounced sententiously.

"Get him away or I'll kill 'im!"

We wrestled Hank aside and Demant went charging in. As he squatted in this dark hellhole, Hank stood over him discoursing on the hazards of faulty sanitation.

Yes, three glorious weeks of wild luxury, shopping, dining, drinking, spending, buying embroidered kimonos, carved tusks, silk pajamas. Hank bought a violin in Thieves' Row . . . singing, dancing, cavorting, drilling with murderous hangovers. We explored the terrain on maneuvers (casually). Twenty-five square miles of confusing mountains, hills and valleys. Three short weeks, with war so far away and life a continual party. Defense? Reinforcements? Five hoary RAF planes in all. Well . . . the higher-ups knew what they were doing. Yes, they knew: that Hong Kong could be swallowed up in a gulp. We were expendable. Bit of a farce, what? Too bad it would all go down the drain. And all those Canadians with it, but — there it was, and pass the crumpets.

Chapter Three

EARLY MORNING, DECEMBER 8. Jenkins, a husky young linesman, was shaving peacefully and frowning at a strange noise. He stepped outside to gaze at the sky and returned with a curious, dazed expression and a tone of mild surprise: "They're . . . droppin' bombs, fellas." This roused snorts and snickers of derision.

"But fellas, they're really —"

Bra-a-am! Baroooom! Windows were blown in, walls cracked, bodies dived under beds — suddenly, unbelievably: *war.*

Man, the most violent, bloodthirsty species on earth, was off again on his favorite voyage of self-immolation. Having learned nothing in a million years . . . . Death, flames, bombs were raining from the heavens . . . . The Rage of God. Earth rocked with the echoes. Sneak attack on Pearl Harbor! Most of U.S. fleet destroyed! Day of Infamy! Salvos of words, fine and fierce and outraged, blasting the airwaves, from the U.S., Britain, Canada . . . .

"Yes . . . fine, fine, but . . . what about *us*?"

We were green, unprepared, happily unaware of how bad it really was. Outgunned, vastly outnumbered, and not a hope in hell of any help. We were caught in an impossible, suicidal, front-line position. The madness was beginning . . . . Some had gotten their first training on the ship. Some were as young as sixteen. Blacky taught Jenkins how to load his rifle as they repaired lines, crawling close enough to enemy positions to hear their voices. Raw recruits threw grenades at the enemy without pulling the pins. An irate Limey sergeant roared, "Whatcha tryin, t' do — 'it 'em on the 'ead wiv it?!"

A war on? How could there be, with me lying feverish in a malaria ward of Bowen Road Hospital? Sunny rooms, clean sheets, friendly British nurses . . . calm, peaceful, marred only by the air-raid siren, that haunting wail of a witches' chorus unleashing curses on the world. Beds filled up around me with wounded . . .

blood, bandages, pain — *the real thing*. Jesus, I *was* in a war! Not one I wanted or expected — man plans, God laughs. What the hell had Hitler to do with Royal Scots and Indians fighting Japanese for a British colony? Crazy. And I might be *fighting* soon — hell, I couldn't fight my way out of a paper bag! But hadn't I dreamed of wild adventure — exotic settings in a foreign land, Gunga Din and all that — and this was it, wasn't it? Then why the sinking sensation, the sense of veins draining away? I'd never felt *that* reading Henty. I thought of the old joke about the dumb recruit in the front lines with shells exploding, saying: "Y'know, a guy could get killed here." Fun-nee. And the guy could be *me*. No . . . it couldn't. Not me. I would walk between the bullets — they were for the next guy. A belief highly unoriginal, yes, but universal.

My bed was needed — too many serious cases now, and I was turfed out the next day with a slight fever. I made my way down to the ferry and over to the mainland. I found our unit at the end of Waterloo Road, prophetic name.

Blacky was patrolling with rifle at the ready, swaggering, clearly enjoying himself. We were billeted in tents, with Matthews strung out and very hyper even before trouble began, heightening the general tension. I was still struggling to believe this was really happening, carried along by a floating sensation as though part of my mind still lingered in an unpleasant dream. The dream would end, of course, as they always do, and I'd find myself back in my Montreal bed.

First, one attack after another on our Gin Drinker's Line — our Maginot — built to hold back the hordes, now cracking, crumbling. Our dispatch riders sped back and forth, returning white-lipped with images: "Thousands of 'em! Pouring in! Crazy suicidal bastards — racing into the wall of Brens and Lewises, the barrels going steady, getting too hot to handle. They drop and drop and die and pile up in a hill of dead and keep coming — climbing over the dead, screaming their murderous *Banzai-ai!!*" The situation was soon hopeless, and after four days we were ordered to retreat to the island of Hong Kong.

We loaded our heavy No. 11 radio sets on two trucks with Matthews shouting commands, his voice edged in hysteria — a man meant for a Boy Scout camp, not this. Me too. Trucks dashed by, brakes screeching. Wounded men limped down from the hills, dazed, disoriented. A British officer threw our Chinese driver out of our second truck and drove off yelling, "Need it for wounded!" Matthews fired his revolver in a rage, shrieking, "That's my truck!" Everything was falling apart as Sergeant Sharpe brushed him aside, shouting, "Climb on the equipment! — *on the double* — they're coming!"

We leaped up, elbowing Matthews aside. The scalp-tingling siren went off. "Get cracking!" Sharpe yelled at the driver "Go!"

Matthews panicked, shrieking, "Don't you dare leave me!" Sharpe pulled him up beside us.

Someone yelled, "Aircraft overhead!"

"Lie flat!" Sharpe ordered.

"We'll bust our ribs!"

"Better than getting your head blown off!" he replied. "We're going through town and it's lousy with fifth column!"

Sirens wailed, the truck jolted, bouncing, its horn blasting. Blacky cursed, bombs crashed. Black smoke. People ran in blind terror in opposite directions, silently, mindlessly, in mute intensity, like herds of deer, instincts gone awry, dashing nowhere, pursued by the demonic siren.

"Look!" Hank pointed to three men reclining on a bench, relaxed, serene, grotesque, no wounds visible. My first dead men. "Concussion," Demant pronounced. Weirdly prophetic of his own death.

At last the Kowloon docks came into sight, Hong Kong and safety across the waters. We were swallowed up in a jostling, shouting, churning sea of bodies. Terror and madness trembled in the air. Sharpe took the truck back for the others while Blacky and Hank went off, shoving a way through the crowds with a tommy gun to find a boat. Orders: "Everything not portable must be destroyed." Flames rose on all sides. Truck tires were slit, windows shattered, engines smashed, the docks rocked with the explosions — sappers blowing up dock facilities. Mass destruction on every side. My head was spinning — only three weeks ago we'd landed right here in triumph, now we were trampling one another in our haste to leave.

A coolie running with a sack of rice was shot down by a policeman. "Looters," said a Cockney voice nearby. We craned our necks. "Looting what?"

They were rifling the *godowns* — a row of warehouses beside us, with police at the doors. Demant was astonished. "Why don't they let 'em in? The Japs'll get it anyway!"

"And start a bleedin' riot?"

Matthews was emitting little moans and meows of distress. Somehow his terror lessened mine. A drunken white policeman was firing bursts from his tommy gun into the air for the hell of it, then he opened a *godown* door, shouting: "Go to it, mates!" Demant shouted his approval. Then the drunk began shooting down each coolie as he emerged and roaring in delight. "Breakin' the law, mates!" he hooted as we gaped in horror. More than anarchy — pure lunacy!

Blacky and Hank were back, breathless. "Let's go! Two men to a set — smash de rest!" We staggered, straining through the thickening crush . . . mothers dragging children, shouting for lost ones . . . strange uniforms, frantic schoolgirls, dialects, turbans, bedlam — then onto the boat at last where we sprawled on the deck exhausted . . . "strategic withdrawal."

Under way at last — in time to meet a fresh wave of bombers, diving at us like shrieking vultures. Boats were blown out of the water. The harbor rocked with fresh explosions — theirs and ours. Fear was expanding within me like a luxurious tropical plant. I knew I was a goner if we were hit since I couldn't swim. My scorn for Matthews's abject terror was slipping away — only a matter of degree, after all.

The planes left and I stood at the rail looking back at the feverish crowds along the shore, listening to their clamant chorus. They were trapped, waiting to meet their fate. Would it be another Nanking? Sounds and shouts grew fainter and became one bitter, fading dirge . . . haunting, clinging . . . like those first clutching, beseeching fingers . . . hello *cumsha* one cent. Why hast Thou forsaken us?

Safe at last on the Hong Kong side, we arrived at Victoria Barracks, shrewdly located beside an ammunition dump, a prize target. We experienced our first direct shelling — bombs were powder puffs by comparison. The skull-shattering blasts seemed to explode inside and outside our bodies simultaneously. My helmet was blown off my head — I looked up to see Blacky waving it victoriously on the point of his rifle. We were sprawled in a corridor that was filling with clouds of blinding dust. Some idiot yelled, "Gas!" We clawed in panic for our masks and lay like stricken, groveling monsters.

After a hasty meal of bully beef, hardtack and tea, we were off in a packed open truck in the dark, jouncing through the hills, headlights blacked out. Singing. Letting it all out — the pent-up hysteria, the joy at being alive. The old words sounded so new: *"Fuck 'em all, fuck 'em all! The long and the short and the tall!"* Song after song as we roared defiance at the stars — charging boldly ahead into the menacing future — let it all out!

We were led into a dimly lit house to sleep on the floor of some room, minds and bodies abuzz, swapping news, stories: Sharpe got across on a sampan after dark . . . Beaton on his motorbike was waylaid by fifth columnists and barely escaped. My mind was a surreal swamp of smashed trucks, sitting corpses, running coolies shot down, enveloping crowds — was all this really happening? What were they hearing, thinking, feeling at home? They must be glued to the radio. It was all so impossible. Wasn't the war supposed to be in Europe? Where troops, training for years, were itching for combat — with an evenly matched enemy. Here we were ready for bugger-all, in a place as familiar as Mars. The future? A dark forbidding mass, suffocating hope. Too much — *too much* for one puny brain.

Darkness and silent thoughts. I heard Jenkins's querulous voice: "Dya think we'll ever get outta here alive?" A long pause. Penny's quiet voice, at last, drifting through the dark. "Can't see how."

And so to sleep.

Chapter Four

I AWOKE INTO A NEW ASTONISHING dream. I was lying on a soft carpet under a gleaming baby grand piano. Morning sunlight sparkled through huge windows. Tall portraits adorned the walls, and a stately chandelier hung above me from the beamed ceiling. Soldiers slept on their kits between fine leather furniture. It was a bloody palace! Offered to us by the owner. Bizarre.

Hank and I wandered about, finding Jenkins shaving. "Six showers, if you please!"

Demant was in the library, languidly draped in a large leather chair, puffing a cigar. "I'm stayin'. Need a nice quiet place to retire. Have a ceegah."

"Scrounging bastard."

"It's okay, the owner's a personal frienda mine. Met in Bombay, y'know. Oh, oh, oh, it's a luvully war." A jive tune was coming from a shortwave set beside him. He was back to normal. Only yesterday he had been battered and jolted to the core. I envied that. My own spirit was weighted, jittery, as I feigned normality.

Outside, a superb view of fairy-tale islands below, swimming in sun and mist. An enchantment out of a Chinese scroll. A place for a wandering poet in long robe and staff, dreaming in harmony with earth and sea and heaven . . . . How could war in all its thunderous darkness be so near?

Our stay in these sublime quarters was all too brief. Our next stop was a lowly pillbox with Brigade HQ at Wong Nei Chong Gap. What names! Kipling again, as exotic as Khyber Pass and destined to play out its own tragic drama.

Pillboxes — small cement cubicles wedged into the hillside. Made mostly of sand, thanks to homegrown graft and greed. Triple bunks lined three walls, with a steel slot in the fourth for machine guns. A long, narrow air vent above the center bunks brought sand and pebbles shooting down when a shell or bomb landed. Just my luck to draw the top bunk directly under the vent. It was a cozy, stuffy, smoky little igloo offering a false sense of security. Rations were drawn from Grenadier lines across the road. We worked four-hour shifts on a telephone exchange and the No. 11 radio sets.

Fifth columnists were everywhere, dressed as coolies, spying, filtering through the lines. Orders were given to shoot them on sight. Strolling over to get my rations, I paused to stare at a young lieutenant interrogating a coolie caught wandering by. He was held firmly by two Grenadiers. There was no interpreter, no communication. I sensed that the young officer was out of his depth, confused. There were orders, you know . . . . The prisoner was in rags that could be fake or real. What to do: let him go? shoot him? An innocent man! Eyes wide in terror — or bewilderment — did he know his life was at stake? How could he if he'd done nothing? Just taking a shortcut through his own hills, to reach his family? A little one-room shack, where children played, his wife over the supper pot? Supper waiting after a long day's toil?

The lieutenant's face was blank, masking his conflict. "May be fifth column." His voice was flat and deliberately hard. "Guess . . . we'll have to shoot the sonofabitch." *We* meaning *they*. He nodded to the teenaged-looking Grenadiers. My own heart pumped heavily as they began pulling him away. The victim drew back, resisting, talking volubly, explaining, questioning — *What did these armed foreigners want?* — as he was dragged around a corner. I steeled myself, shouting inwardly, stop it! But of course there was no stopping it. None of my business, in fact, but — how could they? This wasn't the heat of action — it was cold-blooded murder! I heard a burst of bullets and fought back nausea. The Grenadiers returned, alone. The younger one was pale, breathing heavily through pinched nostrils. The job was done. And we — they — would never really know. Orders were, after all, orders.

I returned, trembling, in confusion . . . . Who or what was responsible? The enemy? The war? Us? *I* . . . was part of *us*. And I hadn't uttered a peep.

We ate, slept, smoked, did our shifts, played cards, speculated on how or where it would come. There was feverish activity — Japanese troops massing on the Kowloon shore. Aircraft took leisurely photos, licking their chops at the coming feast. Bombing and shelling increased. Fires started. Would it be a direct frontal assault? A sneak play from the rear? Or both? Day or night? These myopic barbarians who "couldn't see in the dark" had turned out to be amazing night fighters. At night, amid mounting tension, our searchlights raced nervously over the waters.

On December 13, the Japanese flag went up over Kowloon and their demand for surrender was refused. Planes and artillery pounded the island harder. On the fifteenth, a feint was beaten off by a Royal Rifles platoon. The enemy was behind schedule and growing impatient. On the seventeenth, they demanded surrender again, threatening indiscriminate bombing. Time was important to both sides. Our own encouraging orders were to hold out at any cost, which didn't improve my scant sleep. Nor would I have slept any better knowing the Japanese were planning a three-pronged offensive with the main thrust aimed at Wong Nei Chong Gap. Tensions were growing unbearable.

On the eighteenth, the whole area from the harbor straight up to Wong Nei Chong Gap was devastated with a deadly and incessant shelling that seemed about to blow our measly little pillboxes to smithereens. We lay on the floor waiting for shells to land. Our pitiful pillbox walls seemed suddenly paper thin. We listened to the artillery and I joined the count — *pown, pown, pown, pown, pown:* five — the swift rhythmic pounding drumlike sounds kept pace with my heart. Here they come: the first sickening *whoooosh* of air hissing *death!* Then the deafening blast of all creation ripped apart — missed — next — breath frozen, muscles coiled — life or death in a split second — pride stops me from shrieking *stop! let me live! Whoooosh* — CRASH! Then another and another and another, then silence . . . . It's over for now, for a few precious minutes . . . .

With shaking fingers, Demant passed me a cigarette. He forced a sickly smile. "Time," he said, "goes so fast when you're havin' fun."

Below us we could see fires out of control. The whole harbor and shore was full of drifting smoke. What was happening? Conflicting messages were coming through from different sectors. Confusion increased as darkness fell. Were they coming? Where? How many? The Rajputs and Middlesex were being overrun by swarms of Japanese coming over the water on anything that could float — rafts, boats, sampans, junks, tubes — or even swimming. For every ten brought down by machine guns, a hundred would replace them. On they came in never-ending thousands, fanatical, irresistible, fanning out across the island, east, west, south. "Wait till daylight," some of our messages read, "this may be a feint." Orders were countermanded again and again.

Behind us and around us, carnage . . . chaos. Friends battled friends. Rajputs mowed down dim figures who were yelling, "We're Canadians!" as they died. My friend Tommy Marsh fought desperately in the hills behind our pillboxes, where platoons were being slaughtered. A Japanese officer sprang at him out of the dark, screaming "Banzai!" He shot the officer dead, then caught a bullet through his throat and jaw, another in his leg. He was blown up by shellfire, blacked out twice and was finally captured.

A spirit of madness took over the night. The whole island seemed secretly transformed in the darkness into some strange volcanic mass that was erupting and burning at a hundred points, like flaming mouths, gobbling up everything — earth, bodies, guns — invisibly. What was happening out there? No way of knowing we were the enemy objective. Matthews, knowing more, was beside himself, but now with good reason. He appeared at a quarter to twelve, hardly coherent, to tell us — when it was almost too late — that our situation was impossible and we'd better get away as best we could, leaving a crew to man the sets to the last. Four men to stay — stay being a euphemism for die. Yes, but . . . which four?" He paused.

"Whose shift comes on at twelve?"

"Ours," I said in a quavering voice.

He gazed down at my face, knowing only too well, as we all did, that this could be virtually a death sentence. Only war can place men in such devilish positions, forcing life-and-death decisions to be made at high speed. Strange emotions chased over his face as he stared at me. I saw his struggle. What did he think at that moment? What did he see in my eyes — a wordless, hopeless prayer for life? Did he picture me lying in a pool of blood, my face mangled by bayonet wounds? He was an imaginative man. Whatever thoughts raced through his brain, Matthews could not face them.

"The present shift will stay on," he said breathlessly.

I nodded thankfully, full of guilt. A man I had no use for was saving my life. The men left behind were, in fact, trapped and overrun.

We left our gear, everything, took only our rifles and hastily left the pillbox, feeling naked, abandoned, bewildered. Matthews's fear and mine were one. Fright left me weak, so weak that the rifle itself felt heavy. Fog and drizzle had thickened the darkness . . . it throbbed with violence and bloodletting. Men were dying all around, invisibly, horribly. *Go!* Where? No one knew. *Run!* Forward? Backward? Right? Left?

I dashed into the blackness, pursued by a crazed beast of panic that set its claws in my skull and clung tenaciously — riding me, driving me, this way, that way . . . . We staggered away in all directions and were soon hopelessly lost. I ran into George Grant, a fellow operator, disoriented, panting — which way were the Japs coming from? I didn't know. We found a path that seemed to wind into the hills — it led nowhere. We tried to retrace our steps but everything changed in the dark. What to do? No orders, no leaders, no equipment, no information — I felt adrift in a threatening sea of dark, undefined masses, my mind charged with tormenting Kafkaesque images. Frightful things were going to happen. The beast of panic sank its claws deeper as we crashed around in the wet underbrush, which tore and slashed at us, driving us in circles.

After several hours of aimless, exhausting wandering, we found a tiny abandoned Austin and crawled inside out of the rain. "Let's sleep here till daylight," Grant suggested. He was a rosy-cheeked youngster of twenty-one, just married, a man whose lack of fear was an unexpected comfort on such a night. He was really more angry and disgusted than afraid.

He promptly fell asleep in the front seat. I tried to doze in the back, rifle across my chest, electrically jolted awake at every suspicious sound, a slave to the wildest forebodings. How could the bastard sleep in the middle of all this? What was he made of? What was I made of? Disgusting stuff. And I suffered for it — serves me right. Well, cowards or heroes, we'd all share the same fate, only *they* wouldn't suffer this much, damn them . . . . Of course, I may be lucky — one bullet, *fast and clean,* no bayonets, no torture, no pain, *zip* and it's all over . . . . The night was interminable.

At last a gray dawn began to lighten the windows. I leaned over to peer out. Sounds of gunfire were increasing. Looking down I blinked and peered and blinked again in unbelieving horror: *dim shapes, bodies, faces of Japanese soldiers, kneeling in firing position all around the car!* I threw myself back as though stabbed. My heart seemed to implode inside my body. Oh God! My worst fears come true!

"George! Ssst! Wake up!"

He was in an amazingly heavy sleep. "Mm? Lemme be."

"Sh! Look! For chrissake, look out the window — *we're surrounded by Japs!*"

"Eh?" He leaned over groggily to look. "Holy Jesus!"

We both lay in frozen silence. "What do we do?" I asked.

"God knows," he muttered. "We make a dash, they'll grab us. We stay put, they'll soon see us."

My body felt drained of all blood. Instead of adrenalin flowing, I was paralyzed by a great fit of terror that was squeezing away my last resistance. Do we die fighting? Do they take prisoners? Not in battle. *Would they torture us?*

The light grew ominously brighter. Grant edged cautiously to his window for a second look. He stared and stared.

"Well, fuck me dry," he giggled loudly. "Look!"

I gazed uncomprehendingly out at Grenadiers crouching beside the Japanese. It dawned on me. These were Chinese soldiers I'd never seen before, but they were definitely on our side. I half laughed, half wept, having aged ten years for nothing.

We crawled out of the Austin to begin the longest day of my life. The hills were spotted with clumps of soldiers. Units were fragmented, mixed, leaderless. The Japanese were too close for comfort, covered in masses of leaves and branches, humped, like dozens of hairy turtles trotting along the crest of the hill. A young soldier beside me was firing methodically, calm and authoritative. I squatted alongside, trying to mimic his comfortable position.

"Where'd you learn to shoot like that?"

His eyes were unwavering. He fired and replied in a flat voice: "Spain."

"Hey! Really? Spain? The Mac-Paps? No shit!" In the middle of all this? What was he doing here? What did he make of this war? Ever ready for a stimulating discussion, I was quickly returned to the here and now by the zing of bullets. Everyone but me seemed able to crouch behind adequate rock cover as I settled in disgust behind a threadbare bush, aiming my trusty rifle. It had enough pebbles and sand up the spout to blow my head off, as the first shot nearly did. The recoil cracked my shoulder like the kick of a mule. I tried again. A figure was dead center in my sights . . . silhouetted against the sky as I pulled the trigger. He dropped. The thought vaguely registered that I had just killed a man. And so *easily*. I only had to line up the sights on the center of the turtle, tighten my finger — *bra-a-am!* Down went another. A duck-shoot booth at a county fair. I thought of the books I'd read of the young soldier's emotions at the first kill. What did I feel? Nothing. I was sleepwalking through an ugly fantasy, a phantom in a surrealist dance. At another level every crazed act seemed sane and normal. Killing three men, getting away with murder was . . . okay. Natural. Had gone on since time immemorial. And anyway, if it was written that my life should be dangling by a thread, what did *anything* matter?

There seemed no rhyme or reason to the anarchic battle going on around us. No orders, no leaders. Grant called over: "Let's get the hell outta here."

Grant, Wes White and I went scurrying down the hill to a road. There was an officer at last: a British major, red tabs, brass buttons, pips, belt, barking orders — at least *somebody* knew what was going on. He assigned us briskly to one side of the road and we settled in, heads down, organized at last, admiringly watching him giving orders, calmly ignoring bullets. Courage to burn. Actually he was mad as a hatter, busily inventing his own storybook war. He struck a dramatic stance as he shouted: "Men! We're going to hold this position . . . *to the end!*" The *end*? My God — a suicide stand! We, a puny dozen men, were to turn back the whole goddam Japanese army! Grant shook his head. "Loonier than a bedbug!" But we were stuck with him.

Waiting . . . . With a mounting sense of calamity, I watched wounded stragglers thin out, heard the firing die down and an eerie silence settle over the road. Waiting . . . . So this was it. Was this where I was to die? There was no other way. The end of everything. Dreams, plans, ambitions . . . stupid, stupid, *stupid*. I was to die, idiotically, meaninglessly, invisibly, on a distant Chinese hill. Waiting . . . and feeling a need, a call, from somewhere deep in the obscurity of my agonized soul, for dignity, for calm, for a proper mental frame in which to meet death. It was strength I craved, not this numbing, whimpering dread. The need filled me like a powerful prayer.

The Angel of Death was here . . . reaching out to me, entering me, allowing me, with a prodigious effort, to accept and defeat him. Did I die? In an uncanny way, yes. Feeling my own death, allowing it in, digesting it, I could now *move beyond*. Rising higher and higher above these hills, into the heavens, hovering over continents, I saw men fighting and dying by the thousands on battlefields, in Europe, in Asia, in Africa — young men with wives, sisters, mothers all moaning in pain, heartbroken for loved ones . . . . I saw families destroyed, my own mother weeping, and realized she was no different from the rest. Why should I expect special favor? I truly understood that my death didn't matter in the overall scheme of things. My tragedy was no greater than any other. In fact, dying here might be saving another life by somehow filling in the ranks of the dead. No, my life was nothing, my death was nothing. Grasping that, believing that, brought a curious calm, a total acceptance. I had shed Self. It was some kind of sharing, a transcendent leap into another plane of awareness that left me if not at peace, then free at least of that abysmal clinging terror. It was easier to die now.

But we were not slated to die. We braced ourselves at what sounded like stampeding cattle. A wave of retreating soldiers came pouring around the bend in total disarray. The wounded were helped by others, some with bloody makeshift bandages, staggering, limping, trotting, running, some carrying machine guns, a chaotic rout, totally out of control. Our officer was overrun, swallowed up in the mêlée as they swarmed over us. We were soon caught up in the flood, running with the rest toward what seemed like safety, part of their single-minded driving panic. But it was too late. We rounded a bend in the road — the only avenue of escape — and found it totally covered by enemy machine guns.

Safety lay half a mile ahead where the road curved away. And death was waiting in between, all along the way. We went dashing forward in groups, a half-dozen at a time, diving as machine guns rattled. A deadly rhythm of *dash-dive-dash-dive*, with heart outracing feet and head bursting with fright. I dived under a bush and heard the gentle raindrop patter of bullets through the leaves overhead. I braced for the next dash with the Chinese soldier in front of me leading. He leapt to his feet only to catch a bullet in the neck and drop in front of me, blood gushing from his throat. Now I was leading, but not leading, hypnotized by the bubbling gurgle of blood, unable to budge — with jolting cries behind me:

"Who's in front?!!"

"*Move!!*"

Me in front — and not moving at all, at all. I felt one-ton weights on each leg.

"*Go!*"

"What's the hold-up?!"

Then, with failing will screwed into a tight knot, I leaped up, knowing I could never repeat this. No more leading, dashing or diving — I *flew*. The old cliché "Fear lent him wings" was never more apt. Bullets flew, machine guns rattled, I ran, ran, ran — revealing hidden talents in the art of retreat. I ran like a wild-eyed runaway bronco galloping through flames — on and on forever, bludgeoned into a state of idiocy, powerless to duck or dive or pause or stop — till the road turned to the right, curving its welcoming, loving arm about me . . . . *Made it!*

As we had feared, the pillbox (where I should have been) was soon overrun. Hills were captured, held, lost, retaken and lost again. Isolated units fought to the end, dying uselessly. Heroic acts, cowardly acts — nothing could change the outcome. Brigadier Lawson, head of our mad expedition, was trapped at the Gap and was shot trying to fight his way out.

Grenades were lobbed down air vents, turning pillboxes into death vats. Pillboxes filled up, packed with fleeing victims vainly seeking shelter in a world gone berserk. Grenade after grenade came down the vents, exploding, killing, blinding, with those still alive screaming, twisting, clawing, crawling over one another, mingling torn arms and legs and entrails in a hellish chamber of Dante's Inferno.

Volleys of bullets raked the steel-shuttered windows and rifle butts pounded them — "*Banzai-ai-ai!*" Johnny Little, a signals operator, joined a dozen others in a desperate dash to escape — seven were cut down but Johnny got through. The rest were captured, the wounded slaughtered, the others beaten, bound and marched off.

Our retreat brought us to a hospital in the fishing village of Aberdeen. Troops rushed to and fro, exhausted, ashamed, astonished. A makeshift kitchen offered bully beef and hardtack to hungry mouths, but my churning stomach was too tortured to handle food. I found Grant, White and a few other Signals, but no sign of Hank — where the hell had he gotten to?

Harassed nurses were trying to attend the wounded, piled everywhere. In a courtyard Grant and I were hailed by an orderly to lend a hand with the dead. I gripped the cold blue legs, Grant the shoulders. "Pee-yoo, what a stink!" The face was an eerie theatrical blue with a red beard. Then the air-raid siren sounded. We hurried, laying corpses quickly in a shallow grave. The minister's last rites were swift and garbled, with one eye on the diving planes. We shoveled earth over the corpses pell-mell.

Inside, the troops were recovering. How dare those little bastards do that to us! A decision was made to counterattack and away we went, dashing out to two open trucks. I tried to clamber aboard the first one — too late, it was pulling away. I turned, with Grant, to leap onto the next one, and the two trucks roared off in different directions. The first, I heard later, was wiped out in an ambush. The second was going to a place called Sushin Hill under the command of Mad 'Enry. Mad? Yes. His men, who hated and loved him, confirmed it. What was this gift we had for attaching ourselves to insane British officers? Or were they *all* bonkers?

He assigned us to one of the trenches on Sushin Hill, awaiting attack. It was a long day in which I made entries in the small diary I carried over my heart. A day in which I had a bad bout of diarrhea and was forced, during a bombing attack, to evacuate the trench to avoid evacuating *in* it. A day in which a deadly snake came crawling down my arm. A day in which Mad 'Enry, forgetting us, decided to ride back to retake a place he'd lost. Reminded of the dozen men up there in the trench as he pulled away at dusk, he left orders for us to defend Sushin Hill against the Japanese Army.

We went down to his shattered pillbox and went to sleep for the night. No guards were posted — no point. We knew fatalistically that if we were overrun, it would all be the same in the end.

I lay gazing up through a shell hole in the ceiling at a circle of sky, with the stars — my Greek chorus — gazing back, aloof, derisive, enjoying the antics of this crazy, tortured planet. Where were the others? Hank? Demant? Blacky? Where, O stars, would I sleep tomorrow night? If I slept at all. No . . . please don't tell me. Only the present matters — this hour of peace, with no flying bullets, no throats gushing blood . . . peace . . . and let that be all, oh please, let that be all . . . .

Only the present? There was some wisdom in that, because tomorrow would be worse.

Chapter Five

WE AWOKE TO A FINE SPARKLING morning with the pleasant surprise of finding ourselves still in one piece — no attack during the night. Unknown to us, Japanese mortar and machine-gun units had moved past us as we slept. We conferred. Mad 'Enry's men followed him on foot. A few of us decided to walk back to Aberdeen and look for the Sigs.

We set off in high spirits, passing in front of an enemy machine-gun unit, who held their fire. Too small a target to give away their position. We met and saluted an open car full of high brass, who returned the salute — their last. We heard the rattling blast of machine guns and stood transfixed. That could have been — should have been — *us*. Another of the nine times, by later count, my fate was dangled playfully by a thread.

At the hospital, the air of bravado was gone, the tension, fear, despair now palpable. Our spirits sank. Snipers surrounded the area, and we had to crouch to pass a window. We found a few Signals, and went off to find a telephone. After many tries and a long wait I finally got through to Matthews in China Command. Hah! Sixty feet underground, the safest place on the island — naturally. Still, it was good to hear that voice again — a return to some kind of order in a disintegrating world.

He told me most Signals were together at Wanchai Gap, four miles up in the hills behind Aberdeen, and we should try to get up there. I said we'd try. Fine. A *plan*. And back I'd be with my unit at last. I'd see Hank's homey, comforting puss again and feel Demant's sunny spirit. And Blacky — hah! — that bugger would be in his element.

I returned to the hospital to find everyone — Grant, White — gone. A sudden alarm had sent every armed man out to turn back an attack. Hand-to-hand fighting? Holy Jesus — bayonet fighting to the death? And I'd never had a fistfight in my life. The demons of fright, in all their debilitating fury, were back. My stomach churned, my brain turned to mush.

I found a fellow operator, a man I'll call Joe, cowering behind the kitchen, squatting in a circle of coolies, peeling spuds, traumatized. "Someone grabbed my rifle," he mumbled. "I'm . . . helping out." The first swift rush of contempt that I felt dissolved into pity, guilt, gratitude that I could still stand, gazing down angrily. Here was a mirror being held up forcibly to my soul, to one who had always lived in fear of fear, of a descent to . . . this. The image was so naked, so blatant, it induced enough self-hating rage to offer strength. Never — *never* would I sink to this. Joe saved me. What was cowardice, after all? A failure of pride? Weren't heroes afraid — of how they looked to others? To themselves?

My tone was savage: "Get up! We're getting outta here." And he obeyed like a whipped dog.

We ran into a furious head physician, his eyes bloodshot. "Get out, damn you! *I'm surrendering the hospital!* No arms! I want no one here but the sick and staff! You heard what happened at St. Stephen's? *Slaughter!* They found arms — *get out!*" He rushed away. No, I didn't know about St. Stephen's . . . where arms were found and troops had been turned loose in the hospital wards to go berserk, murdering the entire staff, raping nurses, bayoneting patients.

A limping Grenadier joined us. "I ain't waitin' for *them*." At the sandbagged gate an orderly stopped us.

"We're surrounded. Go out now and you've 'ad it, mates." The Grenadier cursed. Joe moaned. My world was tumbling down around me again — oh God. "But we can't stay! What can we do?" The orderly suggested hiding in the basement. The Grenadier agreed, doubtfully. We hurried back, with a leaden terror weighing down my brain, my stomach nauseated. We ran into the head physician. "We can't leave now," I implored. "It's suicide."

"*Get out!* Damn you! Do you want us all killed? It's your lives against hundreds! *Get out!*"

He escorted us this time to the gates. We passed the sandbags . . . into the silent street.

"Gimme your bayonet knife," the Grenadier said. I detached it. One rifle, one limping Grenadier with a knife, one trembling unarmed signalman. Great.

Our *clump, clump, clump* echoed thunderously along the deserted streets in an unearthly stillness . . . everything was bleached in the white light of a hot blinding sun. My heart crashed against my ribs like a caged tiger. Chinese faces, eyes, peered out from behind doors and windows . . . . My body grew weak with the deadly drug of terror. I'd be worse than useless in a fight. I almost wished for a sniper's bullet to hurry, hurry and end it quickly.

Nothing.

No bullets, no snipers . . . street after street . . . empty, silent . . . not even a stray cat visible. I began to breathe again.

"What the hell was that bastard talking about?"

"Crazy sonofabitch! He had me shitting bricks!"

"Where are we?"

"Christ knows. We're still in this world, that's all I know."

We were, but hopelessly lost . . . knocking on silent doors that exuded a fecal, rotting stench. At last there was some movement at the end of a long street. We crept closer till we could make out a truck . . . figures . . . *British!*

We went dashing forward, hailing them as we would Earth men on Mars.

We made our way up a winding road into the hills toward Wanchai Gap, dodging bombs and shells. There was news from someone coming down: "A whole slew of 'em killed up there by a shell — Signals, I think. Helluva mess."

Hurrying on up, we found the Signals billeted in the basement of a house. Grimston, Rose, Gerard, Speller, Damours — faces pale and gloomy but a joy to behold. My unit at last, the closest thing to a family. Their presence suggested the known, the stable, the distant world of sanity. "Where's Hank?" I asked eagerly.

Tony Grimston answered, blank-faced. "Dunno. Maybe in another sector."

"Well, shit. Demant? Normand?"

He shook his head. Tony . . . tall, lean, intelligent, deep-voiced, with narrow, avian features and a sharp sarcastic tongue that was now still and gently sober. Yes, it was true about losing a lot of our bunch this morning. It had been sheer inexperience that led them to set up their sets in the front part of a house instead of the back. A shell would have to hit the front or pass over it. Yes, it had been a direct hit and few got out alive. Then his halting litany of names, carefully edited, fell on me like a succession of body blows. "Sharpe too?" Brave, handsome, efficient Sharpe, running things with Matthews holed up at China Command.

Speller nodded: "I warned them. I said every time they set up those damn sets the Jap artillery beams in on them like flies to honey." Had I arrived a little earlier I probably would have been in that room. The dangling thread again . . . .

A Middlesex sergeant appeared in the doorway. "Need some help digging the graves up top." I rose with some of the others. Tony looked uneasy. "You'd better not," he told me. "You — uh — look like hell. Better rest up."

"I'm okay."

The sergeant passed around a jug of rum, saying, "It's dirty work." Then we followed him up to the villa's front yard, now pitted with graves. Slightly woozy from rum on an empty stomach, I joined in the digging while the sergeant disappeared inside to continue sorting the dead. I dug my shovel into the turf, trying sadly to visualize the faces of the dead men, too young, too vibrant to picture dead. My reverie was interrupted by the sergeant emerging from the house. "Anyone here know a Greenberg?"

"Hank Greenberg? Yeah, me." I blinked at him. "But he's not here, he's in another sector."

A curious glance. "Well . . . there's a respirator with that name. Better have a look."

"Okay, but it's impossible. Someone must've borrowed it." I followed him into the dim interior, my heart beginning to beat rapidly. The stench of dead bodies, laid out in rows, was thick in the air.

"This one." I leaned over a body, peering at the face in the semi-darkness. It was beyond recognition: nose and chin sliced away, leaving flat gaping wounds still wine-colored and glistening, catching a faint light from the doorway. Part of the scalp lay open beside the face, attached by a strand of skin. In it, as in a red saucer, lay what seemed part of the brain floating in blood. Nausea rose in me with the heavy stink as I bent lower, trembling . . . closer, seeking anything familiar in the slashed contours, gripped by a terrible irrational dread . . . peering desperately, inches away. No. . . I shook my head, relieved. *It's not him.* It couldn't be.

This is crazy — someone's borrowed . . . my glance fell on his sweater as I stared at it uncomprehendingly. How the hell . . . oh, God! The finely knit officer's sweater his uncle bought him — the only one in the unit . . . . This corpse — this mangled *thing* — was him! A shellburst crashed inside my skull and walls, roof, floor gave way. I was sinking, dropping into a pit of darkness — hands grabbed me, pulling me away. I was staggering . . . reeling drunkenly into the blinding sun. It was too much . . . the suddenness, the completeness of the surprise, the nightmare atmosphere of the room, all combined to tilt my brain. I was going mad. I was under attack and had to stop it — block it off — shut it out — stop it, stop it, *stop it!*

I was crawling over a fence, through a blur of agony into a room where liquor bottles sat on shelves . . . . I seized rum, pouring it into a large mug, filling it, gulping it down in a frenzy . . . burning my chest, scorching my empty stomach. Grabbed another bottle — whiskey — filling the mug again, forcing it all down . . . faster, faster, more and more to drown out this awful torment. I wanted oblivion — to kill the savage truth of it all, to escape the terrible guilt . . . the haunting image of his mother at the station as I hugged her, promising, offering my sacred word, my glib assurance — *don't worry, I'll look after him* — to counter her tears, her premonition. He was dead, as she had known he would be; he would never shoot a puck down the ice, play ball, giggle crazily, blink his long lashes in astonishment at a wonderful world. He was cut to pieces for no good reason, condemned for his stupid innocence . . . *nothing to worry about* . . . . I didn't want to think, feel, see, I didn't want a brain, I wanted to burn it out.

Then, as the liquor took effect, I entered a nightmare world of total disintegration. I stumbled back to the Signals room in a haze of dizzying, twisting objects, head spinning, stomach in revolt . . . weeping, babbling. Pity turned to revulsion among the others as I vomited over everything.

"Get 'im ta hell outta here."

I went stumbling drunkenly into the hills. Faces, uniforms passed in a blur of sky and bushes. I was driven, pursued, enclosed in a bedlam of noise . . . voices I couldn't recognize, only feel, induced pain, despair, guilt. The stench of the bodies was heavy in my nostrils. The outline of a distant house became the respirator with Hank's name on it, framing his mother's accusing face. *You let him die*, you promised, you slashed off his nose and chin. You must drink his saucer of blood in penitence. *Why him, why not you?* You have destroyed us with your promises — guilty before God and man. You are an enemy on the side of death . . . .

A voice, kindly and new, directed words at me, the cadences of a priest asking what was wrong. "Wrong? My shoelaces," I blubbered, "I can't tie them." He helped me tie them and vanished in a bleary mist out of which Normand appeared. "Ally! Hiya! I'm just outta hospital. Where's the bunch?"

I blinked at him. "All dead," I informed him.

"What? What's wrong with you?" He led me back to the unit. I was growing sober now, returning to the horror and to a fresh blow, one that didn't quite register. Demant: he was up there, one of the corpses. Concussion. But my brain could not encompass that. I sat in a dark corner listening to spurts of gloomy conversation. How would it all end? I stared at the blank plaster wall before me, trying to become part of it, to make myself as flat, as blank, as inanimate.

The next day we decided to make our way down to Victoria Barracks in the city, closer to China Command and Matthews. A British Signals officer suggested we check the lines up to Magazine Gap. The sun had emerged after a rainy night, and the clearing sky offered us a bright and glistening morning. The scenery was stubbornly lovely in its pristine unwarlike beauty, leaves and bushes moist and fragrant. The empty bombed-out villas we passed spoke another language. My brain received the new day with a desperate relish. Yesterday was gone, unthinkable, and could never have happened. The moment, again, was all. The thoughtless resiliency of youth was taking over, washing everything before it. The dead were retired to a locked compartment of the brain. I took counsel from the frolicking leaves. Mustn't think of the dead now, they said. You may be joining them soon enough — don't waste a glorious morning, it could be your last. And our young blood responded, rising toward the sun, not death.

We strode along, diving for cover occasionally when spotted by a plane. Grant and others repaired the lines. I could only watch. At one point a huge camouflaged artillery piece went off beside us and I nearly jumped out of my skin, clutching my ringing head. We discovered the British gun crew holed up in an amazing bunker below the big gun. We gaped at the splendor of the decor and furniture, looted from empty villas, the finest larder, record-player, bookshelves, lamps. They had no intention of fighting. They lounged in colorful bathrobes, riding britches, wearing the finest of silk shirts, cravats. "Fighting? No point in that, mate," our genial host explained languidly, reclining on a soft pillow. "Too few to defend ourselves. Besides," he added casually, "we've been spotted already and we've only a few more days at best."

"And then you'll bugger off?"

"And leave these lovely digs? Go rolling in the muck with the bloody infantry? We're all for it in the end anyway — we and you and all the rest. They've never taken prisoners. We're going out in style, chums, soft bed, clean clothes, fine stock of liquor. It's the only way."

Life and death seemed to be some glorious sport played for ultimate stakes. There was a terrible logic to the casual words. And . . . it sort of worked. By thumbing their noses at the Angel of Death, they were reducing him to an ineffectual clown.

We grew tipsy together on exotic liqueurs. "What happens if the Japs get here before you're blown up?" I had to know. The cheerful reply came from a cigar-smoking corporal. "Shan't be taken alive. We've all agreed to shoot each other first." Quite simple.

It was a glimpse into an old world, a far-off heroic time. Of Hector and Lysander, of admirable insanity. And very British. Gallantry, it used to be called — that nineteenth-century syndrome, so chillingly sensible here. Inspiring, terrifying, sublime.

Chapter Six

OW EACH DAY SAW THE inescapable net spreading wider and wider over the island. Isolated units, starved and exhausted, fought on, divided, captured, crushed under the advancing juggernaut. Hair-raising accounts of gruesome deaths and narrow escapes came in from every side. Friends in Victoria Barracks were astonished to see me — my own death having been recounted in detail. Apparently I had a look-alike fighting with the Grenadiers, who went berserk with the horror of battle. I — he — suddenly leaped up screaming and ran blindly down a hill, directly into enemy hands. They described how I was hung by my feet from the branch of a tree and bayoneted in plain view. My shrieks echoed across the small valley till our machine gunners opened up and riddled my body. It had the sound of one of my nightmares. No, it was some other poor bastard, not me. But it might have been.

At about this time a Grenadier friend, Doug, as he later told me in prison camp, was left lying on a hill after his platoon had been wiped out. An experience to remember. They were bayoneting the wounded. His buddy hissed: "Play dead!" Then Doug heard him groan when kicked, then scream when bayoneted. Doug braced himself, but a whistle blew and footsteps receded. Later he crawled away and jumped over a wall, only to land among a group of Japanese soldiers. He was then forced to dig his own grave and lie down in it to be shot. But an officer drove up and stopped the execution. Luck. Yes, but there were no stories to be heard from the luckless . . . .

We did guard duty, talked, listened, and moved closer to despair. There was no water, little food. We shaved in beer. We slept fully dressed, rifles on our chests, in case of a sudden stand-to in the night. Snipers shot at us in open places. Guard duty was a form of Russian roulette — standing out in the open, a target for snipers, an ordeal that left the victim half alive. Talk . . . and more talk. Our problem was hopeless. News? Yes, Churchill and Mackenzie King were offering high praise, but nothing else. We had been written off.

What were they thinking at home? The family must be hunched around the radio every day, sifting the latest bulletins. "Hong Kong's gallant resistance continues . . . . " No real information . . . it was worse for them in some ways, knowing nothing, imagining everything. I knew at least that I was alive. They didn't.

But this was no time to think of home. Hard enough not to succumb to the morgue-like atmosphere here. Faces once pink and young were now aged and gray with the smell of death on them. I struggled against the pervasive air of doom — with words, even with song, with whatever hope I could muster, but found no response. The despair was total. We were creating our own tomb, waiting for the door to swing shut. I looked into each bloodless face and saw fatalistic acceptance. Well, hadn't we been brave long enough? We were, after all, only eighteen or twenty or twenty-two, with a whole future yet to be tasted. How could it all end now? When would it come? Tonight? Tomorrow?

Matthews came over from China Command nearby, jittery and twitching. But he could help a little: I told him we needed a pep talk badly. *Anything.* We gathered around him, firing questions.

"Any news from the Chinese?"

"No. No help there."

"How long can we hold out?"

"Not much longer. They . . . have the whole island."

"Any orders? Any plan?"

"Um . . . no. Well, yes. Just to . . . fight to the last man . . . Churchill's orders, I think."

We stood there digesting the words, the judgment.

"Is there no hope at all?"

No answer. We waited . . . as he looked helplessly around at the eyes, full of desperation, anxiety, need. His jowls trembled.

"I'm sorry. You've been . . . fine and I've been . . . terrible. I wish . . . I'm sorry I got you boys into this. You see . . . . " The nose flattened, the chin quivered, the face twisted into a grimacing mask of pain as he began to weep unashamedly. It was the contorted face of an old man whimpering childishly. Spirits plummeted. I felt myself sinking, sinking with him into a bottomless pit. I felt anger too — at him for making everything worse, at myself for expecting more. At the implacable forces deciding our fate.

We turned away slowly and wandered back to our quarters. "That's what I call a real pep talk," I said to Tony. "He really has a knack."

Still, I struggled. There was vibrant life within me screaming denial. I couldn't die! I wouldn't die. It was too *wrong*. There was too much bottled joy and laughter, there was explosive desire, there were unattained dreams, there was a universe to explore, goddamit — it couldn't all be extinguished in this hellish, idiotic farce! Yet all these faces proclaimed the end of everything. I was surrounded by dead souls. I refused them. I had to get out of there. I wandered into the next room where the linesmen slept and found Blacky, Jenkins and Ted Kurluk. Here was a different spirit. They were alive. They still joked, they could grin, they sang. Blacky seemed to welcome every situation as a challenge to his manhood. He told how he had sat calmly on a bridge cleaning his rifle as the English dove for cover from a dive-bomber . . . showing how a French-Canadian acts. Proud.

He prodded us to laughter. He dared me — shamed me — into walking down a dangerous path, within range of snipers, to reach a better toilet, just for the hell of it. Frightening, but therapeutic. He led us to the empty recreation room to play billiards, refusing to quit when bombs started dropping. With them I felt myself reviving, breathing live air again. A bit like the artillery crew. Yes, the Angel of Death may be arriving soon, but we were not beyond choice in *how* we would go.

I decided to move into their room to sleep. Night was always the worst. Lying in darkness, in the chill of the bare walls. No talk, no faces, no diversion . . . the battle was on against thought, the enemy, lying in ambush inside my skull. It dredged up the same images, the same lacerating logic: first Hank's face, before and after, blinking away at the snowy vastness of the Rockies, in wondering awe . . . his throaty baritone singing Deanna Durbin's songs . . . his startling giggle . . . . Then the face: nose and chin slashed clean . . . *no* . . . . Demant's Santa Claus face, once alight with mischief, now blue-gray, devoured by worms . . . . Was that my fate? Whatever it was couldn't be held off much longer. Our time was up. We all knew that. Don't think of the end — think of anything . . . Blacky's face, strong, alive, challenging . . . washing with beer . . . the bird I saw, hopping along, its wings blown off . . . on and on while sleep, with its tantalizing promise, kept its distance.

The alarms were coming in more frequently now. The city was surrounded, the water supply cut off, the population rioting. Small isolated units were being mopped up. Resistance was growing more meaningless. All that was going on now was a continuing slaughter. On Christmas Eve we lay down to sleep on the concrete floor with our Lee-Enfields clutched to our chests. This had to be the gloomiest Christmas Eve on record. There were several alarms during the night with machine-gun fire close by.

On Christmas Day there was a fresh alarm and a strange hubbub. Bodies charged to and fro — Middlesex, Punjabs, Canadians — confused cries I'd never heard before, with a new and terrifying timbre to them. What were they shouting? Were they attacking? Where? I couldn't catch it! *Something had changed!* I grabbed a Middlesex soldier dashing by. "Hey! What's up?"

"Packin' in!" he yelled in a panicky voice and rushed away.

"What's that mean?" But he was gone. I didn't know the phrase. The corridor was a bedlam of smoke and dust and incoherent shouting. My heart raced.

"Surrender!" a voice cried. "Throw away your arms!"

"What?!"

"The *end!*" someone yelled. "It's all over!"

Over? Could it be? What did it mean? I couldn't think — couldn't grasp it. The Signals gathered in a cluster, faces registering disbelief, relief, foreboding. Lay down your arms? I couldn't! It was all wrong. But the others *were actually doing it.*

"Pile them here!"

My precious Lee-Enfield? My security? My protector through all the mad chaotic events, my faithful friend, the only thing I didn't discard. Without it I was half a man, helpless. The others were laying theirs down, man after man. Slowly I followed suit, overcome by a terrible, alien sensation of nakedness, of being totally helpless, an act of ritual self-destruction. I was trying . . . grappling with the enormity of what was taking place. A faint glow flickered in the recesses of my being and expanded . . . . *It's over* .... The idea was filtering into my brain: no more terror, no dying, no fighting to the last man! It spelled "life," hope rekindled, a respite at least. I would not die today. The frightful weight was lifting and a flood of light filled me like a joyous roar: I was *alive*. To hell with tomorrow!

Tony's face was stiff with anger. "What's wrong with *you?*" I demanded. "This is great!"

"Great! It's a goddam disgrace! It's disgusting. We should have fought it out."

My irritation was mixed with admiration. "And died? No thanks. Look — we're beaten. Face it. Prolonging it just means more killing — what the hell for? What's so honorable about suicide? They did what they had to do!"

"Bullshit."

I walked away. Stupid, stupid . . . life was life and death was death, and the choice seemed simple. And here he was loading me down with guilt. Then fear took over.

There were suicides here and there by those who had no hope, no faith in the mercy of an enemy who had never taken prisoners. Would we be slaughtered? And how? It was *unconditional* surrender. We had no rights, no appeal, none of the dignity that was the essence of being human.

We gathered to watch the victory parade. Thousands of triumphant troops tramped past, flags flying, officers on white horses strutting proudly, imperiously, down these British-built streets, tasting the sweetness of power unlimited, impervious to the curses lavished on them on all sides. Wasn't this how we had marched down these streets a few weeks ago? How easily one was brainwashed, hypnotized into a belief in the false god of permanence. We assuaged our wounds with vengeful thoughts. Well, have your turn, you bastards. Someday, somehow you'll pay the piper too.

The day passed with no soldiers, no takeover. They were still disorganized. We sat around, waiting, wondering. Blacky took a chance on going into town alone. I wouldn't dare. He came back in high spirits, having met a lovely Parisian girl who chatted with him in French in a delicious accent — a romantic adventure, an enchanted moment.

Orders came through to prepare for a march next morning.

Where to? How far? No one knew.

Grant found some fresh water. He led me to a tap sticking out of a wall in an adjoining building. I filled a cup twice and drank greedily, stupidly, the first water in days. A mistake. By evening I had the runs and was rushing to the toilet every half-hour . . . on and on through the night.

There were only two toilets, one at each end of the barracks. Dashing to one, I found it occupied. Frantic, I rushed down the long corridor — *hold tight* — reaching the other one only to find it locked and out of bounds. Shades of the S.S. *Awatea* — the sonsofbitches were at it again! What a time to pull rank! Seized by anger, need and a sense of good theater, I gave vent to all three. Whipping off my pants I left a pungent deposit on the doorstep, dead center with the sign above it reading "For Officers Only."

By morning I was in no shape for a grueling march. Weak and faint, I reported to the medical officer, who said it was dysentery. I had to get to Bowen Road Hospital, several miles into the hills. No, no transportation, only your legs. And he asked me, as a topper, to take them a heavy suitcase packed with medical supplies he couldn't carry on the march.

Our goodbyes were not easy, as we wondered how our fates were to be decided. There was always comfort in the company of friends, even in misery, and now I was on my own, facing the unknown with a sinking heart.

Heaving the pack on my shoulder took great effort, as did lifting the medical suitcase. What the hell did he have in there — dead bodies? I set off on the road into the hills, enfeebled and wobbly. This would be fun. My strength waned quickly as the road grew steep and the sun grew stronger. I was soon bathed in sweat and began to doubt if I could make it. Struggling on, I cursed the doctor, cursed the water, cursed my failing body, cursed the curse I was under. It began to feel more and more impossible. And still miles to go. On and on . . . . Stopping to move my bowels and loading up again . . . gasping, panting with each step, staggering blindly up a road that seemed to stretch to infinity. I bent lower and lower under the increasing weight. What was I doing here, alone, a prisoner of war, a pitiful fainting wretch with tortured bowels, crawling up this road to Calvary? What terrible expiation was I paying out?

My blurred gaze saw a woman coming toward me, an old crone, bent under a bamboo pole with heavy loads of wood on either end. She was clothed in black rags, her back permanently curved from a lifetime of bending. She glanced at me dully as she passed, like a vision of death, accepting me easily as part of the existence she knew. She saw no barriers between us. There *were* none. And with a shiver of foreboding I knew I had stepped across a mystical line into her world. We were now one. All my past — family, schooling, dreams and aspirations — had disintegrated, vanished, and I was being born again into a new dimension, a new life, a new identity that, like this weight, I was to carry with me through the coming years.

Chapter Seven

I ARRIVED MORE DEAD THAN alive at Bowen Road Hospital . . . and what a change! Doors and windows were damaged and scarred. Gone were the crisp linen and motherly nurses, the scrubbed walls and floors. It had a prison atmosphere now, unspoken but tangible, with neglect speaking out of every corner. Most patients in the dysentery ward were Royal Scots and Middlesex. The cure was simple: starvation. No food, only tea, for four days. Then I was placed with the others on quarter-rations. The only catch was that the entire hospital was already on quarter-rations because of the uncertainty of the food supply, and we were allotted one-quarter of that quarter — meaning one-sixteenth of the normal rations. We were expected somehow to stay alive on that. As a clincher the Royal Army Medical Corps — medical orderlies, hungry themselves — were pilfering what little we had. With us on the fourth floor, there was ample time for them to nibble on the way up from the kitchen. RAMC, the Middlesex told us, stood for Rob All My Comrades.

We grew thinner, more feeble each day. One morning breakfast arrived: cornflakes and cheese. When we got ours, we found about a dozen lonely flakes spread along the bottom of each bowl. And there was a $1\frac{1}{2}$-inch cube of cheese to be divided among eight men. In a feeble fury we took the cheese down to the officer in the kitchen and displayed it in the palm of one hand. "Can you tell us how the fuck eight grown men are expected to live on this?"

The answer was ready and glib. "No new supplies coming in. We'll just have to tighten our belts. Nothing *we* can do."

Nor we, but swallow our bile.

Days passed . . . . We were starving . . . prowling through nearby houses, scavenging for anything edible. Everything was stripped clean: only schoolbooks, photos of healthy smiling faces remained — where were they now? Then a bathroom medicine chest and an empty bottle of Eno's Fruit Salts with a layer of white at the bottom

— a score! Something edible — drinkable! Some water, quick, diarrhea be damned . . . . I stirred up the powder and guzzled it down with gusto.

Learning that Matthews was here, I hunted him down to find him ensconced in a private room with a fireplace. He greeted me with pleasure. What was he doing here? He was wounded, he said, with a straight face. Diving under a bed? . . . . Ah well.

Somehow he'd managed to scrounge a bag of flour. He was busily mixing it with water into flat biscuits and baking them on a fire. Showing a fine instinct for survival. I watched with my salivary juices freely flowing. Homemade matzoh — great! Lead me to it, ol' Mose! Let us make unto ourselves a holy Passover with this unleavened bread! I am ready and able! Were the Jews wandering in the desert ever this hungry?

We chatted as he worked, gossiping about the latest rumors, the possibilities, the future . . . . The Canadians were mostly in a camp called North Point, in Hong Kong; the British were in Sham Shui Po. I watched him munching the crisp biscuits as he spoke, waiting for some to be passed my way . . . nothing. I had described our desperate food situation. He had listened sympathetically. Nothing *he* could do. Seemed to me there was one hell of a lot he could do — a go at those yummy-looking biscuits would be a good start. Damned if I'd beg the bastard. But no. He had somehow separated his existence from the outer world. Such self-centeredness, so total, might have been, in less dire circumstances, fascinating.

I left with an empty stomach and his friendly goodbye. He wished me luck — and meant it. Leaving me, for a change, a confused mess. I owed this man my life. This goddam creep. This very strange man . . . .

To add insult to injury we were ordered, in our enfeebled state, to form work parties to repair damaged parts of the hospital. We told them to go to hell. This brought a British colonel over for a dressing-down. Several wards of patients were gathered in a compound to listen. The colonel was heavy-set and looked very well fed, a no-nonsense type, all spit and polish, shoes and belt proudly gleaming. He was puffing on a briar pipe, which accented his air of immense self-satisfaction. This wouldn't take long; he would make short shrift of these petty malingerers. He had the gall to give us the belt-tightening line, with his own close to bursting and he painted a terrifying picture of conditions in prison camp. So many grams of moldy bread per man, so many grams of filthy rice, outright starvation everywhere. Now how would we like to live in those conditions?

"Fuckin' bullshitter," someone muttered.

"Now there's to be no more grumbling about work parties. The place needs sparking up and there's no one else to do it, so we'll have to roll up our sleeves. So far we've enjoyed a great deal of freedom here in uncrowded conditions — no harsh punishments. The Jap has left us on our own, not crowded us into rat-infested huts like sardines, surrounded by vicious guards and barbed wire. Of course if you feel well enough for that, it can be easily arranged. You either stay and follow orders or get out. It's as simple as that. Now. How many choose to leave? Raise your hands."

His eyes widened and his rosy face grew rosier as most hands went up. "Pack your damn kits!" he barked. "You'll be on the march in the morning."

I collected my belongings, wondering about his description. Was it all bluff? Was it really that awful? How could it be worse? Could I handle the march? I sensed a true beginning. This had been a brief interim, floating weakly in limbo, no Japanese, no war, the world had paused. Now it would continue. Down or up? I would soon know.

In the morning we feebly shouldered our kits and set off under guard. I looked wistfully back at the hospital, still in its proud outlines nestled in peaceful greenery, still echoing its old promise of rest and solace, of gentle hands and comforting voices. Goodbye then . . . .

We made our way down into the city and marched in a straggling line through the streets, no longer crowded but bleak, neglected, their lifeblood drained away. We looked around us: war damage everywhere. The buildings, still standing, watched like mourners at our wake, empty, desolate. We staggered under our loads, straining, feeble, sweating. The passers-by looked away, taking no satisfaction in these bedraggled, dull-eyed, unshaven creatures, former masters. Strange it was to pass down these broad streets again with their hint of bygone days — but what *contrast*. On that first triumphal march we were jaunty, full-bodied, our blood roaring with explosive energy, delight, shock, excitement and the crowds were teeming with bustling life . . . . Now they were cautious, eyes averted as they glided out of the path of these guards, with their volatile tempers and their Greater East Asia Co-Prosperity Scheme. Fear was in the air around us and a prescient awareness of horrors to come . . . of days when they would be eating their own babies.

A white woman slipped a pack of cigarettes into the hand of a marcher out of sight of the guards and flicked a heartening V-for-victory sign as we passed. Victory . . . yeah.

We stopped at last, exhausted: North Point Concentration Camp was a pathetic-looking cluster of long wooden huts lying between a wide street and a sea wall. Guardhouse and gate at one end, guards patrolling inside a high wired fence . . . . Some huts with bullet-scarred, vermin-infested double bunks, others bare and crowded with prisoners sleeping on cement floors.

Units were mixed, scattered, disorganized. Sanitation ghastly, nights bitter cold. I was placed in a Royal Rifles hut, sleeping on the cement beside two Newfoundlanders who shared their meager blankets. Amazing Newfoundlanders. The hut, dismal as a crowded morgue, was transformed by the jibes, vitality, gallows humor and goodwill of men who had just passed through an inferno. The air vibrated with the spirit of open sky and field and sea spray. "Is she cold enough for ye, b'ys?" "Hoo-oo! Freeze the shit in the ol' barn tonight!"

Food? A cup of rice — maggotty, moldy and full of mouse turds, true, but *food* — twice a day, with a thin soup of vegetable tops dubbed Green Horror. A bonanza after Bowen Road.

We gave the guards a wide berth. They were battle hardened, deadly, trained to accept brutality as normal. Their treatment of the Chinese was worse. One day I watched them pounce on a well-dressed middle-aged man in spectacles, white suit and panama hat. His crime was passing on the wrong side of the street — an excuse for judo practice. They tossed him to the pavement again and again till he was too weak to rise. He didn't cry out as they kicked him where he lay. What was he: a professor on the way to a class? doctor on the way to a patient? ordinary citizen on the way to his family? Then they dumped him into a cart and pulled him into camp. There they hung him by his ankles and charged at him with battle cries as he swayed, bayoneting him to a bleeding pulp.

Another time I watched a naked woman die slowly on a cold night after being raped in the guardroom. Things that filled me with fear, rage and . . . wonder. I was forming a twisted loathing for all things Japanese, judging — misguidedly — an entire nation . . . planting poisonous seeds that would take a lifetime to root out.

In a few weeks I moved in with the Signals in the hut assigned to Brigade HQ. Our group was made up of Postal Corps, Ordinance, electricians, cooks, dental assistants, MPs and others from all corners of Canada. We were sadly reduced in number. Canadians had by far the highest casualties; our Brigade HQ had taken the heaviest punishment, with a third killed. What a comfort to be back with familiar faces. Living, as I was, like a rudderless boat tossed along on crushing waves, this was my only tenuous promise of a safe harbor.

Guards paced to and fro beside our hut near the barbed-wire fence. Windows and doors, shattered or looted, were crudely boarded up against the cold and rain. The double bunks were well infested with bedbugs that sucked our blood by night while lice lived on our unwashed bodies. For light in the bleak evenings we rigged up small tin cans with lighted strings soaked in peanut oil. There was no heat in our undernourished bodies and we lay shivering in the cold January nights, huddled together for a glimmer, an exchange of warmth, staring into the tiny flame before us, absorbed in its imaginary heat as though it were a roaring fireplace. If there was a cigarette, four or five men shared it, then kept the butt.

Conversation was sparse. Thoughts were barren and desolate. No one was strong enough to avoid indulging in endless descriptions of food that set our salivary juices flowing. Home was a golden haunting dream that pursued us night and day, inflicting its own subtle tortures. Time stood still, allowing the world to go its way, passing us by as it went, denying our existence, confining us to limbo in this dark, forgotten hole. Was there still life out there? Were there really healthy, laughing, carefree beings, loving one another, eating lustily, shouting, running, dancing? What were people doing right now? Winter in Montreal . . . people walking in lighted streets, warmly muffled in scarves and thick clean clothes

. . . windows revealing cozy, brightly lit interiors. People entering a warm house and — *click* — with a flick of the finger, a whole room is flooded with light. A snack? Crackers and cheese? — magical phrase — oh God — peanut butter on toast? Hot chocolate and cookies? Oh murder . . . and then a hot bath, fine-smelling soap, soaking in heavenly warmth, clean towel . . . . And so to bed — a mattress, billowy softness, soft pillow, white sheets . . . sweet dreams. . . .

The wind moaned, the bare rafters creaked, rain leaked through the cracks. Yes, but dreams at least were free and couldn't be imprisoned — they were treasures, private, owned by me alone. They could wing me away to exalted moments . . . summer days, two couples biking down a country road . . . . Stopping at a little country store, ordering a quart bottle of milk and cakes — biting hungrily, gulping thirstily, faces glowing from the wind. What's that under the dusty glass — penny candy! Let's have some for old times' sake — sure! Caramels, marshmallows, licorice plugs (old and hard), coconut balls, chocolate coated . . . all dropped in a dusty brown bag. Small acts of ordinary living were swollen to glorious vibrant drama in the darkness. Christ, was all that continuing? Had we once been part of it? Incredible. Yes, that was being alive. And life had stopped. Ended. We had been lowered into a crypt, embalmed in silence, cold and darkness.

Time to sleep. Out went the miserable little wick with the three of us huddled close in the darkness. I in the middle, being the weakest, Blacky on the outside, warding off the gusts of wind blowing through the cracks. Tony on the right. Each alone with his thoughts and his growling empty stomach. Blacky lay pressed against me, locked away in his own bitter world. He spoke little these days. If there was longing, sadness, self-pity in him, he would not give it voice. I knew there was frustration, anger at the uncontrollable forces that had stolen his pride. He had been geared for war. Unlike me, nearly destroyed by it, he had reveled in battle, stood ready to be tested in any challenge of courage and strength. But it had been all too brief, and suddenly his solidly built base was sinking in quicksand. Decisions were made, events occurred, beyond his power to fight. He'd been sold off into slavery, humbled, locked away in this goddam leper colony . . . no place left for pride. We didn't know that there were to be ample tests of courage and strength and, yes, pride too. Only they were arriving in different guise, hard to recognize or understand. A new unseen war was unfolding. And we were not prepared.

I kept my precious diary in my greatcoat pocket. One day at the latrines I hung my coat on the door in the semi-darkness and absentmindedly left it behind. When I rushed back, the coat, with my diary, was gone. I was inconsolable. Blacky said I looked like I'd lost my best friend. He helped me construct a bigger diary, sanding down two strips of wood with holes bored through them and looseleaf sheets of paper bound with a shoelace drawn through paper and wood. The paper came from Porteous, the YMCA officer. It remained with me throughout the war, hidden in many strange places.

Now during the day I busied myself with my diary, recording the details of our daily life, noting the vagaries of the types around me, each life a book itself. There was Beaton, the dispatch rider, who could not or would not eat the moldy rice. He lived on the small bun served at noon and traded his rice off for smokes, not giving a damn if he lived or died. A walking ghoul, top-heavy with his large skull and exophthalmic eyes, how long would he last? There was Mitchell, a Sudbury miner, a brave fighting man in battle, now unable to face the ugliness, the emptiness, the non-life . . . lying staring at the ceiling in his heavy winter underwear, which he wouldn't remove, probably crawling with lice . . . refusing to leave his bunk to walk, refusing to talk or even listen. Would *he* last?

There was Erny Dayton, captured (in my place) at Wong Nei Chong Gap, subjected to gruesome obscenities recounted with soft masochistic relish. A coterie of friends sat around him as he lay on his bunk, a dull shaft of light on his black hair and white bloodless face, discussing recipes with a mirthless unearthly grin, a Christ figure, lifeless, wraith-like, with pain-filled eyes.

To watch the cautious trading and exchanging of recipes in the hut was to sense the creeping madness in the air. Men had taken to compiling whole recipe books. They would even trade some article of value for an enticing new recipe. They would venture outdoors, braving the cruel wind and rain, to meet another collector and work out an exchange, returning shivering and victorious with eyes alight. Depressing.

But a little light did appear here and there in the gloom. There was Red Barlowe, boisterous, irrepressible, charming, giving the lie to his surroundings. He had found clippers and scissors somewhere and set himself up in the barber trade, cutting hair in exchange for IOUs to be collected someday at home. The very act was a defiant declaration of faith in the future, played out with a brash confidence that was a tonic in itself. With the heart of a lamb, he loved, with his fiery red mane and beard, to come on as a ferocious battler, Barry Fitzgerald style. "This bunch o' fives," he would say, gleefully brandishing a fist under my nose, "is the Clincher. And this" — up came the other fist — "is the Finisher." To enter his aura was to feel the gathering clouds banished. Had he blundered on the secret of survival, I wondered? But the man had an inner radiance that defied imitation. Still, it could be studied . . . .

I wrote and wrote, bent over my tome, absorbed. People found their way to me, bringing their troubles, sorrows, confusions. I listened, trying to be objective, play sage, but failed. I felt all the pain. My soul had always been wide open, trading laugh for laugh, tears for tears. All this was to change radically in the years ahead. But at this early stage I was totally vulnerable. It was the actor in me, betraying me, making me play their parts — a knack, or curse, of transference. They sensed this and poured it on, making me their outlet, their instrument easily responding to their fingering.

Everyone was struggling, fighting blindly for balance, clinging to straws, trying to look normal, think normally. But everyone was acting, desperately. Each lost in a maze of shapeless corridors, with no markings, no names, no guidance. The officers, themselves swimming out of their depth, offered nothing, their glitter, their symbolism gone. Their authority was a sham in our eyes, their posturing ludicrous. We accepted the make-believe army structure only because the alternative was worse.

Every hut had its fill of bizarre histories, of tragedies, of minds hovering on the brink. Some had already passed over the edge. Morgan, a young Royal Rifle, tall, heavy-set, raised in luxury, was one of these. He wandered over the camp, digging out small clumps of earth and grass to eat. I watched him with pity, horror and envy. He would not survive, but he had escaped.

And there was the elephant man, who waited patiently beside

the water tank to get water for his elephants. Life had become very defined and very simple.

Wasn't the whole world reflected here in microcosm? The whole earth was caught up in this madness, running out of control. An image came back to me of a man in a bowling alley I had seen, at age fifteen. He was having an epileptic seizure — a large, heavy-set, middle-aged man. He lay writhing, convulsed, gasping blindly for air. That was the state of the world as I saw it, recording some of its convulsive agonies. The man in the bowling alley didn't die. Nor would the world. But . . . what about *us?*

Chapter Eight

ORAGING PARTIES ALLOWED out of camp brought in many books, and a library was set up in a small hut. Books! What a magic elixir to fill the brooding hours, to lure the mind away to distant worlds far from the groaning gut! I rushed over and found a huge selection available and returned with my prizes. What a blessing for all of us, I thought, hurrying back. But no one could be roused to go over. Hell with that . . . too much trouble. They didn't seem to understand: this could be the key, dammit! Our bodies may be locked away to rot but our *brains*, our precious brains were still free to roam! I recalled the song of the German political prisoners: *"Die Gedanken sind frei"* — thoughts are free. All action had stopped, true, but why not turn inaction into a period of mental activity and growth?

I recalled my first "important" book. At seventeen, I had decided on some serious reading. No more novels. I read Freud's psychoanalysis of dreams — and found it idiotic. How could people believe such guck? Walk through a door — look out, it's a bloody vagina. Lean against a tree, it's a pecker. So much for Freud. But I was not discouraged and pushed on to better things — and was happy. Reading, any reading, could be a vital lifeline here.

I decided that the mountain had better come to Muhammad and appointed myself librarian for the hut. I gathered a great stack of books and went from bunk to bunk peddling my wares.

"Okay: *now* will you read the goddam stuff?"

"Well . . . maybe . . . what've you got?"

"Everything. Mysteries, crime, romance, history, politics, which is it?"

"Crime."

I fell into a pleasant, oddly satisfying ritual of making the rounds every morning after "breakfast" to collect any finished books, discuss them, return them and bring a fresh supply. Slowly, over the weeks, the reading habit took hold. Even Mitchell accepted a book, showing the first sign of returning life!

Gradually the period of shock, gestation, was drawing to a close, and new shoots of vitality began to appear here and there. The instinct for survival asserted itself. Rolly Damours, who spoke Chinese, was a language freak and gathered a few cohorts to study Japanese. George Grant and Jack Rose joined him, taking lessons from Rance, the Eurasian interpreter.

"Wanna join us, Al?"

"No," I said, "waste of time. We should be outta here in six months."

This was a common belief I shared. We *had* to be out by then or we'd all be dead at this rate. It was an illusion that followed us for years. A whole year always seemed unthinkable. My optimism, though idiotic, prompted a decision that proved right for the wrong reasons. Grant and Rose eventually became interpreters in the camps in Japan and lived to regret it. It brought extra duties, extra beatings and no extra benefits.

The days grew warmer. The latrines were clogged, drawing hordes of flies that spread dysentery everywhere. Whole walls were black with flies that descended like a pall of evil. They covered our rice as we ate and flew into our mouths. Matthews came up with a fly-catching campaign, using fly traps and awarding a cigarette for every thousand flies caught. I watched him as he happily repeated the rules in his schoolmarm cadences. He was in his element — back in Boy Scout camp. No bullets, no bombs, a weekly salary and an officers' canteen with lots of goodies — yes, he was adjusting nicely. I noticed this curious talent in Joe, too. In the absence of danger he was flourishing, while the Mitchells of this world were falling apart, unable to accept slave status, the loss of self-worth.

Hunger intensified resentments and backbiting. Anger against officers ran deep. The spectacle of their extra food and privileges was salt on a raw wound. At first they ate in the open for all to see, but then they decided to move their mess indoors to enjoy the special dishes prepared by their cooks. They played baseball to keep in shape, running, shouting, laughing, with a row of weak skeletons hunched on the ground along the baselines, watching wistfully. A common sight was the tableau of a husky officer strolling on the parade ground with an emaciated figure stalking him, waiting for him to flip his cigarette butt away.

"The good officers," it was often said, "died in the hills."

"Not all," Tony would say. "Look at Corrigan and Black. Real men. Corrigan's a bloody hero." He liked to recount how Lieutenant Corrigan in a hand-to-hand fight shot an officer, grabbed his sword and used it in his free hand to attack and slash and kill. Yes, a hero. And we could use a few.

To replace the faulty latrines, boards were rigged up, protruding from the sea wall at the camp's edge. The boards were spaced to allow the prisoner to squat between them with one foot on each plank. We hooked our belts over a post to keep our balance in a high wind. It was best not to look down at the water below. Sections of bloated bodies floated up to the sea wall, awash in the waves of dysentery shit and corruption. I couldn't help looking as I peed over the edge, and the delectable sights varied each day. I saw a swollen leg with a high heel on the foot, the skin dangling like a loose silk stocking. There were bodies, sometimes whole and evil-smelling, with hands bound and rope about the neck. Tides bore them off and replaced them with new goodies each day.

And one day, yes, the inevitable happened. Many had grown too lazy or overconfident to fasten their belts to a post and depended on their sense of balance. At one point several men sat squatting on the boards. Suddenly one man slipped, and over he went. When he was fished out, he found he'd won himself a lot of privacy.

Weeks passed. Dysentery was taking its toll. Men began to die, and a hut was set aside for the worst cases. It was called "hospital" at first, then Agony Ward, more fitting, a charnel house of the living dead. There was little the doctors could do. The stench was ferocious and made visiting a friend an ordeal. Men emptied their bowels where they lay, too weak to rise, awaiting their turn to die.

Ted Kurluk had a bad case. He grew weaker and weaker. He was a gentle, soft-spoken soul. There was a doglike innocence about his large brown eyes, which gazed out of their deep shadowed sockets with an air of uncomplaining hurt. He wanted no part of the hospital. Blacky and Jenkins, fellow linesmen, took turns half carrying him to the latrine through cold, rain or heat, waiting patiently, wiping him, cleaning him up. Sometimes they carried him on their backs. Blacky's resources of power and strength seemed limitless. I could not foresee the day when *I* would be carrying *him*.

As the weather improved I began my nightly walks, strolling between the huts under the watching stars. The huts were silent, the inmates asleep. It was good to step out of collective living and be alone. Time to think, to assess the day, week, month gone by and weeks to come . . . . Life here was a war, a new one. I had recognized the many faces of the enemy by now: hunger, boredom, despair. Some men were winning, some faced defeat. I must develop new combat weapons and, harder still, give this life shape and meaning. How could I fit all this into what I'd learned?

My philosophical and political views were refreshingly naive and clear-cut at the time. The Utopian day seemed so near when all racial, class and national barriers would be broken down. Just change the base of society, the ground rules, and — *voilà* — everyone, I believed, would become angels. And I had wanted to play my part in it all. How simple it all was in those days. Today, when revolution has had time to show how it produces the worst kind of thought control as it congeals, all that can never be simple again.

But what could be done in a dump like this? Was there a role to play? Well, I couldn't change the world here — I'd lost all contact, in fact. But maybe I could start, like Confucius, with those around me and work outward toward enlightenment — drop a pebble in the still pool and watch the ripples expand. How?

The books were a start. I replayed the heady sensation of breakthrough as hard-boiled, blank-wall Mitchell reached for a book. I'd won something, scored, beaten back the ogres of darkness — a tiny victory, yes, but delicious. And the others, who responded grudgingly at first, now called for my books with quickening enthusiasm. This was the vaunted working class, mythical heroes of *Das Kapital* — me too — destined to rule the world. But what the hell could *I* offer? Well, I could entertain, and I had skills, erudition . . . . Could I help to fill the empty hours, interest the mind, expand thought, fight the enemy? Was that why I was here?

Though introspective, I was not honest enough to question my motives. Few do. We always enjoy a good photo of ourselves, truth being incidental. Was I play-acting? Well, if I was creating a noble persona, I could do worse. After all, one can *become* good by doing good often enough, as the sages say. And if I was a fool . . . well, if it weren't for fools there'd be less progress.

I walked on under the stars, planning an offensive, a way to turn defeat into a victory of sorts.

In the succeeding days I began nightly programs of debates, spelling bees, concerts, lectures. I combed the camp, tracking down experts on various subjects, inviting them to prepare talks. Singers were happy to perform. The audience grew. Soon the whole hut was gathering for the nightly entertainment. Hunger was soon forgotten in the heat of debate, prison boundaries dissolved. Minds, dulled and atrophied, were roused, set in motion. Prisoners from other huts wandered over to see what was on that night. Soon we were too crowded and moved outdoors. I found myself back in show biz, playing to packed houses, with truly captive audiences.

What had begun in a spirit of heady altruism became for me a secret of survival. I felt alive again, spurred by a lofty sense of mission. People depended on me. Here was purpose, here was meaning. Was all this a blessing in disguise?

There was another skill I could put to use here: art. Since the age of fourteen I had taken art classes, three nights a week at the Monument National in downtown Montreal. We had drawn from busts with instruction in French, which I couldn't follow, but it was *some* training. There were painting classes in high school, life classes later on and a period as a commercial artist. Here was a chance to use these elementary skills. I began a weekly art class, open to the whole camp, with pencil and paper the only requirements. Surprising talent came to light. Some worked tenaciously all week and anxiously presented their drawings for criticism with an air of the fate of nations hanging in the balance . . . great! Some had never drawn before and glowed with a sense of self-discovery. I was planting seeds, watching the emerging crop with fascination: again, a giving and receiving. I was winning.

One day, watching my art class, Blacky suggested I do some painting. "Love to — but with what?" He asked what I needed.

"Hah! Canvas, board, brushes, paint — fat chance."

Unfazed, he chewed on that and came up with a thought. The musicians practiced in a canvas tent nearby — how would that be to work on?

"Fine, but how could I get some?"

"Leave that to me."

Next day a large section of the tent was found mysteriously missing in action. Blacky cut it up into the proper sizes, then scrubbed and dried it. I pinned one canvas to a board. Paint was a trickier proposition. We put our heads together and decided that oil from the Japanese ration truck might work. With Blacky, taking chances always seemed easier somehow. I engaged the Japanese driver in an animated dicker for Blacky's watch while Blacky emptied the crankcase. We couldn't agree on a price and I left. It turned out to be wonderful oil, with a good variety of shading in olives and browns.

For fine lines Blacky whittled a stick to a point. For brushes he took the bristles from an old shoebrush and wired them to a stick. We were in business.

I painted the harbor with its half-submerged sunken vessels, a passing junk and the hills of Kowloon in the distance. I did a starving prisoner gazing at his empty mess tin with another ghostly specter in the window. Another of a bombed-out ruin, with guard and barbed wire in foreground. Some stark, some downright corny, but Blacky proudly sold them to officers for yen, which were happily converted to "extras."

The humidity in these hot tropical nights made sleep difficult, as did the mosquitoes. A few taps of cold water had been rigged up as a makeshift shower at one end of the camp. It was a chance to cool off. A new friend, Bob Warren, and I made it a ritual to shower every night before sleep. He was the youngest of the MPs, tall, with rugged good looks and a fine dry wit that drew us together. Humor, I had learned, was a powerful weapon here.

Bob was to become my best friend in the years ahead. He was a keen observer of human folly, and we spent hours dissecting our fellow man. We also shared a great appetite for movies and, with hundreds of other milling cattle, moved round and round our parade ground forgetting our hunger, reliving our favorite films, re-enacting memorable scenes and lines. A great obstacle was recalling names, now that beri-beri was affecting the brain, and this affliction increased over the months. Mind and vision had begun to blur to a frightening degree. At one point we came upon a friend in the Ordinance Corps sitting on the ground weeping. We stopped, thinking he was in pain. It turned out that he could not remember his son's name.

"Ain't never so bad but what she can't git worse," went the old Newfie saying. And sure enough, to add to our trials, work parties were called for to rebuild the Kai Tak Airport. The number needed far outnumbered the camp stock of healthy bodies, so the sick men were sent out.

Work parties lined up before dawn to be counted and recounted for hours before being ferried over to Kai Tak. It was dull, grueling labor in the murderously hot sun, draining what little substance we had left.

With pick and shovel, we slowly pulled down two sacred Chinese hills used as burial grounds, with thousands of ancestral ghosts screaming silent protest around us as we sweated away. The dislodged earth was shoveled into baskets attached to bamboo poles that rested on the bony shoulders of two prisoners, who carried it away. Wally Normand and I were a team of carriers. I needed him. Humor was in short supply out here. One had to work at it. To attack the fatigue and monotony of the long hungry hours, we turned our job into a rhythmic conga walk-dance, singing: "Coolie, coolie, con-*ga!* Coolie, coolie, con-*ga!*" The Ritz Brothers in Kai Tak . . . part of the peculiar battle.

Time passed with no sign of change. The future held no promise, only further deterioration. Sgt. Johnny Payne, Tommy Marsh's buddy, decided to escape. He was a talented artist and poet and had done some fine sketches of the life around him. He had the handsome good looks of a matinee idol and seemed moved by the same spirit — probably believed himself cast in that role, certainly his plans had that quality. He urged Tommy to join him.

"They only mean to starve us to death or let us die of disease. What have we got to look forward to? Years of slavery and finally death. Why not take a chance on escape or a quick death? We should try while we still have our strength."

Tommy thought it hopeless, and it was. With three others, they escaped but were caught, tortured and executed. The camp was in an uproar. Beatings increased. Guards dashed to and fro. Tommy was interrogated by secret police. "Why," he was asked, "did they want to escape? Were they not happy here?"

I myself was to be asked that very question by a Japanese psychologist in 1945. When I admitted, standing hungry, naked and shivering in winter, to not having discovered the bluebird of happiness in prison camp, he pondered this for a moment and asked: "Why?"

Johnny Payne had lived out his own romantic dream. I could admire, even envy the courage it took. He was all of a piece and found completion in a hero's death.

All further escapes were prevented by a canny move. We were divided into sections of seven and told that if anyone escaped, the remainder of the section would be shot. This meant that all seven had to escape together, which was impractical. It also made everyone spy on the others in his section since his life was at stake.

One evening as I strolled past the Indian huts I heard a faint chanting that intrigued me. I glanced through a window and saw many turbaned heads and some ceremony under way. The Indian culture had always enchanted me with its richness and mysticism. I remember being hypnotized by the strange terror of the Malabar Caves in *A Passage to India*. I had also plowed through Keyserling's *Travel Diary of a Philosopher*, an impenetrable tract on Indian religions. At nineteen, I had a grandiose outline for a play set in India but, happily, never wrote it. Here, in the middle of all this misery, I felt a stirring of the old romantic lure.

I went around to the door and decided to enter. No one stopped me. I removed my shoes and placed them with the others. Inside I squatted on the floor in the dim light, pressed against the others, and saw an amazingly opulent and exotic canopy at one end. Seated under it on a dais was a fat beautiful old man in rich robes with a fine turban and a long flowing white beard. It seemed miraculous. Where did they get all this splendor, I wondered, in the middle of a prison camp? There was a heady scent of incense. Candles fluttered silently. The priest, oozing confidence and relaxation, was chanting in a soft mesmeric cadence, waving a large feathery wand from time to time, waving it before my eyes till my senses seemed to dim and take me drifting off into some soft and comforting twilight. Voices around me rose in a gentle soporific murmur. I was released . . . . Spacious thoroughfares opened before me . . . white resplendent temples rose about me, echoing the soothing rhythmic chanting . . . white-robed figures moved slowly by with quiet, graceful tread. I lost track of time, squatting there, becoming one with the turbaned heads. Once again I had found an escape hatch — the unbridled imagination. Religion understood it — knew how to use it successfully. I would too, consciously, by letting it burrow a passage to freedom. Impermanent, yes, but ever-present, ever possible . . . without risk, without violence, something they could never rob me of as long as I had a brain to set in motion. "No one can deny, *die Gedanken sind frei.*"

Blacky, not a man for communal living, built himself an amazing bunk high above us among the rafters of the hut. Made of scrounged boards and rice sacks, it was fixed to the roof and made an ideal isolated roost free of bedbugs and humans. He swung down by a rope, like Tarzan, startling visitors.

At one point Jenkins ran afoul of a guard for breaking a rule. The guard bellowed at him, firing questions he couldn't understand. It looked like a beating was coming up. Jenkins was backed down the center aisle of our hut at bayonet point, trying vainly to explain. Blacky, watching from his roost, came swinging down on his rope like a dark thunderclap, bursting from the heavens. He landed between them, his fierce wall-eye bulging, and roared: "*Nanda* [what's going on]?" in his powerful basso.

The guard was so startled, goggling at this apparition, that he backed away, turned and buzzed off. This was the real Blacky I choose to remember. Not the humped, pain-wracked figure I was to live with in the months to come.

The pitiful daily rice ration remained the same, 900 calories, too meager to sustain life and health as the months wore on. Malnutrition began to take its toll. More men died. We seemed marked for the seven plagues of Egypt. A disease called pellagra brought open, running pus sores to many parts of the mouth and body. One of the curses produced red, swollen testicles, dubbed "strawberry balls." Another turned them into huge melon-sized monstrosities called "Hong Kong balls." Wet and dry beri-beri stymied the medics. Men developed "electric feet" — painful nerve shocks in the toes that continued relentlessly day and night. This curse attacked those with large feet most. Blacky, with large feet and hands, developed a severe case, while mine was mild. It progressed in stages. First came the pain-filled sleepless nights, which produced exhaustion and lack of appetite. In time, at the middle stage, the misery gradually drove men mad. They could neither eat nor sleep. Finally they wasted away and died.

A hut was set aside for the advanced stages, again dubbed Agony Ward. Their gaunt figures bent double on the floor, weaving and bobbing and rocking back and forth in pain, like penitents at the Wailing Wall, rubbing their tortured toes and weeping, made a haunting sight. I had never seen grown men cry. It roused pity, disgust, horror, fear — fear that this was awaiting me. When we visited a friend and recognized the mad faraway look in the eyes, we knew it was a matter of time.

Syd Varcoe, the talented camp poet, was an advanced case. On a visit he asked me in a voice of plaintive appeal: "How long do you think the war will last, Ally?"

Thinking to reassure him with a note of hope, I said: "Three or four months, I would say."

He flew into a rage. "You heartless sonofabitch! You dare to tell me that? Look at me! Do you see me lasting three goddam months? And you've got the gall to say that to my face?"

I beat a hasty retreat. How stupid — not seeing time from his point of view. Three months could seem like a death sentence.

Blacky bore his pain stoically, rubbing his toes silently during the night, groaning in his sleep. With no change of diet, would there be any hope for any of us? We needed Vitamin B badly, but there was none of it to be had in this moldy, polished white rice.

I continued my nightly strolls between the huts. I was stripped to my *fundoshi*, the narrow cotton undergarment we all wore, and caught the faint fetid breeze from the water. Yes, we needed a change in diet badly. But what a hope. Colonel Tokunaga, in charge of all Hong Kong camps, was a human horror, a fat hog of a man, full of so much venom he seemed to exude it as he passed on parade. He appeared regularly to review the prisoners.

Each night on these walks I assessed our prospects, struggling for an idea, a path, a way out. One night it came to me with all the force of a religious revelation. The pigs could save us! On our work parties we'd seen the pens where the Japanese kept a large number of pigs, fattening them up with sacks of brown rice. Brown rice was not thought fit for human consumption by the Japanese, but I knew enough about nutrition to know it was loaded with Vitamin B and could cure all our ills. But how to get it?

Well, after all, even Tokunaga could see how he could save in white rice if we switched to pig feed! It was in his own interest, wasn't it? One decision like that could reduce his ration budget and cut down on all the deaths he had to report to Tokyo. How many deaths by "heart failure" could he get away with?

Ah, but who would bell the cat? The officers? Hopeless. They walked around Tokunaga on tiptoe. They'd never go for the idea — it would make waves. They'd refuse, or table it . . . . No, it had to be presented to Tokunaga directly. By me? No, not Chicken Willy . . . . By someone with courage. Blacky? No, he couldn't explain it properly. Tony? No, he would smile his languid cynical smile, pick it to pieces and ask why I didn't do it myself.

Yes, why? How could I ask someone else to do something I was afraid to do myself? Yet — it was staring me straight in the face — if I didn't do it, *it just wouldn't be done*. That was the ugly truth. The whole idea would go down the drain. And it couldn't, goddammit — it was too good, too important. Our fates, our future, our lives were at stake. It was bigger, more important than my petty fears, my private terrors, my safety, really. It just *had* to be done. And I was elected. I hated it. I was a man of peace, dammit, and here comes trouble again . . . . Shit! Why did the gods insist on horsing me around? This couldn't be done without risking my bloody neck — if it could be done at all. I had to bypass the officers, the guards, in one shot. How? When the colonel inspected the camp, he began at the gate and made a full circle. He was surrounded by officers, guards and an interpreter, a slow, stately procession full of empty pomp and circumstance with guards clearing a path before him, haughty, arrogant, a fine nominee for Lord High Executioner. But this wasn't Mikado stuff, this man was uncomfortably real — a palpable Pooh-Bah who could mean it when he drew that long sword and sang:

> . . . *the short sharp shock*
> *from a cheap and chippy chopper*
> *on a big black block . . . .*

Would it be my head on the bloody black block?

I'd wait at the gate for him to leave — that would be the time and place. I planned the scene: I would step out before them, bow, salute, kowtow, a very picture of abject humility — *that* would be true enough — and respectfully request an audience, quickly getting in the idea of great promise and benefit, like a super salesman with one foot in the door. That would be the toughest moment. Once past that and into the details, I'd be home free. And, I foolishly reasoned, once he got the idea — well, greed, self-interest, logic would move him to see the light. Bound to. It couldn't miss! What a glorious victory! Of course it wouldn't happen overnight — he'd have to mull it over before it sank in. But the more he thought about it, the clearer it would become: lower the death rate, feed the scum pig feed, save rice and look like a benefactor. I saw it all unfolding before my starry eyes.

I told the others my plan. Some thought it fine, logical. As I expected, Tony took a dim view. Fat chance — I wouldn't get near Tokunaga in the first place. And if I did, he wouldn't listen. And if he did, he'd ignore me, and so on. And I'd be lucky to come away in one piece for daring to interfere. That didn't improve my sleep, but I had the bit in my teeth by now and there was no turning back.

For a few nights I rehearsed the details of my foray, screwing up my courage. Then I was ready — or as ready as I'd ever be. I knew if I delayed too long my blood would turn to water.

I made my way over to the gate and waited for the inspection party. Some of my friends followed at a distance. I couldn't chicken out now. I was shivering from head to toe as they drew nearer, suddenly afraid of my fright — afraid that I might faint dead away when the moment arrived. And it was drawing closer and closer now. The inspection was over, they were making for the gate . . . . Here it comes . . . . What if I goof? Will the words come out clearly in logical sequence, or will I gibber like an idiot? I could feel the words gathering, coagulating in a gummy lump on my tongue. The shouts of the guards sounded like battle cries in my ears. I watched their stomping boots raising dust as they struck the ground . . . I could feel them stomping on my skull as I fell . . . Tokunaga's sword whistling through the air . . . . *Let them pass, let them pass, let them pass*, my voices cried. *Don't be a loony!* This was some kind of hallucinatory stage entrance . . . . *Now!* I plunged forward in front of the group, half flying, half leaping, with my scalp pulling at my skull — saluting, bowing . . .bowing, saluting . . . .

"*Nanda!*" the colonel barked.

The column stopped in surprise, the guards leveled their bayonets and I pressed forward to the interpreter, saluting, bowing obsequiously. The officers gaped. "Excuse me, please! Important message for Colonel Tokunaga! Message of great benefit to the camp!"

The interpreter eyed me uneasily — one must be careful with lunatics. He turned to translate to Tokunaga, who grunted.

"What message?" The interpreter asked. *Over the hump!* I spoke at high speed, expecting to be cut off by a blow at any point, making it as short and simple as possible, trying to point out all the benefits. Tokunaga listened irritably, restively, scowling . . . till an angry wheeze gurgled up from his chest and he growled an order that must have meant: "Get rid of the stupid bastard."

I was brutally butted and shoved aside as the group resumed its progress. I was quivering with tension, feeling no pain — *did it!* God Almighty — and still in one piece! I turned away, swollen with relief and success. He had listened, damn his fat hide — he *did* listen! Drank it all in!

I walked slowly away, replaying my victory . . . got all the points in — great. Yet . . . did it sink in? Did we really win? Only time would answer that. Let him think about it — he's bound to see reason, he's not an idiot . . . .

No, he was not an idiot. He knew he could make a profit by selling our rice on the black market, and no harebrained scheme about pig feed would be allowed to impede that little enterprise. There wasn't a hope in hell of influencing Tokunaga, and the self-deluding brainstorm conceived in my fevered dream world should never have been allowed to see the light of day. That is not the way of the world.

Chapter Nine

MONTHS PASSED. THE camp grew more crowded with new arrivals. Hong Kong Volunteers were a great boon to the camp — civilians from all walks of life, including old China hands, professors, students. They had knowledge, experience to share. Classes were set up. I tried studying Chinese but gave it up. I took Chinese history — that was better. We sat, paper and pencil in hand, weak and emaciated, probably the world's hungriest students, filling our minds as we tried forgetting our empty bellies.

I made new friends among the Volunteers. It was here I met Shura, Mike and Henkin, three students — of Russian-Jewish parents, like my own — from the university of Hong Kong, studying medicine and engineering. They were born in China and spoke Chinese and Russian in addition to English. Their parents had fled the revolution in Russia and settled in Harbin and Shanghai. Shura was a poet of rare charm and a delightful raconteur. He had had a Chinese amah to raise him, and he regaled me with accounts of discovering ancient dust-laden tombs and mummies while playing with friends, of going to exclusive Chinese houses of pleasure frequented by the rich sons of high families, where the courtesans had to be courted to win their favors. Later he studied at a Chinese university.

Shura was an oasis, a kindred spirit. My mind revived in his company. He was well versed in philosophy, my special interest, and we could take off on the loftiest themes: how Nietzschean amorality had degenerated into Nazi gibberish, how Hegelian dialectics had led to communism. He recited reams of Chinese poetry, translating as he went. He had a much-valued talent for inducing total forgetfulness.

And there was more and more that needed forgetting. Illness and death increased. Johnny Little was dying in the dysentery ward. He and Erny Dayton were two of the four operators who had been left behind at Wong Nei Chong Gap when Matthews told us to get away. Matthews was supposed to have stayed with his men, but he had gotten out fast. When they were overrun and trapped, Little had joined eleven others in a desperate escape through a storm of bullets. Johnny and four others got through. They reached a machine gun, held off attackers till nightfall, then slipped through enemy lines to safety. Valor worthy of a medal, but Matthews wanted to forget it all. Johnny now couldn't stomach plain rice without flavor, and we passed the hat to raise two yen to buy a small tin of jam from the officers' canteen. They were now receiving Japanese officers' pay and had many goodies there. A few spoonfuls of jam to flavor Johnny's rice made it edible and kept him alive. We did this twice but our money ran out and I tackled Matthews for a contribution. Two yen was peanuts to him on his high pay. He was about to consent when he asked who it was for.

"Johnny Little," I said. "The one who made that daring escape from Wong Nei Chong — remember?"

"Oh." He squirmed. Johnny was a living witness he could do without. "I'm afraid I can't help," he said shakily.

"Oh, come *on!* You get what — twenty-five bloody yen a week? You can spare a couple to save a man's life!"

"Our funds are tied up in a canteen fund — um — and a mess fund and I just don't have anything extra to spare . . . . Sorry."

"So am I."

I left empty-handed. That was my last source and there was no more jam for Johnny Little. In about a week he was dead. A makeshift box, a makeshift grave . . . gone, with no family to notify, no one to know. Death here had its own plane of horror. No real mourning — a willed forgetting. Even thinking of it was devastating. You placed one foot before the other and didn't look back.

Shortly after that I was strolling with Matthews on the parade ground. He had pangs of conscience.

"I don't suppose the boys like me very much," he said.

"No," I agreed. "I don't suppose they do."

"But *why?*"

No point saying, "Because you're such a miserable shit." Couldn't change that anyway . . . once a prick, always a prick. I merely shrugged. Conscience? A bit late for that. Johnny was dead. Was a faint breeze of remorse filtering into that mass of jelly?

"I . . . *want* them to like me," he said plaintively.

"Well," I said, "you have a funny way of going about it."

"What should I do?"

"I don't know." What could I say — stop being you?

"I mean — I really *had* no money . . . . It isn't as though I've done anything wrong."

"Oh?"

"They just don't understand."

He was hurt. I was baffled. This man always managed to justify his actions by some kind of inspired legerdemain and came up smelling like a rose — in his own eyes. A common talent, I suppose. Again I fought my unhealthy brew of emotions — disgust, pity, resentment, together with the ever-present indebtedness that dogged me — and reminded myself that this sonofabitch had saved my life.

I walked away in a state of befuddlement . . . one more chapter in the human comedy.

Weeks passed. The Indians were removed to a camp of their own. The Volunteers were moved to Sham Shui Po, and with them went a large slice of richness and color. Classes ended. Free time disappeared. Malnutrition diseases increased everywhere and diphtheria showed up. The Canadians sank into a bog of gloom and monotony. Three cases of cholera appeared, with two men dying of it, but it was kept a close secret because the doctors feared the Japanese might exterminate us all to prevent its spread.

In September we too moved to Sham Shui Po, our first home, once a proud symbol of power and glory, now a sorry, decrepit-looking boneyard with doors, windows, even window frames stripped away and replaced by patched boards and packing. Still we welcomed the move: it was spacious, with its broad avenues and white cement huts. At a distance one could half close one's eyes and catch an echo of former splendor.

There were Middlesex here, Royal Scots, Volunteers, Russians. I looked up Shura again with his two pals and had a happy reunion. They were quartered in a small hut full of Russians.

With thousands crowded into the huts, disease flourished. It seemed doubly treacherous, the way it lurked behind this stately facade, reaching invisible fingers into the huts, marking this man and that for death. There was no serum, no defense against diphtheria, which reached epidemic proportions. The death toll rose ominously. At first makeshift coffins were built of odd boards. Burying parties left each day for the graveyard nearby. As deaths increased there were no boards left and the corpses were carried on stretchers and laid unprotected in their graves. Thirty-one Canadians died in October. The sick lay crowded in a rundown hospital hut. Without serum the doctors could do nothing but watch men die. Although Lieutenant Saito, the medical officer in charge of all camps, was irritated by the death toll, he did nothing. All serum had been shipped to Japan. As an inspiration he beat the doctors and staff for their negligence, but that seemed to have no curative power.

This was a new enemy, invisible, merciless. We moved in an atmosphere of fear and danger. It could be hovering at your side or attacking you as you spoke to a friend.

The man who slept beside me fell ill and died. Others around me died. I thought of the plague in the Middle Ages. I was spared by a lucky fluke: I had had a severe case of diphtheria as a child and probably was immune. Again, someone up there liked me.

Kai Tak Airport took its toll too, increasing its demands for labor. We rose in darkness at 4:30 a.m., groggily ate our bowl of rice, then lined up for the endless confusion of counting heads in the dark. At dawn we crowded onto a ferry, sitting or lying across one another as we caught a precious half-hour's sleep before facing the dreary interminable day of sweating in the sun. We returned to camp at 8:00 p.m., in darkness. Exhaustion and hunger led to more deaths. We seemed beset by faceless vampires sucking out our life's blood. Morale sank to its lowest ebb.

One morning we left the ferry as usual to walk to Kai Tak. This was the worst time, with the whole day ahead of us. Wordlessly the Canadians dragged their emaciated frames down the road in a straggling group, faces fixed in permanent grimaces of fatigue and misery. Some limped, some were carried on stretchers to fill the bureaucratic quota. We walked as slowly as possible, prodded by the guards like reluctant cattle. My ear caught the sound of singing up ahead. *Singing?* I perked up, pushing forward to the front of the line. A group of Russians was marching ahead of us, marching in step, singing with verve, loud and clear, a rousing march that lifted my spirits. Incredible! They were as thin and haggard as the others, but here were men actually enjoying themselves! They were as low on the totem pole as us, yet somehow they had created a life force that charged the air about them with joyous energy. Now *there* was morale, dammit. I felt drawn to them like a plant to the sun. I couldn't understand the words but I didn't have to. We will live, their spirit sang, to love and laugh and drink one day when these dark days are past. If only *we* could sing and march like that — how different the day ahead would look.

That night when I visited Shura I asked about the singing. Yes, they sang everything: old Gypsy songs, old classics like "Volga Boatman," new Red Army songs. They had a fine choir, four-part harmony, and practiced on days off. They called over the choir leader, Jan Solecki, a handsome Polish student, educated in Russian. I felt the zest and optimism bubbling out of this man.

"Can I join your choir?" I asked him on impulse.

"Why not? Do you know Russian?"

"No, but I can memorize the words."

"Fine, I'll teach you."

"Can I bring a couple of friends? They're good." Blacky had a fine bass and Bob Warren had a special talent for music.

"The more the merrier!"

This choir was to open a new dimension in our lives. The spirit and high morale were manna to us. There were barrel-chested sailors, White Russian emigrés, Volunteers, all with music in their bones. We performed around the camp in the sick wards, watching stricken faces light up as we belted out our songs with infectious enthusiasm. The Russian words didn't matter; the spirit of song made its own transcendent language. Sounds, melodies, rhythms spoke of life and joy and found eager response in the rapt listeners. Our voices arrived like trumpets, blowing down walls and ceilings, lifting suffering souls to the heavens, defeating pain. I felt this power as we sang, this joining of ourselves to the others and to these gaunt faces, this giving and receiving.

But there were places we could not, should not, penetrate. Areas of the dysentery ward where our sound, with its gaiety, its verve, seemed a disturbance, a desecration. Where men moaned and wrestled with demons . . . where God didn't venture. Men there lay in the last stages, in total neglect, abandoned by orderlies whose interest was with the living — why waste time and energy on the ones who were too far gone? Too weak to rise, they lay reeking and rotting, covered in shit, crawling with lice, the living dead, some with barely enough energy to weep, though weep they did.

But Jan Solecki reached them in his own way. Not through song, as I later learned, but through giving of himself to them, in a way I knew I never could. What he did made any meager altruistic ventures of my own pale by comparison.

Entering these dismal alleyways of hell, no one could come away unaffected. The sights roused guilt, among other things, at being so hatefully, insultingly alive and healthy. But Jan was not one for useless introspection — he was a man of action and optimism. One didn't walk away from a problem of haunting guilt, one met it head on. Joined by a friend, George Yaholkovsky, they approached the head doctor, Colonel Ashton-Rose, a physician in the Indian army, and volunteered to help in the dysentery ward with no pay. The colonel snorted with surprised approval, accustomed as he was to haranguing lazy RAMC orderlies. He himself was a colorful, abrasive character who made enemies by stepping on toes and who tackled the Japanese fearlessly. He was an imposing figure with a dark, handsome Indian head, silvered at the temples, and a huge black handlebar mustache. The Japanese respected him and granted many requests that otherwise would never be filled. He berated guards who interfered in the "hospital" and on one occasion slapped one for trying to trade for the watch of a patient who was too sick to think. We expected him to be shot for it, but the incident was ignored. He did, in fact, save more lives than all the other doctors combined. Now he gruffly promised Jan he would get anything he needed. Jan asked for soap, a tub for boiling water and disinfectant.

They came to the dysentery ward each day, pushed their way through the thick stench, selected the worst-looking patient and set to work. First they carried him outside in the warm sun, stripped away his fouled clothes and tossed them into the boiling water. Then they scrubbed the crusted shit and corruption from head to toe — ears, armpits, feet, hair, under the testicles where the shit was glued in layers — scrubbed and scraped with rags and fingers, nearly drawing blood, till all the skin shone pink and fresh and glowing. A glimmer of light crept into the dead eyes, wary, beaten-dog eyes at first, then filling with confusion and disbelief. The soiled clothes were ridden with lice and many parts of the underwear were white with thick patches of lice eggs. They scrubbed the clothes with disinfectant and boiled them. Then they washed all the bedclothes, the filthy sheet and blanket, and took out the black iron bed with no mattress and attacked the bedbugs with disinfectant. They laid the patient in the sun to dry, gently placing towels over him to avoid sunburn, pampering him and handling him like a porcelain doll. Needless to say, he must have felt he was dreaming, after so much brutal disinterest. Then, while he rested, they went in to get the next patient. In the course of the day, they gave two or three men this elaborate treatment.

It was only with prodding that I was offered these details. I listened with a growing sense of envious wonder and awe. I knew I could never do that. "How did they react?" I asked. "What did they say?"

"Hah!" Jan grinned with unalloyed enjoyment at the thought, as though recalling a fine meal. "The faces, the faces! They looked years younger. We carried them back to their clean beds — shaved, shampooed, so relaxed, so happy, so peaceful — amazing. They didn't know what to say — what could they say? Some cried, some kissed our hands — the look in their eyes, in their faces, was reward in itself."

They returned every day for a month till we had to go out on work parties to Kai Tak.

I thought of that ward, that terrible stench, that cesspool of shit and filth where innocents were condemned to molder and die, alone, in criminal neglect, and fade into oblivion . . . . And then I considered this act of — what? Love? So out of its element? Where did it come from? Imposing itself, asserting itself, in the middle of all the ugliness, violence, sadism, dog-eat-dog jungle law. Yes, it was all here, in man — everything. The depths, the heights . . . for us to witness, to absorb. All possible.

The greatest event in this period was the first mail. For months our families had had no word from Hong Kong. They were left in limbo to wonder, hope, pray. Was he alive? Missing, wounded, dead? No one knew. For months my mother kept my photo under her pillow as though her very physical warmth could breath life into the image, willing and praying for my safety. It was half a year before any casualty lists were received — nine months before a letter reached me. By this time, many listed as alive were dead. And I was luckier than some. Larry Dowling, a fellow operator, was listed as missing in action, by mistake, and his family had to live with that. Wally Normand's parents had no word from him for several years.

I gazed at this wondrous rectangle of paper with my name on it in a familiar hand. Contact! There really was a living world out there, loved ones rooting for me. This paper had actually been in my home in Montreal! It had been touched, handled, folded by loving, compassionate hands. I wanted to kiss the envelope. Touching it was touching them, an invisible embrace, a reunion, a banishing of all the grime and horror and ugliness. I was home. Safe . . . clean . . . full. What had they been feeling? It must be a kind of torture I didn't know. I knew all along that I was alive, but they didn't. What agonies of uncertainty they must have suffered.

I opened the letter with trembling fingers and stared uncomprehendingly at the first sentence: "We were overjoyed to know you are a prisoner of war." Overjoyed! There I sat — in shit up to the eyeballs, half dead, crawling with lice, exhausted, starved, disease ridden, jolted by electric feet, a bloody walking skeleton — and they were overjoyed? Had they all gone balmy? It took a while to see it their way.

I cherished that letter like a good-luck talisman. Banal phrases, ordinary news of everyday life. I sucked up the life-affirming images of real and civilized people doing the make-believe things I dreamed of. Here was proof that it was all truly happening, all possible. *Someone* at least was living this way and this knowledge enriched me, gave my own circumstances new meaning and purpose. In the months following, I read it again and again, over and over, to retain the secret tenuous thread that still bound me to a dimming reality.

At last a little serum came in via the black market, and the doctors had to choose who was to receive it. They were forced to play God, pronouncing life to some, death to others. Lieutenant Saito refused to allow any sick men to go to Bowen Road Hospital, but eventually he had difficulty explaining to Tokyo why there were so many deaths from "laryngeal croup." Tokyo had very little idea of what went on in these faraway places. By the time Saito made up his mind to bring the epidemic to a close, 130 Canadians had gone to their graves. But he was more army man than doctor and was only behaving in standard army style. Prisoners, after all, were beneath contempt and should have died in battle with honor anyway. In fact it was an honor to die at *any* time — illness offered a fresh chance — so what were these stupid whites complaining for? Disgusting creatures . . . let 'em rot.

A fresh curse to be visited upon us was "hot feet," a form of beri-beri that made the bottoms of the feet burn like hell's fires. Men soaked their feet in water for relief, but this led to secondary infection. They walked as though tiptoeing over hot coals. Only good food could cure all this but since there was no such hope, the prospects looked grim. A few Volunteers got parcels from families or friends in Hong Kong, but for us there were no extras to be had.

In Sham Shui Po the roll call was a big affair with lots of hoopla. A Japanese inspection party made the rounds and received the count from the officer of each unit — in our case, Matthews. This close contact with the enemy always had a traumatic effect on him. It was a spectacle. Most of us despised him but I was embarrassed for him. I felt pity, of course, not being a stranger to fright myself. But in this case it was too much. He would go rigid, all trembling and quaking, and work himself into a state of near hysteria as they drew near. He merely had to call us to attention as they approached, then turn, salute and present the numbers. Simple enough — but not to Matthews. His "Parade! 'Shun!" came out as a shriek of pure terror. His report was a mess of broken screaming sounds as he shivered and palpitated. Blacky, who always referred to him flatteringly as "dat big tub of shit," would shake his head sadly with an *"Oh mon Dieu,"* or an irritable growl of *"Ferme ta grande gueule, grand plein de marde."*

The Japanese eyed Matthews as though he were a madman. And he was, for a moment, living the horrors of his private, invented hell.

One day as they left, I tried to ease the tension with a satirical comment on the scene, which drew a guffaw from the others.

Matthews, still in a tizzy, decided we were laughing at *him* and chose to assert his authority.

"Very funny, Allister. One day on honey-buckets. Laugh that off."

That was a horror — no laughing matter.

"Oh goody," I shot back angrily, trying to blunt his sadistic little victory. "At the going down of each honey-bucket I shall remember you."

This drew another titter at his expense, which spurred him to greater heights of wittiness.

"We'll make it three days then, shall we, since you like it so much."

There was silence. The bastard. That was vicious. Everyone knew what one day on the dysentery pails entailed. He smiled, pleased at having bested me in our little repartee. I chafed. In a way this teacher-pupil relationship we had fallen into reminded me of my Baron Byng High School days, where the daily sport lay in baiting our teachers, a collection of weird eccentrics who made each day a lark. But this was no schoolboy stuff. This was playing for keeps. Honey-bucket duty was the worst job in camp.

I reported for duty next morning at the latrines. The stench was ghastly. The three-foot-high buckets were full and covered in flies, brimming with fetid dysentery mucus. My senses reeled as I gazed into this noxious soup of corruption. This was not feces, not excrement, it was Shit, a sickening reddish-brown, bloody from tortured entrails and floating in piss. We hoisted the buckets onto a crude cart. When it was loaded, we pulled and pushed the cart a half-mile over uneven bumpy ground to the sea wall. With each jolt of the cart the liquid contents would slosh over the edges and splash onto the cart, spraying our hands and faces and clothes. At the sea wall we dumped the contents into the wind. Then we trundled the cart back to the next outhouse.

This was repeated all day until all the toilets were emptied. By the end of the day I felt I'd had an excremental bath, leaving enough turd residue in my nostrils to flavor all my supper. Next day the toilets were full again, the flies, the pails, the mephitic blood and pus, all there awaiting my tender ministrations. After three days on the honey-buckets, I felt my soul submerged beyond recall in some evil-smelling fecal quicksand.

Dear Matthews . . . the sonofabitch who saved my life. Forgive them, Father . . . .

One day, a dark day, a new interpreter arrived. He spoke English fluently, with all the vernacular, having been born and raised in Kamloops, B.C. The Canadians welcomed him with open arms, feeling that his arrival heralded a new period of greater rapport and understanding. What we got was an education in race relations. The Kamloops Kid, as he was dubbed, was a monster, driven mad somehow, somewhere. Mad with hate for all things white and Canadian. His craving for vengeance was awesome.

"The Japanese flag," he told us, with venomous delight, "will soon be flying over Ottawa. All Canadians will be slaves as you are now! Your mothers will be killed. Your wives and sisters will be raped by our soldiers, and anyone resisting will be shot!" He raved on and on, painting lurid pictures of mayhem and destruction for our future and our loved ones, working himself into a sadistic frenzy.

His punishments were swift and murderous and brought into play at the flimsiest excuse. We were totally at his mercy. He was a being fulfilling himself, attaining rare orgasmic happiness. What, I wondered, had they done to this man in Kamloops? I conjured up visions of a timid child, isolated, insulted, jeered at, beaten up on the way to school. As it turned out, I wasn't far wrong. Sometimes he was almost friendly. Some nostalgic part of him craved our company — a dichotomy, torn. After all, he was born and bred in Canada, he probably couldn't feel at home in Japan — maybe he didn't even speak the language properly. He had the classical angst of the expatriate.

We enjoyed, in an odd way, the sight of a fellow Canadian, free and well fed. His boots were beautifully polished and he smelled of clean, strong soap — perfume to me. Slender and sleek, he fascinated me and drew me with the hypnotic power of a handsome, magical boa constrictor. His face was soft, smooth, his features delicate. I could see him as a boy, adored and nurtured by doting parents as their pride, their graceful flower, a fine student, as they saved up to send him to Japan to study his roots — except for this darkness, this blight, this fatal virus that poisoned his blood and doomed him to an early death. I felt for him: trapped in an alien culture, cursed, never to find peace, knowing he was hated on our side, probably unaccepted by the other. In his depths he still sought acceptance but his lust for revenge always won out.

"They called me a dirty yellow Jap," he confided to us one day. "When I was ten, they invited all the other kids to a party, but not the little yellow bastard — he wasn't good enough. Beat the shit outta the little rat, that's all he was good for, a fuckin' punchin' bag!"

Silence. What answer could we offer? Apology? It was all done. The deeds, the sins piled high, tallied somewhere, the debts accrued. All done and not to be undone, the psyche slashed, scarred, mangled beyond recall. Now the bill had arrived for us to pay, and pay we did.

It was all new to me. Was this how other Japanese children fared on the West Coast? How loyal could they be expected to be? At the outbreak of the war, he had leaped at the chance to join the Japanese Army. Now he could exact revenge at last. He was ready to kill, maim, destroy everything in his path. After the war he was hanged for his war crimes. A life gone full circle. It was a sentence we were, in a way, pronouncing on ourselves, destroying our own Frankenstein creation.

One memorable day he found all the excuse he needed. It was one of the strangest days of our prison life. Truckloads of shiny new sports equipment came zooming into camp one morning. Baseball gloves, bats, balls, boxing gloves, sports togs. Ration trucks arrived with meat and other exotic food supplies. Crews set up a baseball diamond on the parade square. We were ordered to clean up, shave, organize teams, sports squads. The Agony Ward was cordoned off with barbed wire to look as though it was outside the camp.

The mystery was soon solved. That afternoon a party of Red Cross officials arrived to inspect the camp — our first living contact with the outside world. We were full of cautious optimism. At least we were not forgotten! Apparently stories of this "hellhole of the Pacific" had finally gotten out. Tokyo had bowed to international pressure.

Emaciated prisoners donned boxing gloves that felt too heavy to lift and were ordered to swing them at each other under threat of dire reprisal. Baseball players, their bony shapes swathed in bright new jerseys and shorts, were set in motion hitting and chasing a ball. Volleyball teams seemed to be having a fun day at a holiday resort as the party passed. The inspecting party was accompanied by our officers, who were warned by Kamloops to keep their mouths shut. He would do all the talking, thank you, and God help anyone who dared utter a false note. Good health, happy games, jolly sports, general contentment all around. A heartwarming picture to take back to the outside world and silence all the malicious calumnies circulated to give Japan a bad name. Shame on those nitpickers.

Captain Norris, a Grenadier officer in the party, was jockeying closer to the Red Cross officials as they walked. He was hoping for an opening, an unguarded moment when Kamloops's attention was diverted, to whisper the truth in an official ear, to explode the whole charade by telling him to look at the Agony Ward. But Kamloops was, as we knew, crazy but not stupid, and he stayed glued to the officials throughout the afternoon.

The day wore on, the inspection drew to a close. The officials were completely taken in. Captain Norris chafed at the bit. If only, if only . . . it was all so tantalizingly close. How tragic, after all the effort, to send them away in ignorance. No, he couldn't let it pass, come what may. He stepped over to the head official and said: "This is all a fake! The prisoners are dying of disease and starvation. There's the hospital — behind those barbed wires. See for yourself!"

Kamloops went livid with fury. "That's a stinking lie!" he snarled. "You saw the camp — they get the best treatment!"

The Swiss official stared at them, astonished. "I insist on seeing that hospital," he snapped.

There was no avoiding it now. In the uneasy stillness the barbed wire was removed and the group entered the Agony Ward. The Red Cross officials stared about them in shock at a scene we knew too well. Nothing had been prepared for the visit here. Prisoners crowded the floor, lying in pools of their own reeking dysentery shit, staring up at the party out of dark, hollow eye sockets. The open buckets, the airless stench was staggering to the cleanly laundered spectators. Other cadavers sat on the floor, madness staring out of their eyes, rocking and moaning with the pain of "electric feet." Kamloops was silent, swallowing bile. The official turned angrily on the Japanese officers.

"This is scandalous!" he fumed. "We intend to report these shocking conditions to the International Commission and send a formal complaint to the Japanese government!"

The party left the camp.

The sports equipment was removed. The rations and meat were loaded up and driven away. All returned to drab normality. But there was an air of immense satisfaction in camp. I could taste it . . . at last the world would know. We were no longer forsaken. But with the calm came a strong if subdued tension, palpable, as before a storm. We knew Kamloops. And we knew there would be a price. We waited.

We were not kept waiting long. We lined up for our daily roll call with Kamloops joining — stalking — the inspection party. Captain Norris was on duty, taking the count. We eyed him with new respect. He had done this deed for all of us. It took remarkable guts. When he reported all present, Kamloops took exception to his numbers and accused him of lying and sabotage. We listened as he worked himself into one of his hysterical rages, seldom far from the surface, then leaped at Norris and knocked him to the ground. The beating began: kicking, pounding the silent figure on the ground, shrieking with each blow. We stood at attention, lined up, silently, helplessly watching as it continued, on and on. He would not stop. Norris must be unconscious by now. Would he kill him? We felt the blows as though they were our own bodies. Red Barlowe couldn't stand it any longer — cheery, clowning, happy-go-lucky Barlowe suddenly yelled: "You goddam murderer!"

We jumped on him and shut him up, wanting no new victims.

We were dismissed at last, with the limp body left lying on the parade ground. Later he was carried to the hospital and revived. Norris didn't die but was never the same . . . a quiet, slow-moving figure limping along with a cane for the rest of his time.

In December work at the airport was stopped and we had time on our hands again. More men grew sick. The death toll mounted. Blacky's "electric feet" grew worse and he went downhill alarmingly. Walking had become an ordeal. He refused to be removed to the Agony Ward, where he could be looked after. I did what I could for him, fetching and carrying, but I couldn't relieve his pain. He spoke little, living enclosed in his own narrow universe of agony. It shut out talk, food, friendship — all were irrelevancies interfering with the total concentration on pain. Pain sat beside him, a malevolent presence, jealous of any spurt of energy, any pleasant thought come to challenge it.

He grew thinner each day. The proud muscles were gone. The meat left his bones and I watched in dismay as he gradually acquired the blank, dull, faraway look of Agony Ward inmates, a non-caring, introverted look that made me afraid. When a man gave up he was finished. He ate without appetite. But he did cling tenaciously to his routines, forcing himself to walk. All night he rocked silently beside me on his bed space. I felt guilty going to sleep so easily. Every third day he would fall into a heavy sleep, a stupor of exhaustion, with the shocks jolting his feet as he groaned in his sleep.

I sat beside him helplessly, thinking of the pride he had once taken in his body, of his graphic descriptions of Saturday-night fights at the dance hall in Ville Emarde . . . . *Poof! paff! pam!* Girls screaming and jumping on tables, fists and chairs flying . . . he reveled in it all. Or working for "the Bell," repairing lines in a driving sleet storm, climbing a pole in the face of a screaming wind, testing his manhood — that was *living*. What a peculiar combination of gentleness and strength, of quick humor and deep warmth. Only a few months back he had composed a haunting song, an exotic Arabic melody full of desert mystery, to which he added lyrics.

I glanced at his empty pipe, filled so often with his beloved Alouette tobacco, as it was on the train from Debert. Nothing to fill it now. I thought of his stopping a fight at North Point — two weakened prisoners, driven by hunger to anger and violence, ready to spend their strength stupidly in fighting — how Blacky's large paws had grabbed both by the scruff of the neck as he said in his deep basso: "Anybody wants to fight can fight *me*." I thought of the times I had needed his protection in sticky army situations — no one tangled with Blacky. Now *I* was looking after *him*. I pondered the strange but powerful bond between us. Two people who would never meet in normal times had now grown to be virtually blood brothers.

One day we were lined up for rations to arrive. The talk turned to feats of physical prowess we had seen and done. I described how Blacky used to place his hands and feet on four chairs, lowering his body between them, to do seventy-five pushups. Blacky listened sadly. The contrast was too glaring to all of us. Something — pride, anger, defiance — stirred in his breast.

"I'm not dead yet," he growled. I was silent. "I could still put you down," he added. "Want to wrestle me?"

I looked at him wonderingly. Wrestle? In his state? What was he trying to prove? I sensed a tragic, irrational desire to recapture his old physical supremacy over me, his protégé, his weak and fragile artist pal — to banish the present in one dramatic action before all these bystanders who knew and respected him. Was he jealous of my health? Or was it that he couldn't bear his own public image and needed to wipe it out? I refused, pretending, as of old, that I was too chicken to accept. This only goaded him on. He swung his mess tin at me, hitting my arm.

"Come on, fight!" he insisted.

I shook my head, backing away. He swung again. Now we were in front of the line of watching men. Color came to his cheeks and I saw a wild battle light in his eyes as he advanced. He had to continue. Let 'em watch — he'd show them all the stuff he was made of. He struck me again, a painful blow. I backed up, with him following. I felt his hurt, his need. He was lashing out at a healthy man — a lucky man — at all the unjust fates that had robbed and cheated him of his precious manhood. He swung again, without thought.

"You're chicken!"

"You're right!"

My arm was paining. He didn't realize how that steel mess tin could hurt. He was not rational any longer — he couldn't really see me or know me as he charged forward, lashing out fiercely with his last strength. The blows were marking my arms. This was crazy. "Hey — cut it out!"

"Come on!" He was a force again, striking fear into those around him. He was back in a dream past with an opponent backing away for dear life — affirming his old power over life around him. I debated stopping him, putting him down easily. But the humiliation, in front of all these men would be the last straw, a death blow to all he held dear — I had to spare him that. I backed away quickly, fending off the blows with my sore arms until we rounded the end of the hut out of sight of watching eyes. Alone, I grappled with him and put him down on the ground. With a pang of sorrow I noted how easily his poor wasted body succumbed. He felt weak as a kitten in my arms. The effort and the struggle left him limp and exhausted. I lifted this sack of bones with its wounded soul. Leaning on my arm he limped back, returning to the ugly reality of the present.

Going back with our rations, Buddy Dicks walked beside me. "What was all that in honor of?" he asked. "He wasn't kidding around."

"No."

"He was hurting you — I thought he was your pal."

I nodded sadly. "He is," I said.

Shura and company were of the lucky few whose families kept them supplied with food and money. Their shelves were stocked with mouth-watering goodies — cornflakes, cocoa, milk, canned goods. They bought eggs and other foodstuffs from camp traders and ate like pashas. This attracted many eager "friends" who hung around for handouts. To avoid any suspicion of this I decided, painfully, to refuse all discreetly offered leftovers. They must have discussed my diffidence and decided to get around it by a formal invitation.

"We want you to join us for Christmas dinner," Shura announced, "and bring a friend, okay?"

Well, that was different, and I was happy to accept. I hurried off to tell Bob. Blacky was too far gone for any social interchange. He could barely walk or eat and lived in silence. Bob and I counted the days.

On Christmas Day we arrived to find they had been preparing for hours. We drank a toast of sake to our freedom: "May we all be free, in '43!"

O happy day! Succulent dishes flavored with exotic spices were trotted out one after another — *as much as we wanted* of each! After twelve months of musty flavorless rice, tasting of sacking and filled with white worms and mouse turds, this was too impossible to believe. Each glass of sake seemed to banish more scars of the year gone by. We were soon floating in a heavenly mist that was the only reality. I felt my growing pessimism receding like a dark forgotten cloud . . . . The world was no longer askew, it had somehow righted itself, become what it always should be . . . . God was back in His heaven. Blacky's misery wasn't really happening, the dysentery, the diphtheria, the skeletal bodies laid in their graves at the rate of five or six a day — it was all a horror film I'd seen somewhere, couldn't remember where. And hunger, that old intimate that never seemed to have left our side, pledged to stay forever, had retreated, bowed and disappeared through a side door, leaving us a vast banquet table stretching to infinity.

The Russians took delight in our delight. And our delight was boundless. They described the ingredients of each plate and the ingenuity used in the preparation. I almost pitied them their lack of the wolfish lust that drove us on, attacking each new gourmet marvel with unsated desire.

We sang lustily.

"*Sheruka strana maya rodnaya*" and all the other Russian songs we knew so well by now. Bob and I sang duets we had practiced: Spanish Civil War songs, English music-hall songs his father had taught him. And one that most fitted the occasion:

> *O de King of Babylon Balshazaar,*
> *Sat dere feastin' on his golden piazzer*
> *With his court and concubines*
> *Stuffin' in fried chicken and imported wines*
> *Mene mene tekel . . . .*

We sang and drank and ate till our bellies were bloated for the first time in a year — bloated to bursting. We gorged and gasped till we could go no further.

"But the desserts," they protested. "The best parts!"

"Yes, yes," I gurgled. "But I can't! Whew!"

"Hot chocolate and whipped cream?"

"Oh God." I longed for a gargantuan mouth and a bathtub belly.

"We'll eat it," Bob said resolutely. "Only let's take a breather."

Heads swimming with sake we staggered outside and lay full length on the ground, holding our tortured bellies and struggling for breath.

"I don't believe this."

"Gotta go back in there."

"Where the hell will we put it?"

"I don't give a shit if I vomit."

"Like the Romans. Eatin' and pukin' and eatin' — stuffin' in fried chicken and imported wines."

"Yeah, the fat fuckin' pigs."

"Thass us."

We began giggling. We couldn't stop. Strange peals of sacrilegious mirth shattered the air. They rose like joyous birds flying in the face of the dark brooding pall of death and suffering hanging over the huts. All the darkness was invisible now, banished to the past and future, as we lay caught and chosen by the bright rays of the sun, praying for the gods to stop time in its tracks and let this enchantment never end.

Chapter Ten

WE HAD LEARNED THE dialectic of rumors by now. The good ones faded, the bad ones came true. This one sounded bad: we were to be shipped to Japan. And, as feared, it turned out to be true. Two drafts of British prisoners had left in September. The last one, rumor had it, had been sunk. Now it was our turn.

We lined up for a fitness test — we must be able to work in Japan. We were each instructed to walk across the road. Those who made it were pronounced physically sound, A-1 category. Even Blacky, who dragged himself across with a cane, passed with honors.

We were told to pack our kits and prepare for departure. Japan . . . ? My imagination was awhirl with lurid images, anxieties, excitement and a dark amorphous dread that was overpowering. What did I know about Japan? *Madame Butterfly? The Mikado?* Dream imagery, fantasy. It couldn't be any worse, the optimists said. There was no future here, only more illness and death. At least a change held out hope — if we *get* there, the pessimists added. But this wouldn't be *Madame Butterfly* stuff. Japan was the land that had produced our guards, these brutal, sadistic fanatics who looked on death as a piece of cake. Here at least the dangers were familiar. And what about that persistent rumor — that the last draft was sunk by American subs that controlled the seas? Well, maybe it was just another story . . . .

Luckily, I couldn't know how accurate the pessimists were. The 1,800 men in the second September draft had been crammed into the holds of the *Lisbon Maru* under horrendous conditions. After four days, they were hit by a torpedo and the ship began to sink. Lieutenant Wada, the army officer in charge, ordered the 800 Japanese troops to abandon ship; he also gave orders to nail down the hatches holding the prisoners. The Japanese captain protested that they would suffocate or drown, but Wada told him the army was in command. The prisoners were then locked in the holds and left behind to drown. By the next day, conditions had become unbearable and water was bursting into the holds. They managed to break out in some places. In one hold, with water gushing in, men panicked and began climbing over one another, falling back down into the hold on top of others.

Those who reached the deck dove into the sea and swam toward the Japanese boats but they were shot at and turned back. Hundreds drowned. Some seized bits of wreckage and stayed afloat. Survivors later said how one man who spoke Chinese had made it to the rocky shore and persuaded nearby Chinese villagers to sail out and rescue 200 prisoners. They fed and clothed the survivors, but the Japanese arrived next day to recapture them. The prisoners were stripped, then loaded onto other boats. On one boat the prisoners were surprisingly well treated by the naval officers, who explained that they had been trained by the British Navy. The treatment quickly changed when the army took over. When the survivors finally reached Shanghai, they counted 843 men drowned or shot in the water.

These facts, which came out later, would not have given us much comfort as we were poured down into the holds of the *Tatuta Maru*. We noted that large red crosses were painted all over the ship — good idea — a technique much used by the Germans in transporting troops. The decks were crowded with Japanese soldiers wearing great eye-catching bandages on arms, legs, heads, with painted bright-red splotches to simulate a hospital ship full of wounded. We hoped for all our sakes that this would fool the soft-hearted Americans; it was one of many times we were to find ourselves rooting for the enemy.

As the men streamed down into the hold, it seemed to shrink. How in the world could this area, the size of a large room, hold 700 bodies? The answer was simple: it couldn't. These four airless steel walls with a bare steel floor became a giant sardine tin packed with living, squirming human creatures. There was nothing to do but take turns lying down and standing or sleeping in a sitting position. The heat rose. The air was soon foul. The food was pitifully meager. Tommy Marsh said this was what the slave ships out of Africa must have been like. We were allowed up to the upper hold to join a long line waiting to use the few toilets. We were lucky; in most of these "hell-ships," even this was forbidden; instead, buckets were handed down to be used and kept with the prisoners. In some there was no food or water and dozens died. One American survivor described how after several days, prisoners went mad with thirst and began attacking one another in the darkness, biting to draw blood and suck it up to slake their thirst. Most of these ships were torpedoed. Some took weeks and months to reach Japan.

My own imagination was working overtime, full of vivid turmoil. I thought I heard the thunderous crash of a direct hit, or water roaring into the hold, or men clawing one another in the mad struggle to get up the ladder. Even if I reached the deck, then what? I couldn't swim. I'd always had a nightmare fear of drowning. No life-belts, no boats, no raft — I'd have to cling to the ship till it went down, choking, clutching, suffocating in the water, screaming soundlessly for help with a throat full of salt water — what a ghastly way to go . . . . Who would ever know how I died? My family would have no word for months, maybe years — they were still "overjoyed to hear you are a prisoner of war." Well, at least they were spared knowing this . . . .

Being a congenital optimist in those days, I fought these grisly daydreams, pushing for a happy ending as I did, subconsciously, in ordinary daydreaming: finding a discarded life-belt that kept me afloat till all the Japanese boats had left . . . spotted in the water by an American destroyer and picked up . . . . They'd revive me, couldn't do enough for me — delousing, showers in hot soapy water, soft bed, clean sheets, wonderful food . . . admiring faces, friendly, sympathetic, warm. They'd radio home to my family and give them a real reason to be "overjoyed." I would be home in a few weeks!

I swung between the extremes of fear and hope as the days passed. True, I *was* only a speck of dust in a vast universe, but hell, I was part of it still, belonged to it, felt its weird and wonderful pulse in my veins . . . . I didn't want it to stop now.

The heat intensified, the air grew worse. We could only think and talk and wait. We didn't realize how lucky we were. No torpedoes. No one died. We had access to a latrine. We had a little food, a little air, and we made it in four days. Relatively speaking, we were blessed, though that's not how we would have described these horrendous conditions and the mental torment. There is little doubt that we were examined in the periscopes of U.S. subs. This was, after all, the main sea lane for Japan-bound cargo ships. Most ships traveled by night, creeping along the coastlines, resting in ports by day. Our ship, gambling on its Red Cross markings, sailed boldly by day in a direct line for Japan. It worked.

Toward the close of the fourth day we reached Nagasaki, a name well known to us in comic song, soon to become a tragic symbol. We disembarked and gazed about us. A cold, dark February day with a drizzle falling steadily, evenly, permanently, as though this were the nature of air here. The shoreline looked bleak, dismal, blurred as seen through dull murky lenses. The change was too sudden, too startling. After the furnace heat of the hold, the cold was an ugly shock, for one thing. After more than a year in the tropics, our blood had thinned and we huddled, miserable and forlorn, shivering in our thin clothing. In contrast to the packed darkness of the hold, the vast space itself was unnerving.

I saw some ghostly fishermen in boats, dressed in kimonos with huge designs on their backs, white cotton bands around their foreheads. They seemed denizens of another world. I stared at the dreary, rainy shore and was overwhelmed by a sensation of total defeat, of being stranded on an unknown planet. Nothing was familiar. Despair filtered into my bones like the descending rain. I felt threat. A shapeless cloud of foreboding hung suspended over the grayness. Never had I been so hopelessly distant, so cut off from life as I'd known it. Hong Kong had been British, with the conquerors as intruders. Here the transformation was total. Our entire identity was to be removed; we were now chattel slaves brought to an alien land with its alien culture, its alien language. There seemed no escape, no exit this side of the grave.

A tall Japanese officer with Imperial Guard soldiers was on hand to take charge. He asked to see the officer in command. Captain Reid came forward, a Canadian doctor, the only officer on board. He saluted the Japanese officer, who greeted him in excellent English. They shook hands. The Japanese stared.

"Reid? Reid? Can it be true? Don't you remember me?"

Reid gaped in astonishment. "Good God!" They had known each other, it turned out, in their student days at a Canadian university. They greeted each other effusively. A storybook encounter. The bystanders, watching joyfully, passed the word along. What a break!

The officer was fairly beaming. "What an odd place to meet," he said. "I'm to escort you. Is there anything you need? How can I help?" He was heaven sent.

Reid was not slow to answer. "The men are cold and hungry. They need food and clothing."

"I'll look after that." He gave swift orders in Japanese.

The news swept through our ranks like a warming breeze. Spirits rose hopefully. Some were cautious from sad experience.

"A Jap's a Jap. All we'll get is a so-sorry-please."

"No, this guy's different! Sounds like he means it!"

We waited in sorry-looking groups outside a train station, hopes fading with the light. At last some trucks pulled up. We watched incredulously as soldiers unloaded thick warm army greatcoats, and a cheer went up as they started issuing them quickly to all of us.

"Hey — this guy's a goddam angel of mercy!"

"I told you, ya dumb tit!"

We congratulated one another on our crazy luck. A good omen. I snuggled into my new overcoat — roomy, cozy — the first I'd had since mine was stolen at North Point. Now this was more like it! Maybe it wouldn't be so awful after all. If this was a sample of the treatment — Christ, who knows?

More trucks arrived as we crowded around. What now?

"Grub! It's grub, fellas!"

"What kind?"

"Buns, I think."

Yes, buns it was. But not of this world — a celestial miracle. A bonanza of large, wondrously fluffy buns, oval, half a foot long, of pure white flour covered with a thick sweetened crust, the first sweet thing in ages. We expected one per man and were startled to get *five*.

"*Five each!?* I don't believe it!"

"Can't be. Someone musta goofed."

"Eat 'em quick before they find out!"

We gobbled them down in a state of anxious ecstasy. It was no mistake. He actually *meant* us to have all five. Spirits soared. Was this land enchanted? There were gurgles and giggles and animated talk as we stuffed our faces with these succulent marvels. The rain stopped, as though in collusion with all these beneficent powers, and we gathered around a lamppost, snug in our spanking new coats, our full bellies singing with contentment.

It was a moment for song and Bob and I, caught up in the spirit, put on an impromptu concert using the now extensive repertoire we had practiced: Russian songs, army songs, show-biz songs, Cockney songs, Spanish songs:

> *Viva la Quince Brigada*
> *Rhumbala rhumbala rhumbala!*

Strange words and melodies filled the Nagasaki air.

> *I dreamt I was ticklin' my grandfather's balls*
> *Wiv a pint of 'ot oil and a feathah!*

We sang lustily under the streetlamps, sending great volleys of joy and energy up into the silent darkness, proclaiming our irrepressible right to exist, our hope revived. I felt transformed as I sang — an instrument giving vent to the collective craving around us. A grand arrival, grand welcome. For one night we were back with the human race.

We entrained that night, crowded into passenger seats where we slept on top of one another. Blinds were tightly closed. Imperial Guards stood at the doors. These were selected men, it seemed, not the surly, brutal types we had known from the regular army. They were taller, handsome men, pink-cheeked, well fed, well dressed and friendlier in disposition. They offered us cigarettes and chatted. They let us know we would be meeting some very bad men in the regular army — they were so right. We thanked them for the warning. That their type existed was surprising, heartening and, for me, confusing. The sign for war was forefingers bumping.

"War — bad — *domi-domi*, right?" They agreed. We, the common men, could get along quite well together, couldn't we? We wanted no part of the war.

"That's the ticket." I said. "You and us — friends — yes? Let's call the whole thing off."

During the day we peeked through the edges of the window

blinds to catch glimpses of a picturesque dreamlike countryside, peasants in cloaks and broad straw hats. I might have been leafing through the pages of *National Geographic*, but this was frighteningly real — there was no closing the book and settling back in the nice cozy school library. I felt menace and wonder and soft pain at the scenes flashing by . . . tiny rectangular fields and farm buildings that spoke of quietness and the slow steady labor of a world at peace. Strange longings stirred in my depths that day, to lie buried for decades.

We reached a station in Yokohama at what seemed to be the rush hour. I stared about me excitedly, hungrily, enviously. Hundreds of commuters scurried by on their way home to clean rooms, familiar, happy children, a quiet cozy supper, a newspaper and a leisurely cigarette. So close. How little they were aware of their own bliss, their own wondrous ordinariness as they went their precious way.

They stared at us as we barged in among them, a dirty, bedraggled crowd of strange, freakish giants, sickly, horse-faced, some with pale-yellow hair and light-blue eyes — the creatures visible on newspaper pages, here in the flesh! I felt enclosed in the cage of a zoo with a Japanese sign on the bar, describing a rare species of troglodytes, captured on a tropical island, locked in the hold of a ship and brought back alive. They gaped and we gaped back.

They moved at a half-running pace as they passed. Speed, zest, intensity — I felt an ocean of health and energy washing around us in contrast to our own weakened, slow-moving, disease-ravaged bodies, riddled with beri-beri, dysentery, pellagra. My fascinated glance fell on the women, some in colorful kimonos and sandles, tripping daintily out of a stage setting, almost singing "Three little maids from school are we." For a nostalgic moment I was back at the Y helping with the makeup backstage on all the chorus of pretty maidens in *The Mikado*, painting cheeks, slanting eyes, flirting, clowning, drunk with the smell of greasepaint and powder, listening to their sallies and titters — a faraway dream. But this was the real thing! Or was it? Which was the stuff of dreams? Wasn't this more incredible, more fantastic than Gilbert and Sullivan?

The Imperial Guards left, replaced by regular army, and the treatment changed. They prodded, cursed and bellowed. The civilians gave them a wide berth. This was our first astonished view of the public's reaction to the army: fear of their own soldiers? Actually it was a reflection of the traditional division that gave the samurai the right to cut down any offending commoner. Civilians were still civilians, army was army. We were to find this dichotomy commonplace in the days ahead.

We were herded onto another train, which took us to Kawasaki. There, with an officer on horseback leading, we were marched down a dirt road toward our new quarters. The area was ugly with industry and smoke and dirt. No pretty countryside here, not a blade of grass or a tree. We were led into a small compound between two long huts with dirt and coal cinders underfoot. This was Camp 3D, our home for the endless months to come. We were lined up in front of a table to hear a welcoming speech by our camp commandant, who stood on it with one hand resting ominously on the hilt of his sword. The speech was translated by Kondo, our interpreter, who could apply strange surgery to the English language.

The speech could not be called inspiring. Our new camp commandant, it seemed, was no psychological mastermind. He urged us to work diligently with a good heart. As an incentive he offered *severe punishment*. We eyed the sword. Since we were prisoners, he said, we forfeited all rights and now belonged to the Imperial Army. All orders must be obeyed or we would be severely punished. The reward for hard work would be lack of punishment. Punishment seemed to be the only game in town.

We were housed in the two long barn-like huts, built mostly of bamboo, with sliding doors at each end. Each hut had a wide center aisle, crossed by ten narrow aisles. There were no partitions. Each narrow aisle, or bay, held a long rickety table on which we marked our numbers for our rations. On either side of each bay was a sleeping platform raised a foot or so above the dirt floor, on which slept fourteen men. The platforms were made of *tatami* matting, divided by inch-wide wooden slats into sleeping spaces thirty-seven inches wide and seven feet long. A waist-high shelf ran along the back of the "beds." Each man was issued a bowl, four wood-fiber blankets that held no warmth, a small round hard pillow and a cotton bedsheet.

We spent the next four days cleaning the place and learning

Japanese army commands. From now on all orders and responses, including numbering off, would be in Japanese. We were eager students since any mistake brought *severe punishment*. We were given Japanese numbers, our new identities.

The rations were a cupful of rice and a cup of soup three times daily. About 900 calories: a fair enough ration by their standards — almost what the regular soldiers received. Only we were twice their size and needed twice as much. The civilians never believed we were starved, since we looked mountainous, wearing every stitch of clothing we owned to keep warm. Actually, although we called it rice, the ration was mostly barley, and a blessing, being unpolished with all the Vitamin B intact. Over the coming months, this was to reduce the dreaded "hot feet" and "electric feet."

We were issued tooth powder with bureaucratic zeal each month. We didn't know what to make of all this meticulous organization. Everything in Hong Kong had been slapdash, casual, anarchic. Here we seemed to be back in the army, with all the trimmings. But what an army — full of a thousand regulations, with beatings for any infringement.

Chapter Eleven

ON A COLD, RAINY FEBRUARY DAY we were marched two miles to the Nippon Kokan Shipyards, where we were to work. Our footwear, often worn-out tennis sneakers with no socks, was pitifully inadequate as we sloshed through icy puddles on the dirt road. We came through the gateway to the plant and were led into a large shed full of lunch tables and benches. We were divided into work gangs and handed over to civilian guards called *"fu*-men," for the letter *fu* on their armbands, which stood for *furyo*, prisoner. It was a word we came to know very well, meaning the lowest class on the social scale, the outcasts, pariahs, dishonored in their own land for not dying — what could be more shameful? Not only had we lost all face, we had lost the right to be considered human. And now we were about to take our place in this society.

We had been given forms to fill out, with a space for our civilian occupation. Ever the optimist, I wrote "librarian" and "painter." What library I expected to work at was a little hazy, but it was worth a try. As for "painter," I had used the wrong word, as I was to find to my sorrow — I wound up balancing on a thin plank suspended over the Pacific Ocean, painting the side of a ship.

We were issued cotton jackets and pants, our work clothes for the remainder of the war. They must have expected monsters, since all the clothing was so badly oversized we looked like walking tents. We rolled up the pant legs and sleeves. This was no fashion show, we gathered, but it was certainly a circus. The small men disappeared in a sea of cotton. Marching to work, four abreast, we were a wonderful sight to behold — straggling, bumbling, clumping along as though in time to some dissonant arrhythmic music. Japanese calligraphy — our numbers — adorned us front and back, with numbered ribbons hanging from our hats and waving like banners in the wind. We sailed along, a motley flotilla of gaunt-faced freaks in some tragicomic Oriental festival.

I was to be part of the paint gang, along with a dozen others. We compared notes. Tommy Marsh and a few others really *had* done decorating and housepainting. Others were farmers, miners and truck drivers. One had been in the Salvation Army. But now we were all painters. A small, neatly dressed man with an armband came over and bowed to us. This was Kondo-san, our foreman, a man who was to play an important role in my life. We looked him over. He had finely chiseled doll-like features, with wide full lips under a carefully trimmed mustache. He looked to be in his late thirties.

"*Peinto-ka?*"

"Painto-yeah, that's us."

He waved his hand at us, saying goodbye, and paused. Was he leaving? He'd just arrived. We waited. He waited. He waved again. We realized this see-ya-later motion, with palm down, meant "Come." Others learned this the hard way.

He took us to the paint shop, an iron shed stocked with paint materials. There was a stove and small lockers at one end and a tiny office at the other. The *ichiban*, the paint master, came out of his office and gazed at us through thick black spectacles. The zoo look again. We stared back, just as curious. He looked about forty-five but was actually over seventy. He wore a black jacket and khaki army pants, white socks in frayed but shiny shoes, a bow tie with polka dots and a straw boater out of Renoir. He bowed and saluted and we followed suit, not knowing we were expected to bow lower, as befitted our station. I liked this bowing routine, a thing of charm, of theater, of self-effacing good manners — or a reasonable facsimile at least. Be sincere, as the saying goes, whether you mean it or not. He questioned us in Japanese.

"Canada *heitai* [soldiers]," we said.

"*Kanada heitai-ka?*"

"Yup."

"*Sō-ka.*"

This called for another round of bows and salutes. He asked for our leader; Tommy stepped forward.

"*Watakushi gunso* [I am the sergeant]," he said, bowing.

"*Sō-ka.*" Another bow.

We were getting along swimmingly. Bowing was more fun than getting slapped. No shouts? No beatings? Politeness? We could stand a lot of that, but it would take some getting used to.

Actually we were entering an area of Japanese life that was closed to most POWs. In one leap we had bypassed the hated army and were for the first time touching the real body of the country — its people.

There were several interesting characters in the paint shop. There was the man whose clothes were made entirely of ragged patches — no hint of the original cloth, a walking rag rug. He was totally self-effacing, bowing constantly and too humble to speak to anyone. But at the end of the day he removed his rags and changed into a natty light jacket, bright pants, colorful socks, oxford shoes and a panama hat. His stance changed, his gait changed, he straightened up and strode jauntily through the gates, a romantic figure, a ladies' man.

Our general manager was an elderly "three-bander" — he wore three gold bands around his factory cap, each band denoting long years of service (Kondo-san wore two). This man belonged to an older generation, polite, formal, kindly, with an inner dignity at odds with this coarse, rough-and-ready environment. He kept his distance behind a gruff facade, but his high-principled sense of fairness shone through in dealing with us, and we all liked and respected him. He would invite us to warm up at the stove; if a guard looked in, he would order us away in a harsh voice until the guard left, then motion us to return. He was always a little ill at ease with us, and I realized later that this came from an overriding sense of shame. He disapproved of our treatment but didn't dare make waves.

One day I came down with my recurrent malaria. I reported sick to Captain Reid, but he had to send me out to work since the work quotas were too high. I was weak, feverish, miserable. I tried to work but grew worse. Kondo-san sent me back to the shop, where I explained to the three-bander that I was sick. He looked at my flushed face and nodded. He indicated I could quit work and go to the lunch hall to rest — *yasumi* — for the remainder of the day. What a relief. I thanked him and went off.

But the guards at the lunchroom took a dim view of such malingering foolery. I collected a few whacks across the face for my trouble and was booted out. When I told the three-bander, he was embarrassed but tried not to sound critical. A look of discomfort — sadness? — passed over his lined face. According to his tradition I was, in a way, a guest of his country, and the soldiers were bringing dishonor and shame by behaving so badly. He gruffly told me to follow him and led me to a small storeroom out of sight of passing guards. He felt my forehead with a paternal hand and said softly: "*Atsui-na* [hot]."

He told me to lie down on the bench there and try to sleep. He would wake me at the end of the day: "*Shigoto-nai* [no work today]."

I lay back, a mass of confusion. Compassion? Here? It had been so long. We had gradually steeled ourselves to expect nothing. A protective sheath of non-emotion. And with it came a draining away of fellow feeling, genuine sympathy for one another, an invisible hardening of the spiritual arteries. A defense — normal for survival, but a creeping evil, a silent destruction. With bitter sadness I thought of how much I'd changed. Where was the golden youth, that carefree clown who had once cavorted over the decks of the S.S. *Awatea*, who loved all life, all people? And where was the sober idealist, the wise counselor of North Point, the sympathetic listener to whom men brought their troubles? Now, in this dog-eat-dog existence, where was there room for any giving and receiving of compassion?

And here was this old man, this gentle, kindly spirit knocking on a closing door. Where did he come from? This country, this alien, hostile, menacing land had made him. He upset me, induced an unpleasant softening, a dissolving, an urge to weep. I could hug this man. And I could kill those soldiers. Was my view darkened and twisted?

Which was the true Japan?

Kondo-san, we realized later, had been carefully chosen as our boss, our *hancho*, because of his education. Though a ship's painter, he was considered of higher class, and he carried himself that way — nothing obvious, but a certain soft-spoken dignity and innate gentleness that dissolved all my defenses. He wore the standard puttees and rubber-soled split-toed shoes. His clothes were of flimsy, threadbare cotton but clean and neat. His eyes revealed his inner life: wary, eager, insatiate, with a hint of mischief behind their soft effeminate wisdom. There was a fear of the world in him — it was too harsh, too demanding — and this assignment was a spot of luck.

The most upsetting element was his tone of genuine respect. This was almost shocking; again I felt a conflict, as with the three-bander. No Japanese had ever spoken to me as an equal. Hatred, disgust, contempt, disinterest, cruelty — these were their stock in trade; I expected nothing else. I was comfortable behind my wall of solid anger, built brick by brick but now under attack. I had lived, after all, under the army heel. Every day they reinforced my revulsion — that couldn't change. Yet every day I mixed with people, too, spoke with Kondo-san as a friend, a warm, sensitive, concerned friend, as though no war existed. We spoke of life, family, literature. He was diffident at first, polite but cautious, as most Japanese are before they let their hair down.

Over the following weeks we were drawn to each other by a mutual respect and admiration. He had read, it turned out, translations of many authors. Aside from my Russian friends, he was the first man I'd met since entering the army who had read Maxim Gorky. He took delight in my clowning antics, and later we reached the point where we were rehearsing comic routines together. Gradually he established the habit of giving us the day's news during our fifteen-minute *yasumi*. He would read the paper on the way to work and give us a resumé, a lifeline to the outside world.

In the first week we were taken out to start painting the freighters under construction. A crush of workers swarmed around the dark cluttered spaces under the ship with a mass of snakelike hoses, wires, pipes underfoot. We climbed up through the bamboo scaffolding on rickety ladders four flights high. I carried a can of paint and a brush. I looked down and turned green, dizzy with vertigo. At the top, with nothing to hold onto, we stood on loose, shaky unfastened planks slung across the scaffolding. We were expected to keep our balance while leaning forward painting the sides of the ship! I was appalled. Were they crazy? The winter winds gusting off the sea swayed the scaffolding. One slip in my army boots, one wrong move would send me hurtling down to oblivion!

I turned to look to my left at the open sea beside me. I felt suspended in the sky, above earth and water, caught somewhere between heaven and hell — how the Jesus did I get into this? Painter! What stupid, half-witted impulse, what flight of optimistic idiocy ever made me write that down? Brilliant! Euphoric visions of being welcomed as an artist, working among fellow artists in a warm, brightly lit room, seated at a large, clean drawing board — goofball! dolt! moron! Now here I stood with knees quivering, balancing on loose planks in the cold wind over the goddam China Sea, with a paint can in one hand and a brush in the other!

Every day I lived in dread of that scaffolding and those loose planks, some of which rose in the air when I stepped on one end. The experienced Japanese painters had rubber-soled, split-toed shoes that gripped the planks like hands. Damned if I'd go through this trapeze act all day. I placed the can on the plank and leaned against the ship with one hand while I stooped with trembling legs to dip my brush in the red lead underpaint, then brushed it onto the steel sides, always leaning forward to avoid falling backward. It was slow going — almost no going. But I was not eager to win any medals for my war effort. On these rations, I had resolved to expend as little energy as humanly possible. I would move like an old man from here on in — it would be my private battle. Sabotage, yes, and survival. In fact, most prisoners, half sick, moved about slowly, to the bewilderment of the Japanese, who zoomed around with nervous speed and limitless energy.

And among the slow, I was the slowest. If there were any prizes for that, I'd have been right up there. The Japanese painters gossiped about us and I was nicknamed *surōmōshon*, slow motion. I found a tortoise painted on my locker to confirm the success of my campaign.

The winter was bitterly cold. There was no heat in our hut, and none at work since we worked outdoors. Although this climate was more miserable, it was healthier in a way than the changes of temperature that the indoor workers were subjected to, which brought on pneumonia. Men began to die of it. Some, like Bob, were considered lucky to be assigned to a pipe-bending shop, where a forge burned all day. We in the paint gang stole away whenever possible to the tiny braziers heating rivets. We warmed our fronts while our backs froze, then turned to do the back while the front froze. We seemed to be eternally cold.

At night we undressed just to change undergarments, to avoid lice, since we couldn't bathe. I had a pair of pajamas that I did not remove in the freezing mornings but wore all day. Sand fleas from the earthen floors found their way to our bodies, biting all night, driving me mad with the itching and the lack of sleep.

On the way to the *benjo*, the outdoor latrines, during the night, it was a common sight to see hunched prisoners wrapped in blankets, with their burning beri-beri feet submerged in fire buckets. The water in these fire buckets, which lined the center aisle, turned to ice during the night; the sufferer would break the ice to shove his feet into the water for relief while he shivered under his blankets. A more desolate portrait of misery would be hard to find. As I passed, I thought of the rows of crucified Christians along the Appian Way. What were their thoughts, these silent, hopeless effigies? They expected nothing, got nothing. Like stoic Indians, they merely endured. I hoped there was no room for thought on the isolated island of pain they inhabited. I hurried by, thanking my lucky stars that all I had to endure were the fleas.

At mid-morning we stopped work for a brief *yasumi*, gathering around Kondo-san for *news-u time-u* as our new Japenglish lingo had it. We always made sure to ask *where* each event took place so that we could piece together our own ideas on the war's progress. I was sure the propaganda machine here could outclass any in the world, Goebbels's included, when it came to sheer imaginative creativity. I took for granted that Kondo-san, an intelligent man, could read between the lines. He taught me the word *waraguchi*, for untruths, and agreed that war news was full of *puropaganda*, but Japanese newspapers didn't believe in that. I looked at his face. There was no trace of guile or mockery or humor. He meant it.

"Oh, come on," I said, surprised. "Look: *Englando — puropaganda* — yes?"

"*Hai.*"

"True," Alf Cox, a moon-faced painter, nodded, stretching lazily. Alf had been in the Salvation Army and always spoke in flat, even tones with voice and face devoid of expression. "White man speak with forked tongue."

"Shut up, Cox, I'm trying to conduct a serious discussion. Kondo-san, Germany, *Unitedu Statesu — takusan waraguchi* [many lies], right?"

"*Takusan*," he agreed.

"Germany, Italy — *onaji* [same], yes?"

He nodded. They were Axis allies, but he was sophisticated enough to expect them to lie. He was no fool. Good. Now we were back on the same wavelength. I took one step further.

"*Nippon — puropaganda — onaji*, yes?"

"*Nai!*" His face reddened and showed us the first sign of anger. His voice deepened ominously. "*Nippon puropaganda nai!*"

"Aw, Kondo-san, come off it."

"Watch it," Nicholson, another painter, warned. "You're getting his shit hot."

But I couldn't let go. I couldn't believe a man of such intellect could swallow all that bilge. I went over some of his tall stories with him. In battle with an American ship, one tale went, the heroic Japanese sailors ran out of ammunition. Instead of trying to escape, they ran their ship alongside, seized the rice balls from their lunch boxes and hurled them at the enemy, who were so startled they turned tail and ran. There was the news report of an air battle between two fighter planes in which the Japanese pilot's guns jammed and out came the rice ball. He hurled it at the enemy plane and it got in the fuselage, fouling the motor, and the plane crashed. Rice balls seemed to be doing double duty as a secret weapon in this war. Kondo-san listened, nodding soberly.

"*Waraguchi nai-ka?*" I asked.

He shook his head. "*Waraguchi nai.*"

I had run into an astonishing brick wall, probably the root of Japan's greatest tragedy. I was beginning to get the measure of a belief system so thorough — beginning with schoolchildren — so all-pervasive, that no room was left for doubt. All opposition had been liquidated, all avenues of information controlled. Here was a man, keenly perceptive, well read, gentle and unwarlike, who could see the need for propaganda in any war situation but his own. His faith was implacable. The voice of authority was godlike in its truth. I was unaware too that the poetry of this man's soul and millions of others made it easy to believe in the power of the spirit over the machine. A joyous miracle was easily possible to a people who spent so much time in the enchanted forests of the imagination. I wondered if he believed like the rest that the

Emperor was really a god.

Codes of behavior had always come down from above. The samurai precepts, *Bushido* — victory or death in battle was the only acceptable path. Surrender was unthinkable. We prisoners were to be pitied at best, when not despised — pity from the older generation, contempt from the young.

Teenagers were drilled in the martial arts and practiced bayonet fighting with long sticks. They considered us fair game for their high jinks, pointing their sticks with jabbing motions and shouting fiercely. Being shameful cowards, we were expected to jump with fright. We tried to ignore them. But one day a bold young punk approached us, baiting Nicholson, a tall, hard-nosed, no-nonsense Grenadier with a short temper. We were enjoying a *yasumi*, and this kid, showing off to his friends, was getting under Nicholson's skin. He stamped, bellowed, jeered, coming closer and closer, then poked him. Nicholson leaped up with a roar and lunged at the terrified youngster, who took off like the wind. Luckily no *fu*-men were around. We were left in peace after that.

Another preconceived notion was the size of our penises. It seemed logical to the Japanese that such giant-sized men should sport giant-sized peckers. Avid curiosity drove them into the *benjos* to find out. Time and again while I was standing, penis in hand, I would find a leering face nosing around my elbow with the hope of beholding a deliciously, shockingly monstrous organ, only to find their grandiose visions dashed. Always a moment of sad disillusionment.

"*Nanda* [what's up]?" I would ask.

"*Chiisai-na* [tiny, eh]," he would say, raising his little finger and wiggling it derisively.

We always used these exchanges to get in a little propaganda.

"*Chiisai*," was the answer. "Here little *meshi* [food]. In Canada much *meshi*. In Canada" — I would raise my forearm with fist bunched, waving it with rolling eyes — "*ookii-na* [huge]. Nippon not enough *meshi*— *dame dayo* [very bad]."

This usually produced a grinning denial. No one went hungry in Japan. Only those who had close contact with prisoners had an inkling of our plight. Some sympathetic *hanchos* slipped us bits of food. Blacky was lucky. He worked indoors at a sitting job, since he still walked with difficulty and had a generous *hancho* who liked and respected him. He didn't seem foreign to them, being dark, with a broad face, high cheekbones and round skull. Except for the eyes, he was not unlike a Japanese.

One *hancho*, a young student who spoke some English, used to buy a pack of ten cigarettes from his meager earnings and give half a cigarette to each of his twenty prisoners every day. When our first Red Cross parcels came, they showered him with fat American cigarettes. I met him forty years later in Tokyo. He'd read of my visit in the papers and looked me up. We went to a museum together and talked of those days. Now a grandfather, he complained, like Canadian grandfathers, of the lack of respect of the younger generation. We felt strangely bonded to each other. He reminded me of Kondo-san.

Tommy Marsh, working in the paint shop, won a few extras for small services. The paint master had a little soapmaking racket going on the side, soap being very scarce. He showed Tommy how to boil the ingredients, then shape the soap into *daikon* (turnip) shapes, to be smuggled out and sold.

Kondo-san never brought us any *purezentos*; I suspected genteel poverty. But his understanding opened the way to a lightening of the spirit that lifted our morale to new heights. In our turn we brought excitement, laughter and a kind of glamour to what must have been for him a drab and dull existence. When he grinned at my antics, his face was suffused with light and joy. He was so taken with my cornball Harpo Marx act that I suggested we do it together. He accepted without hesitation. The others often watched in disbelief as our enemy turned straight man to my Harpo. They thought they'd seen everything. I added spoken lines for flavor.

We faced each other, nose to nose. I puffed out my chest, raised imaginary gloves and slapped his face. "Fighto," I challenged.

"Fighto!" he agreed

"Tomorrow-day?" I barked.

"Tomorrow-day!"

Then we marched off, turned and faced each other at a distance. It was now tomorrow-day — dawn. Legs wide apart, I stamped my left foot, grabbing my imaginary holster. He followed suit, suppressing giggles. I stamped my other foot and grabbed my other holster. He did the same. I took one pace forward, so did he. Next pace forward. So did he, grinning from ear to ear. We advanced step by step till we were face to face, poised to draw. Then like Harpo, with mouth wide and eyes wild, I whipped out a whisk broom and brushed him down vigorously back and front, with a hand out for a tip, which he gave me. This never ceased to tickle him. In time I grew sick of it but not Kondo-san. He would squat beside me during our rest.

"Arisuta [Allister]," he would say with smiling anticipation. "*Hawpo-ka*?"

"Oh, Christ." And I would wearily drag myself up.

Little did I dream when I first did this in the Catskills that one day I would be repeating it ad nauseam with a Japanese *hancho* in the shipyards of Kawasaki.

I often wondered at his attraction to this routine and finally realized that Harpo was a symbol, Dostoyevsky's Idiot, the antithesis of all that our situation represented — the violent, the vicious, the ugly, the misery of war. It was reordering, restructuring a twisted world. Harpo was the innocent, unwarlike spirit of joy and play and sport and peace, the unconscious balance we both sensed, reached for, a proclamation of sanity in a world gone mad.

Our tasks varied. We painted long, heavy anchor chains with steaming black tar, a messy job. The chains were laid out on the shore and the black tar paint splattered over pants and sleeves and stuck to our shoes. Once dry it would remain for the duration. We coated the bottoms of railcars with black tar. We scraped the rust off steel plates to prepare the surface for painting. We carried heavy sacks of cement from where they were stored in the paint shop. They were loaded into two-wheeled carts, with three men pulling each one by its iron shafts.

Our work clothes were coated with layer upon layer of paint. When we came by pulling a *jakku-kaata* (cart) full of cement, there was never any doubt as to our identity. With my head on Cloud Nine, I was generally, thankfully, unaware of what I was doing in the here and now and was considered the most careless painter in the gang. With no foresight, I let my clothes grow thicker and heavier by the month. Tommy Marsh has me down in his diary as the sloppiest man he has ever met. After two years my pants were stiff as boards and would no longer bend, so that my knees were constantly banging against them as I walked.

One day Tommy put me to the test to see just how "unconscious" I was. We had to carry cement up the gangplank to pile it on the ship. We each had a heavy bag hoisted on our shoulders and I followed him up the steep ascent, sweating and straining with wobbly knees. He led me a merry chase, stepping high over wires, ropes, girders, pipes, slipping and sliding. He circled the entire ship while I puffed and panted, suffering, enduring, ever the mindless drone, not bothering to notice we had circled the ship twice. I only knew I was undergoing a miserable ordeal. After the third round he gave up and tossed his sack on the deck. I followed suit, near collapse.

"You," he said, "are an impossible idiot. A bloody freak."

"Oh?"

"I was curious to see how long you'd go on carrying that goddam thing! You'd have gone on forever! Some people are too fucking dumb to live!"

"That's me. Look, I don't want to dampen your enthusiasm, but next time you try your bloody psychological experiments on me, I'll cut your goddam knockers off."

Actually he had touched on the secret of my success in staying alive.

Our breakfast at 6:00 a.m. was a half-ration of rice, a few spoonfuls of beans and a watery miso soup — nutritious enough but too small to work on. By 10:30 I was overcome by hunger shakes. Unaware that I was suffering from hypoglycemia, I thought it normal to be dizzy, weak and trembling till lunchtime at twelve, when we were led to the lunchroom for our bowl of rice and soup. The lunchroom, a long, bleak shed, was a place of happiness humming with our animated voices, warmed by steaming rice, tongues busy, jaws chomping away. We usually lined up outside first, waiting for the serving to be completed. We sat or sprawled on the ground as we waited, watching the passing scene. Workers produced lunch boxes of rice and pickles, held them under their faces and, with small chopsticks, shoveled the rice in with such speed it seemed to be swallowed whole. They squatted comfortably on their haunches throughout the meal. They could even snooze in this position. Groups of reform-school kids trotted by. They wore thin tattered uniforms and woebegone looks.

Everything was on the double. Their sweating feet were covered by split-toed, rubber-soled cloth shoes that stank at a distance. We were half disgusted, half pitying. They looked dirtier, more miserable than us. What had they done, I wondered? Was there a lower social order than ours?

We were not allowed to smoke on the job, but tobacco did stave off hunger pangs and we had our hiding places for a quick drag. Each of us carried a butt-tin, an old bully-beef can cut in half in which we collected our daily haul. Hunting butts was called "sniping" and we named our brand Lucky Snipes. All prisoners walked with eyes lowered, heads bowed, not out of humility but always on the lookout. Rainy days were gloomy because the pickings, indoors only, were lean. At day's end we opened our butts and rolled the dry tobacco into a cigarette of brown wrapping paper, which held together well when moistened.

In our paint shop Tommy, now expert at scrounging wood, had the stove going at the end of the day when we came in, stiff with cold. We rushed to get a place near the fire. One of the workers, a teenage swinger, high-spirited, jauntily dressed and curious, always peppered us with questions. He laughed a lot and seemed to do most of his laughing at us, not with us, with giggling asides to the other painters. One day he offered me a cigarette, a nice white whole new cigarette, a *purezento*.

"*Arigato* [thanks]." I took it. He motioned me to light it. I shook my head, saying it was a no-no. "*Dame-dayo.*"

He laughed and made a sign that I was chicken. No, no, I explained, it was against the rules. He shook his head, indicating that I could go ahead, I had his permission and he would accept responsibility. If there were any problem, leave it to him, he would explain. Reluctantly, not to lose face, I lit up. A mistake.

Just my luck that a soldier on patrol looked in and saw me. He walked in, surprised. Shit! I saluted, bowed and didn't hide the cigarette, to show that it was all right. He bellowed at me. I tried to say I had permission and turned to the teenager for help, but there was nobody home — he'd gone pale and shook his head, denying everything. He had nothing to do with me. My heart sank. Here we go.

"*Ki-o-tsuki!*" the soldier bellowed. I came to attention, feet together. "*Bakayaro* [scum]!" He hauled off and whacked me across the face. A sharp piercing shaft of pain shot through my head. He was strong as a bull, a corporal, with much practice. My ears rang with the second blow that came from the other side. My face felt numb after the third blow and the pain seemed to retreat. It was a question of keeping my feet and not being knocked down. Another and another. He stopped at last, shouted some more, more as protocol than in anger. He seemed satisfied at a workmanlike job and left.

Silence around the stove. My head was dizzy and the ache was increasing. But I was oddly relieved, elated. This was my first formal beating. Till now I'd only been shoved, kicked, prodded, cursed. I had always dreaded a violent attack where I must stand helplessly and let a mad dog savage me. How would I react, I'd often wondered. Would it change me, blight me, leave any psychic scars? Would the pain be unbearable? Would I go to pieces? I'd never been in a street fight, as Bob and Blacky had. What would it be like? Well, now I knew — to a degree. The blows brought numbness, easing pain. In Baron Byng High School I had gotten "the biffs" — the strap — from my class master, and there were strong similarities: punishment from accepted authority, producing, thankfully, no desire to strike back. Good. I knew there would be many beatings ahead, and I was lucky to respond as I did. With Bob it was a psychic trauma, having been trained by his father, a boxer, to always fight back, harder, and never stop till you've won. He was from Verdun, Quebec, where the code demanded that one be tough, superior, cocky. We'd often discussed this. A beating left him half weeping with anger, frustration, conflict and a desolate sense of defeat. Ironic paradox that I, the delicate flower, could leave a beating with a sense of triumph and newfound manliness. I was no longer Dan Daintydrawers.

I turned to my teenage pal who offered up a sly and sheepish smirk. "*Arigato, tomadachi* [thanks, pal]," I said. "You dirty little bastard."

I wished him no good luck for that knife in the back; oddly enough, my wish came true. He dropped out of sight and reappeared months later, trotting by among the reform-school kids, looking lost and frightened. I waved to him with a friendly, happy smile — from one damned soul to another. Welcome aboard!

The assignment we liked best was the one behind the kitchen, where all the girls worked. Kondo-san would take us there to tar paint the undercarriages of railway cars. But we could ogle and flirt with the dozens of girls streaming in and out of the company kitchen. They were not exactly cover girls in their baggy pants and bandanas, but we were no matinee idols ourselves. And they were females. It seemed ages since we'd had any contact with the opposite sex. This seemed to raise our status, subtly, briefly. Weren't we now a part of the universal mating exercise that bypassed the boundaries of wars and nations?

We whistled, hooted, made wolf calls and tried in general to attract their attention. Like grotesque shades of the dainty Mikado maids, they tittered loudly, some boldly, some shyly, at these giant paint-covered scarecrows with light-colored hair and eyes. Certainly we were no ordinary swains and brought a little texture to their day.

I cavorted and clowned to catch their eye, getting down on one knee, plucking at an imaginary guitar and singing soulful love songs. Kondo-san tolerated it but, as he gently reminded us, there was work to be done, remember? We were spending more and more time goofing off and following the girls. This went on for several days with little work taking place and Kondo-san began to complain. Finally we worked out a happy compromise and declared one hour after lunch to be concentrated, all-out legitimized love-time, or in Japenglish, *rovu-timu*, with the rest of the day for work. Bless Kondo-san — we were probably the only POWs in the Japanese empire ever granted *rovu-timu*.

I noticed how different the relations were between the sexes. In a society so full of restrictions, there was a refreshing openness and freedom about the human body. No His or Hers toilets, we were all one happy evacuating family. Each stall had a hole in the floor and a narrow swinging door with ample space above and below to see the occupant. It was common to see a man lean over the door to greet a lady squatting inside and remain for a nice little chat. "How are the children?" "Just fine, thank you." And so on. Very civilized. After all, wasn't it the king of Spain who held his important audiences while on the golden pot?

Kondo-san turned out, as time went on, to be too good a boss. The paint gang began taking advantage of his benevolent regime by doing less and less work. St. John, a nineteen-year-old, was our youngest and blindest, a weak-willed scatterbrain, tall, freckled, with a prominent nose, a receding chin and an irritating, inane grin. He goofed off at every opportunity, feeling he had a good thing going here — a pushover of a *hancho* that a smart man should milk to the limit. On the other hand, Kondo-san had a certain quota of work to fill, which we generally tried to get done.

One day we were scraping the rust off steel plates. It was dull, unpleasant work, with the rust flying into our faces and lungs. St. John poked away for a while with his scraper, a wide, sharp steel blade fitted to the end of a long stick. He decided it was too nice a day for work and he'd prefer a sunbath. He spread himself on the ground. Kondo-san leaned over him.

"*Ima yasumi nai* [no rest now]," he told him. "Now *shigoto* [work]. *Yasumi atode* [rest later]."

St. John flashed his silly grin. "Fuck that noise," he said. "Me *yasumi* now," and didn't rise. Kondo-san flushed and waved his cupped hand irritably in the negative gesture.

"*Yasumi nai!*"

"Off your ass, St. John," I said. "He's the boss, don't get him hot."

He rose reluctantly. "I've done enough," he whined.

"You've done bugger-all."

"Well, I ain't doin' any more. I'm goin' to the can." He turned to Kondo-san. "Me go *benjo* — bye now."

Kondo-san lost his cool and the blood flooded his face. "*Benjo nai! Shigoto!*"

"Aaah . . . piss off," St. John said contemptuously.

The insulting tone and the direct refusal goaded Kondo-san to a sudden fury. "*Bakayaro! Shigoto!*" he shouted, brandishing his scraper.

"Balls."

Kondo-san went into a frenzy and charged forward with his scraper. I jumped between them, thinking I was the only one who could cool him down now. "Kondo-san — take it easy! *Matte yo* [wait]."

He shrieked at me to get away. His eyes were wild. I held my ground, trying to get a soothing word in, but he went berserk —

we had all become one to him. He lunged at me with the scraper, catching me full in the chest and knocking me backward.

I was furious with pain and outrage. "What the hell do you think you're doing, you bastard!" I threw my scraper down and stalked off to simmer down.

Things were badly strained for the next few days and I stayed away from Kondo-san. He kept a discreet distance and no word passed between us. Finally, during a *yasumi*, he squatted down beside me and tried to make amends, explaining that St. John made him *atsui* — hot in the heart. I didn't accept his apology — there was no excuse for violence but I softened a bit at his tone of genuine remorse, even sorrow. Still, this same bugger had driven his bloody scraper into my chest, acting like "a goddam Jap." Was that what lay under the gentle surface? As he said, he was made *atsui* — were any of us free of that? In Canada, I told him, a gentleman — *jentorumano* — didn't strike a gentleman without losing his friendship, so we were no longer friends. He was crestfallen. But finally I relented and we made up.

Neither of us stopped to realize — I in my pique, he in his abject remorse — that by reaching this level in our friendship we had actually managed to bypass all the barricades that race and war had thrown up between us.

Months passed and our days with Kondo-san finally came to a close. It was too good to last. One of the paint gang blew it by inveigling him into some trade that ended disastrously. It was discovered, and Kondo-san was summoned for questioning by the *heitai*. Whatever they said or did to him frightened him half to death. He was stripped of his armband and removed from the job. He avoided us like the plague, and when I passed him all I could garner was a frightened, sickly smile and a hurried exit. My imagination filled in the rest: some brutal, ignorant bullyboy half Kondo-san's age had, army style, taken a human being with poetry in his soul, a warm-hearted, gentle, cultured man, and reduced him to a quivering jelly in nothing flat. Wasn't this what the *heitai* did to one another? And then to an entire nation? The mindless destruction. With Kondo-san went something more: it was the breaking of a tenuous link to a super-sanity, a higher awareness that was to take me forty years to rediscover.

Chapter Twelve

A T TIMES OUR PAINT GANG was divided up, going off on different assignments. A young painter led a small group of us off to work on a distant freighter. It was under repair, crowded with men working in and around one another. After several hours work we broke off for a precious *yasumi*. By now this word, like others, had become part of our English. It was a pleasant change to get away to a new part of the shipyards, a break in the awful sameness. It was not yet time for my dreaded hunger shakes, and my energy was still with me. The days were warmer now. Spring was in the air and with it all the happy associations of bygone springs. I closed my eyes and walked down the old Montreal street, Esplanade, with the tall maples bursting with sun-kissed new chartreuse leaves against the rich, deep blueness . . . bird song in the air . . . wearing my spring coat with its flaring collar open and loose and dashing, as Tyrone Power wore his, footloose and fancy free, smiling at the world with the world smiling back. My happy feelings always found vent in song and as I sat on the crowded, cluttered steel floor, I bubbled over: *"When we begin . . . begin the Beguine . . . ."*

A knot of workers who had never seen prisoners before were watching and discussing us. One of them glowered at me but I continued singing. To hell with him: we couldn't smoke but we could damn well sing — I knew my rights. Stare away, fellas. I felt too good to mind.

He shouted over at me to shut up but I ignored him. None of his damn business. We were owned by the army and the company and beholden to no civilian. Only a guard or a *fu*-man could tell us what to do.

"It brings back the night of tropical splendor . . . ."

He must have taken it to be some patriotic song of defiance or victory. I was an affront to the unwritten code of *li*, the social order of all things. I was not keeping my place. He came up and stood over me. I looked past his legs and sang on. He began bellowing. I didn't follow it but I understood. It amounted to: "Shut your dirty foreign yap or I'll shut it for you!"

I continued, waiting for my *hancho* to tell him off. Our *hancho* looked away. He didn't want trouble. The man shouted at me.

"Better dummy up," Nicholson warned. "He's a mean-looking bastard."

My pride rebelled. I was damned if I would, or could, back down now. He was a civvy, with no power to dictate to anyone. I knew my rights. I looked over at our *hancho*, and he looked frightened. Not a peep out of him. I sang louder than ever: *"And when we begin the Beguine . . . . "* The man lashed out, kicking me viciously in the ribs. My song stopped. He stood over me, foot poised, waiting for me to open my mouth. I was silent, swallowing my bile. I rose and slunk away.

This was worse than any beating. Rights? What rights? Had I forgotten who I was? What I was? The taste in my mouth was bitter vomit. My body seemed full of it and it would not be released. I must swallow it. I was a worm, there for anyone to step on, to spit on. Rage, blind, helpless, limitless rage roared through me, rage against the relentless gods that tossed me about like a toy. I smashed my fist against the steel plate beside me. The pain was welcome . . . I found myself weeping. Something inside had been broken. The pieces would take many years to put back. What was it — pride? Was there any left? What right did I have to claim any? That was pure make-believe, as illusory as any other civilized emotion I pretended to. That kick was truth. It drove me across a new frontier. It kicked me back into reality. It destroyed every myth, every saving shield I'd managed to build up.

I was learning *li* — my place in the order of things.

The weeks and months dragged by. We were becoming laboring drones, with as much mental vitality. We moved in a catatonic stupor, blocking out anxiety, despair. I became a creature of routine, performing the daily tasks by instinct. Each day the same: the breakfast, the march to work, the assignments, the terror of the scaffolding, the endless hours, the shakes, the hunger, the fatigue, the lunch, the hours and hours of empty, dull meaningless labor, the march back, the same question to the sick men in camp.

"What's in the soup?"

"Daikons."

"Shit."

The supper. Roll call. Fifteen minutes to lights out. And so to sleep, lying on our thirty-seven inches of matting in the dark, each to his own thoughts. This was the best and worst time of day. No chores, no action, time just to rest — and think. Thought could be avoided throughout the busy day but not now. The pulse of the brain still throbbed. It came alive, exerting its own subtle torture. The thoughts of five hundred men rose in the darkness, circling, swelling the air, enmeshed. Images of loved ones appeared like ghosts come to haunt and wound, fading before the closer images of Japanese workers, of *fu*-men, two-banders, guards . . . . Underneath it all like disjointed music rose the farrago of fears, anxieties, the wondering . . . how long, O Lord?

There was little war news. No second front. The world was standing still. Would this ever end? Would I be around when it does? Am I to die? How? There were also melodies of anger and disillusionment. Someone did this to us, shafted us . . . the bastards we trusted sent us off to this. It wasn't war at all — we didn't have a chance, and they knew it before they sent us. They just didn't give a shit, no one did, no one does . . . . No one here cares either — why should they? We're all sick and useless, unwanted, marking time, waiting to die. It's all so weird, so crazy, we're like fish on land still trying to breathe, flapping, growing weaker, hopeless . . . how long, O Lord?

In summer we could bathe in the bathhouse by pouring pails of cold water over one another. In cold weather we didn't wash. The ogre of monotony was becoming a worse threat than hunger. I can even recall reaching a point where I deliberately broke rules, looking for a beating to break the indescribable boredom.

One day I was called into the paint master's little office. He had heard I was an artist; was this so?

"Hai," I nodded.

Did I have any samples of my work? *"Hai. Ashita* [tomorrow]," I promised. We bowed. His manner betrayed an ethical conflict. I was a *furyo*, after all, beneath contempt. And yet I was an artist and, as such, a personage of hallowed, semi-saintly status. Here the artist was no posturing Greenwich Village bohemian but a monklike ascetic, sober, solitary, spiritual, to be held in reverence. The paint master's sardonic glance managed to combine disdain and respect.

Next day I brought three paintings I had done in Hong Kong. He examined them carefully and was pleased. Would I make him a painting? Gladly, but I had no paints, canvas or brushes, and there was the little matter of the army, remember? *"Heitai — dame-dame* [soldiers — bad news]. Bang-bang" — I slapped my face.

He nodded. *"Sukoshi mada* [wait a bit]."

I went off to climb the scaffolding with a lighter heart. To paint again? An artist in Japan? My crazy dream come true?

Days passed with no action from the paint master, and I was ready to lay my dreams to rest. At last, the others went off to work one day and I was ordered to remain. He led me into a storeroom in the rear where a corner had been cleared beside high piles of cement bags for a table and chair. I stared in amazed delight at a spanking new canvas and a set of new brushes and paints. The light came from a high window, too high for a passing guard. My heart leaped — a perfect hideaway!

"Joto [tops]!" I enthused. *"Takusan arigato* [many thanks]!"

He produced a photo of a vase and flowers for me to do — a breeze. We saluted and bowed and he left, both of us pleased and happy. I couldn't believe my luck. This was no break in the monotony, this was smashing it to bits! Bye-bye scaffolding, hello flowers. Bye-bye fatigue and vertigo and cold sea winds and messy tar chains. I caressed the smooth new tubes of paint with loving sensuality. He had even produced a new palette, bless him — this quiet loving man making his quiet little plans in careful detail. No wonder he was top man. I'd make him a bloody masterpiece! But slowly. Yes, this was a darlin' thing I had going here and I'd have to milk it to the limit. If they had called me *surōmoshōn* before, they ain't seen nothin' yet.

I set to work, but at a snail's pace. Word of the enterprise got around and painters dropped in to watch the artist at work. I put on quite a show for their money. Soon other curious workers from adjoining shops came to swell the growing audience. They stood quietly, in awe and respect, with their grime and patches, turning the powdery storeroom into a shrine where I, high priest, performed a sacred rite. I was touched, drawn closer to this land

and its people by this mutual spiritual linkage. I was automatically raised from below to a place far above them by common consent. Where else in the world, I wondered, would one find such remarkable reverence for art among a group of factory hands? It seemed that here a child imbibed a taste for art with its mother's milk. It went so far back into history — in a way, more powerful, more enduring than the ugly violence dominating this dark era.

For my own survival I had to play on their awe and tax their patience beyond endurance, turning each brush stroke into a theatrical production. I would sit in contemplation for a while as they waited, whispering respectfully. At long last I would slowly dip the brush into the paint, lean forward and move it toward the canvas. They would lean forward with me to catch the magic moment — but no, the brush would pause in mid-air and I would withdraw it, leaning back in my chair for another protracted spell of contemplation. More respectful whispering . . . patience — Art must be served . . . it moved in mysterious ways . . . such things took great concentration. It would come in a single swift Zen stroke — intuitive, spontaneous, like the flash of a samurai sword! Or like sumo wrestling with all the preliminaries, rituals, false starts, but then when it finally happens it comes with lightning speed — *zip, bang, heave,* and it's over. They dug that, these fellas. I was slow, very slow, but they knew it was only because of the greater depths that must be plumbed.

I was the stage conjuror fleecing the yokels. I regretted conning them like this but there was, after all, a war on, and there were certain priorities. I eased my conscience by telling myself that they were left with a heightened respect for the arts and no harm done.

By an ironic twist I found my hunger increased with this set-up. Physical labor, I deduced, slowed the digestive action and stretched the breakfast out longer, whereas sitting still, with no interference, the rice digested swiftly and left me ravenous. Also, work took one's mind off the stomach, but I, cooling my heels in the storeroom, had nothing to do but think of food. Still, this was healthier, pleasanter and a welcome rest.

The days passed, the painting grew. At the end of each day, clean and rested, I would watch the paint gang troop in from work, dirty, exhausted, gazing irritably at my welcoming smile.

"Lucky bastard. How long can you stretch this out?"

"Forever, I hope. It takes a lot of work, you know."

"Bullshit. Didn't Barnum say you can't fool all the people all the time?"

"He also said never give a sucker an even break."

"Well, live it up while you can."

I did. Each day the paint master came in to check. He was respectful, patient and uncomplaining. He liked what he saw emerging and offered an occasional pleasant, convivial smile and nod. I enjoyed our little conspiratorial *entente cordiale*, with the added warming thought of a hoodwinked guard passing by outside.

It was also pleasant to savor the luxury of a time period in which every minute was not counted and regulated. The mornings were solitary, with everyone away on busy routines. The cement bags, piled ceiling high, were a symbolic presence, a grim reminder of the heavy labor I was missing. They lent the strange silence an extra muffled, deadened soundlessness. It was easy to feel that the world had stopped and I was marooned in this cubbyhole for eternity, a sensation both comforting and unsettling. I could revisit my mental world and lose myself in reverie, returning to earlier days of peace and promise, making it the only important world, reversing roles. This place was only a passing phase, impermanent, melodramatic, exotic. The true permanence was back there — home, unchanging, stable, sustaining. I would relive high moments of affirmation and ego fulfillment: winning the acting award at the Dominion Drama Festival at nineteen. I coveted the plaque like a precious stone, packing it in my kit bag, resolving to keep it close, to lick and taste this sweetest of sweet triumphs, my expanding ego fully satiated. I would gaze at it from time to time at Sham Shui Po like a miser fingering his coins. Ah, vanity . . . all left behind, all lost, along with self-esteem, dreams of glory, even identity . . . .

I busied myself with the painting, thinking of the love of art here that had brought me privilege. Was it an Oriental trait — endemic? I remembered Laughing Charlie, the Chinese laundryman, gazing at my work . . . when he came to collect the laundry, my mother had proudly produced my drawings, at age fourteen. I waited, grinning, cocky, for a reaction to giggle at, Charlie was so comical. But Charlie grew serious for the first time and studied them very carefully. "Too big," he said, pointing to the horse, "man too small." I stared. My grin faded. Jeez, why hadn't I noticed that? Charlie never looked the same to me after that.

The minutes passed. Hunger pangs. Tommy Marsh would wander in between chores to chat. Having painting experience, he was put in charge of the shop, doing odd jobs for the paint master, mixing paint, cleaning brushes, making pots, tending the stove. We were discovering each other and becoming good friends. I found him keenly, eccentrically observant, intelligent and a man of surprising sensitivity and depth. Our talks ranged over many fields — people, war, love. I had been warned that he was far to the right politically. He attacked my "bleeding-heart liberal crap." I attacked his bigotry. We disagreed on many ideas, and yet by a peculiar chemistry we liked and admired each other and found that sharing our present lot created a unique bond. Not that all these political thunderclouds hanging over the world were not large and threatening forces, it was only that they had become artificial, irrelevant. They involved ideas, theories, to massage the intellect, games played somewhere out there on a faraway planet by those who didn't know *this* — the cold, clear *real*, which cut through to the bone.

Tom recounted his fantastic experiences during the fighting. He showed me the scars where a bullet had entered his neck, passed through his head and come out behind his ear. His broken arm had reset awkwardly and now protruded as he walked.

Hunger faded as we helped each other rekindle the flame and warmth of a life once lived, with all its tastes and smells and richness. Pleasant, stolen hours.

But all good things must end and the final day arrived. Sadly, I presented the finished canvas. The beaming paint master accepted it with a bow. I bowed back. There was a definite respect in his manner now — I was no longer the despised *furyo* but a man of substance, and I reacted with an appropriate courtly style. With a bit of a flourish he produced his cigarette case and paid me two cigarettes for my effort. I stared at them. Two lousy cigarettes? The bloody old skinflint! Obviously his respect had its limits. I accepted with a bow.

"You sure you can spare them?"

He looked quizzical.

"Arigato."

After this spree of wild, headstrong spending, we dubbed him Diamond Jim. But he did save the day by producing another photo of another vase and flowers, my next assignment. Saved. This was lovely — it looked like this could be a permanent and ideal little arrangement we had going. He with free paintings coming his way and I with a continuing holiday.

I started in again next day, working at the usual breakneck speed. The following week he brought me a black-and-white snapshot of my first painting, set in a large ornate frame, making a formal presentation of this *purezento* as though he were handing over the Hope Diamond. A little rice ball would have been more to the point.

For the next few weeks I continued to entertain my audiences with my genius-at-work number. At our completion ceremony, Diamond Jim produced his two cigarettes amid much smiling and bowing and saluting. I watched a little anxiously for a note of finality but there was no sign. Good — there would be more. He produced a magazine, opened it at a marked page with a news photo and indicated that this would be my next painting. I blinked. This was no vase and flowers; it was a group of people sitting around a long table. I examined it curiously. Japanese officers and civilians on one side, British officers on the other. What the hell was this? It could only be the surrender of Singapore!

"Singaporu-ka?" I asked.

"Hai," he nodded, smiling.

"Ah, so." I controlled a flash of anger. The sonofabitch. Rubbing it in. Wasn't he old enough, wise enough to be above such tripe? Glorifying military conquest — even this shrewd black-marketeer was brainwashed. Well, I'd be damned if he'd ever get a painting of that out of me. But a direct refusal would mark the end of my blissful idyll. I told him, in diplomatic style, that I would have to study the matter and took it back to the storeroom.

What to do now? There was no question of doing it. Nor did I relish a return to the scaffolding. After some heavy cogitation I evolved a strategy. I informed him that this was a very difficult undertaking and would need much preliminary sketching in my notebook. Each figure in the painting must be done separately in sketches first. This was stretched out for several luxuriously restful weeks. My plan was to do the painting but "interpret" it my way — making the victors look mean and evil and the British kindly and angelic.

I went ahead with the plan, working happily away as the days passed. Diamond Jim checked in every day as before. There was usually a murmur or grunt of approval. I noticed fewer of these pleasant signs as time went on. I worked away, with my faces growing more ugly and malevolent with each passing day. Soon there was only silence behind me when he came by. The British faces began to look gentle and beautiful. The silence behind me grew charged. Things were becoming uncomfortable. The delicate balance of our happy relations had shifted alarmingly. I could feel things turning sour, reverting to the old master-slave relationship.

Time passed. The respectful watchers still came and went. Then one day the paint master stepped softly into the room and stood behind me . . . not a word. He studied the painting for some time. The tension was palpable, electric. I could almost feel his swollen hostility. He was no fool, he was onto me. A showdown was imminent. The tiny storeroom was bursting with vibrations of fury. I could feel his anger whistling down my neck like a karate chop. Suddenly in a swift violent movement he reached past me, seized the canvas, lifted it high, smashed it to the ground and kicked it viciously. He turned to me and pointed to the door. There are no curses in the Japanese language, but the words he used had a nasty sound. To the scaffold with thee! was the general idea.

Banished.

Ah well, I thought, as I picked up my pot of paint and brush, we'd had a good run anyway . . . . A good house every day, Standing Room Only . . . . Nothing lasts forever, and my stupid impossible dream *had* come true.

I returned to the drudgery, the monotony, the invasive gloom — we were cogs in the great national wheel, turning with the rest, and returning in a circular motion to the same point each day. At times it took too much effort not to accept our alien environment, like the others, as the only reality, sinking into it, submerging. At other times we plodded along, divorced from it all, floating above it in a dazed and gloomy coma. At rare intervals, buoyed up by hope, rumor or news, visualizing eventual freedom, we could accept all pain, all discomfort with ease. There were high and low moments in the day, the highest being the ration of hot rice waiting at the end of it. It offered welcome, becoming home, loved ones, comfort.

We placed our various mess tins or tin cans wired with handles over our numbers on the long rickety table. The volunteer server and helpers brought the large bucket of steaming rice to one end while helpers passed up the tins. We closed in like wolves for our nightly ritual. Hungry distrustful eyes watched hypnotically as the server's ladle dove into the rice, lifted a heaping portion and patted it into a bowl, smoothing it level. Then he shoveled the contents into each mess tin, which was returned to its place. It sat enticingly on its crudely marked number, cooling and waiting for the completion of the ceremony. When there was rice left over, it was distributed as "seconds" in careful sequence — often as many as six lucky recipients won this tiny extra mouthful. When portions were too large there was nothing left for the last few and a recall was needed with the helpers, like obedient priests, relaying the tins to the high priest, who removed a dab from each one to make up the difference. Though the dabs were small, it was always subtle torture to watch your precious ration shrink before your eyes as though the rhythm of your body had been secretly interrupted. At last it was time to reach for that blessed life-giving vessel.

Servers were changed often, because of poor judgment or hanky-panky: some were not averse to a bribe (a cigarette) and could pack one bowl harder than the rest. The soup was a matter of how deep he dipped the ladle, since the sparse vegetables settled at the bottom. In our section, Speller lasted longest and somehow managed to rise above the clouds of hostile suspicion and twisted paranoia.

As stomachs filled, conversation broke out and the hut echoed with the cheering clatter of bowls and mess tins and the buzz of voices. Some filled their water bottles with hot water from the kitchen and drank a quart of it, even two, to feel full, if only for a moment. This left the stomach stretched and mournfully empty through the day. No, thank you. I chose to let my stomach shrink to reduce the hunger pangs.

A further weakening effect on our bodies was the ever-present diarrhea. Several times during the night men would squat over a dark hole in the floor, shivering in the outdoor *benjos*, their guts in

North Point Concentration Camp, Hong Kong, 1942. I painted this with crankcase oil, using a whittled stick and shoebrush bristles wired to a stick.

My drawing of Charley Clarke, Camp 3D, 1944.

William Allister, age tw[...]
in basic training at Hu[...]
Quebec, 1941.

The dispatch riders at Sham Shu[...]
Po Barracks, Hong Kong, Decem[...]
1941. *Top (left to right)*: Thomas,
Beaton, Normand, Demant.
Bottom: Mitchell, Speller.

Self-portrait, Camp 3D,
1944.

Horis G.C.R. Grant
Sumidagawa Aug. 18/45

Muckers in misery.

George Grant at
Sumidagawa, Japan, on
August 18, 1945.

William Allister, age twenty-six, in the Laurentians, Quebec, 1946.

Back at the Nippon Kokan Shipyards, 1983. *From left to right*: William Allister, Ichiro Koyanagi (son of the interpreter Koyanagi), Naotaka Kuroda.

a knot. Then, weak and empty, they would march out to work the next day with little to sustain their wasted bodies. They could get nothing from their food. Captain Reid kept the worst cases in camp in a special section. But the rule was no work, no ration. He fed them the crusty burned rice left at the bottoms of the rice pots. Blacky, one of the worst, could not stomach even this delicious treat and kept it for me when I visited in the evening. I saved it for the period of my mid-morning shakes, stealing off to the *benjo* for this tasty snack that kept me going till lunch, a heavenly blessing. Although Blacky and I were still partners, I found myself gravitating more and more toward Bob, a never-ending source of entertaining and stimulating talk. Blacky had grown more morose and uncommunicative over the months of illness and pain, inhabiting his own private world of gloom, anger and depression.

Bob and I led an active cerebral life, seldom at a loss for a topic for discussion. We walked side by side on the march to and from work, talking constantly. By now we knew every member of each other's family and friends intimately, every colorful event in each other's lives. His was a Montreal working-class, street-smart existence in Verdun, something totally outside and opposite to my sheltered realm of experience. In him I found remarkable mental powers unacknowledged, unstimulated, a raw vein of gold awaiting discovery. He sucked up the rain of new ideas in books, theories, authors I offered like a dry thirsting plant. Plato, Socrates, Aristotle were tasted, licked, swallowed, and he seemed to find the very act of absorption a novel form of happiness. We fed each other.

Marching along we visited each other's habitats. He joined me in my bohemian days in New York, doing satirical skits at the Village Vanguard in Greenwich Village or wandering down 42nd Street past the rows of cheap movie houses and porn shows. For twelve cents I had seen three wonderful French films there when French cinema was at its height, with Harry Baur, Louis Jouvet, Michel Simon, Jean Gabin, all the greats. I described how I was hired as a serious actor to join a troupe of players in the Catskills, where there was a great demand for comedy in a society coming out of a depression, and soon found myself a zany comic. Carefree days full of hilarity and adventure. Could anything be more opposite to this dreary, anxiety-ridden, hunger-filled existence?

With Bob I rode the rails across the country. One had to be tough, resourceful, quick-witted. Life moved quickly. At nineteen he had married a French girl and ended up working in a factory, a father of two children at twenty-one. Going overseas must have been a grand release, a glorious return to freedom. The fighting had been a thrilling adventure right out of his father's British Army stories of India, so different from my own response. We were certainly a "unity of opposites."

We talked on. The guards, the dusty cinders, the ragged cadavers around us vanished as we walked. When we reached the shipyards we joined the now-familiar crowds streaming through the wide gates to the tune of the scratchy, blaring factory march. Meant to lift the spirits, it fell on our ears like a funeral dirge, a mournful call, demanding a new portion of our blood, our energies, our life juices. Workers in old garb — capes, cloth shoes, bits and pieces of old clothing, masks, caps, battered fedoras — all hurried in. The inevitable reform-school kids, menacing symbol of crime and punishment, would trot by in formation, buglers tooting on the run, bringing their fetid stench with them like a malevolent wind.

Another hungry day beginning.

Blacky's "electric feet" improved on the diet of brown, unhusked rice. Beri-beri never completely leaves the body, contrary to what doctors believe. Former POWs know better. I can still leave an indentation on any part of my body — wet beri-beri. I still get occasional tiny shocks in the toes — dry beri-beri.

But Blacky was well enough to be sent out to the shipyards and soon fell smoothly into his new way of life. I began to note subtle changes in him over the months. He grew more cheerful. There was an adaptive process taking place in the minds of many. He was one of those. For such men the present loomed large and gradually took over. Past and future faded and finally disappeared. They became an organic part of their environment. Blacky's conversation only carried vitality when he spoke of his shop and his work and the people around him. This was now his all. When I spoke of home, he listened politely with little interest.

Was this healthier? There was, after all, a certain contentment, a comfort in that path. It could be that the mind was protecting itself

— setting up a survival shield. I, on the other hand, was tormented by a past I could not let go . . . longing, nostalgia, escape were the melodies that sang in my head. I could not adapt or adjust. Nor could Bob. That was dangerous. True, our path offered a rich inner life, but it demanded a painful price.

These were not conscious choices. Other forces — subconscious, intuitive, environmental — guided our footsteps. Though we slept side by side, I felt Blacky moving away from me, a quiet separation of spirit. In a way his acceptance was normal, pragmatic. His work engrossed him, even to the point of enjoyment. I felt envious of his inner peace and faintly appalled. There was an element of surrender here that stuck in my craw. "There must be more than this," my soul cried out. "It doesn't matter," his spirit answered, "this is all there is for now, let's not play games. Take each day as it comes and that is that." He was definitely making himself at home, as others did. I watched petty details of camp life become enlarged, distorted, as they do for long-term patients in a hospital ward. These men were full-time *furyos*, imprisoned totally, suffering an indefinable loss. The others, the tormented resisting minds, were passing through the entire furnace of experience with open eyes and wounded hearts.

These were not, of course, black-and-white differences. Each strayed across the other's borders from time to time. As I stood swaying on the scaffold over the Pacific, my imagination often failed. My mind would go blank, dull, numb. I slapped the paint across the surface of steel before me, stroking vertically then horizontally, then filling the blank spaces, and I often felt that this square panel was the sum of all existence. I became an automaton, a thing at the end of a brush, fated to dip, brush, spread, dip, brush, spread this red lead paint forever, because other unpainted panels waited, stretching all around the ship . . . . And after that another row, and another, and when the entire freighter was painted there would be another freighter to begin again, like the hill of Sisyphus . . . and another . . . and another . . . .

The summers were as hot as the winters were cold. There was little shade, no escape from the tyranny of the sun. When we painted long girders with their steel latticework, the surface felt like branding irons on the skin. They were laid out horizontally in a wide-open yard like stricken smoldering monsters to be prodded by our scrapers, painted and awkwardly turned over with rods. We worked sweating, stripped to the waist.

Another job hazard was Harpo. We had gone through many *hancho*s by now, some tough, some distant, some resigned to our poor production. To give us Harpo, our latest, was scraping the bottom of the barrel, implying we had been written off as useless. He was the best and the worst — best in that he let us get away with murder, worst in that he was a sex maniac.

And I was his sex object. I named him Harpo because he was just as mad and chased me the way Harpo chased blondes. He was easily the ugliest creature I'd ever set eyes on. So grotesque, in fact, he was almost beautiful — an artifact, a temple ogre to ward off evil spirits, with his huge crooked fangs widely spaced in discolored inch-high gums, circled by heavy drooling lips. The whites of his eyes were blotched with yellow stains like nicotine. A tiny four-foot clown, he was amoral, kind-hearted, mad, bold, humble with not an ounce of pride. He had passed a sort of Nietzschean frontier beyond Good and Evil. He was all over me bounding like an excited dog with a slavering tongue, leaping at me and kissing my bare arms till I could shake him off. My insults flowed off him like water. He just lapped them up and giggled. I shoved a fist in his face:

"See this, you bloody creep? This is a buncha fives! You want this?"

He blinked at me and the fist, grabbed it and covered it in slobbery kisses. When I cursed him, he loved it and imitated the sounds. Sometimes he would play the penitent unrequited lover. He would sidle up to me as I worked and ogle. My white skin turned him on.

"Get lost."

He would put on a sad doleful face and moan like a sick calf to catch my attention. I ignored him. Then he would lean close and whisper my name:

"Ar-isu-ta-a-a . . . . "

"Piss off."

"Ar-isu-ta-a-a . . . . "

"Oh, Christ."

Then he would kiss my arm again, clinging like a slimy octopus, and I'd jerk it away, turning threateningly.

"Watch it!"

"*U-u-uchitu,*" he mimicked.

"You are a maniac."

"*Manyaku.*"

"Drop dead."

"*Dopidedu.*"

"Oh God."

"*Oga.*"

There was no reaching him. He was one more cross to bear. He was comical, loony, lovable, horrible. Needless to say, he had no authority, and with Harpo around we all declared a kind of Labor Day holiday and let him do all the work. He didn't mind, didn't complain, doing it with cheerful good humor.

He didn't last long. As a slap-happy clown he was a complete success, but as a foreman he was a disaster and soon got the boot. The others were sorry to see him go.

In some way, so was I.

One of the most tangible escape routes came through the medium of letters. One day in late fall, miracle of miracles, mail arrived. The unmoving world had stirred like a great slothful beast and inched forward. Most received nothing. Some received one or two. I drew four! A bonanza! I felt blessed by the gods. I fingered them gently, struck by the amazing fragility of the airmail paper and envelopes. To have made such a journey undismayed! Flung into bags, trains, planes, crossing mountains and oceans to reach, after long months, this soiled, grubby matting . . . sitting here before me, lovely and defiant — pearls before swine.

All were from my sister Rhea, a special bonus, since she could *write.* She'd written short stories, belonged to a literary club and wrote the kind of letter a prisoner prayed for — none of your Mary-had-a-baby numbers, these were long, detailed, descriptive, textured. I fell upon them like a starving prisoner at a four-course meal. But this was such an abundance of riches that I decided to stretch it out, hoarding the letters with miserly cunning. Each *yasumi* day — every fourteenth day — was our precious day of rest, although it was rest in name only, since there were plenty of camp chores to be done and I had to organize a compulsory concert. I read one letter each rest day, over and over, not touching the others. In this way two months went by before it was time to reread any. This gave a special tang to *yasumi* day, which became not only a welcome relief from drudgery but a little secret celebration, a bit of illicitly connived renewal.

At the paint shop we were becoming a permanent fixture. Proximity had broken down the barriers. We were no longer frightening giants, no longer foreign, despised, untrustworthy, curious enigmas. We were adopted as part of the work force, not exactly one of them but — like the Koreans, the students, the reform-school kids — united in a common family. For our part, aware of the good and bad among the Japanese, we sensed that as a people their moral ratio was no different from our own.

One of the bad apples was Little Napoleon, a mean, sadistic, strutting little peacock who delighted in baiting us at every turn and making a bleak life bleaker. He was even domineering to his peers, who frowned on such unnatural behavior and discreetly gave him a wide berth. He'd learned this style in the army, we were told. The others had a way of seeming not to hear his ranting. Making waves, in this country, was not the way to get along. It was he who insisted that *furyos* not be allowed any heat from the stove, that we took the space of shop painters and should be taught to keep our place — in the cold dark sheds behind the shop. That stove was our only chance to warm up after being outdoors all day, with no heat in camp to look forward to. Even when there were no others around the stove, he kicked us out.

Over the months we developed a healthy loathing for him, which he returned in spades. At the end of each day he insisted on Tommy brewing a special kettle of toasted green tea for him and serving it to him — his own private little tea ceremony. There were no thanks, no reward for the service. He had a ritual of placing a cigarette in his holder and lighting up luxuriously, almost triumphantly, as he unfolded his newspaper. His little porcelain cup stood beside the kettle and he filled it from time to time with purring satisfaction, sipping away slowly with sensual delight as he read . . . *puff, puff, sip, sip* — a portrait of lordly enjoyment.

One day, after he had driven us out of the shop like shivering dogs, we watched him from the doorway as he went through his hateful little caper — *puff, puff, pour, sip, sigh*. Someone said:

"I'd love to fill that fuckin' kettle with piss."

"Yeah." There was a silence as we savored the pleasant fantasy.

"Oh man, wouldn't that be something."

Then Nicholson voiced the fateful words: "You know . . . we might."

"What — *piss* in it?"

"It's possible — why not?"

"We'd get strung up by the balls."

Others took it up. "How would he know?"

"The taste, ya dumb tit."

"With lotsa tea? A good strong brew?"

"Sure. He could never prove anything if it tasted a bit — salty!"

It was beginning to seem real. "It's an awful chance."

"Let's have some fun. Life is short."

"Be a damn sight shorter if we're nabbed."

We agreed. We resolved to do the doctoring the following day. It became a conversation piece all day, relieving the monotony as our fear and excitement grew. We could hardly wait for the hours to pass.

We finished work at last and came trooping into the paint shop. This time the *furyos* didn't make for the stove as usual but for some reason went on out to the back. The kettle was produced and we gathered around it, unbuttoning quickly. Tommy left in disgust. Out came a pecker, then another and another. We opened the lid.

"Giv 'er here!"

"Me first!"

"No — *me*."

"Doesn't matter, there's room for all — stop shovin'! *Take your silly prick away!*"

Several jets shot into the kettle and over it as we jockeyed for position like hockey players in a scramble around the net, voices hissing in frenetic whispers.

"Hey, watch it, fer chrissake — it's going all over me!"

But enthusiasm was running too high as we shouldered each other, pushing and jostling as streams crossed and splashed and missed — the kettle overflowed. "Hold it, you stupid fuckers — that's enough!"

"Get the boiling water!"

We poured some hot piss down the drain to leave room for

water.

"The tea now — *lots* — it's gotta taste good!"

"It'll be fuckin' yummy!"

Little Napoleon was settling in at the table but we waited, giving it lots of time to brew. At last the kettle was placed before him with his dainty porcelain cup. We waited breathlessly in the wings for the ceremony to begin. Our faces, luminous with anticipation, hung in the back doorway like lanterns.

Out came the cigarette holder. The cigarette was fitted carefully into position and lit. He raised the kettle and gracefully filled the porcelain cup. It sat there, cooling, as he opened out the newspaper, folded it into position and relaxed. He puffed at the cigarette, inhaling deeply, exhaling leisurely, then reached for the tea. We held our breath and crossed our fingers as we watched him raise it to his lips . . . sip it luxuriously . . . swallow it . . . and set it down with a sigh of deep contentment.

"The bugger's doin' it!"

"*Sh-sh!*"

He continued slowly, inexorably — *puff, puff, sip, sip, swallow, sigh* — we followed every motion with hypnotic delight as he completed his "pee ceremony," draining cup after cup till the kettle was finally empty. We hugged each other in a silent orgiastic celebration. It was almost as good as a T-bone steak. No need to get to the stove that day. Little Napoleon had left us warm all over.

Our compulsory concerts on *yasumi* days were pathetic affairs. The camp commandant ordered us to enjoy ourselves, like it or not. Captain Reid gave me the job of getting a show together and I labored mightily, vainly, to entertain with the same old singers, musicians and tired songs. The men were as wearied of it all as I was.

One of our acts was a tap dance by René Charron, a Postal Corps sergeant, tiny, intense, with large dancing brown eyes that seemed to stare out at the world with a mix of deviltry, mistrust, guilt and anxiety. His dance, to the tune of "Sioux City Sue," was enjoyed most by the guards, and one in particular just couldn't get enough of it. He took to coming to Charron's bed-space, which unluckily happened to be on the main aisle, and he made special requests for more *tapu-dancu*. And with a bayonet blade a few inches from

René's butt, it was an offer that was hard to refuse. One night at 2:00 a.m. on my way to the outdoor *benjo*, I came on the startling tableau of this uniformed groupie standing at Charron's bed with Charron standing on it in his underwear, warm blankets pulled aside, bent double in agonized exhaustion, eyes half-closed in sleep, hopping up and down in a tap dance as the guard, bayonet in hand, beamed his approval, prodding him on to greater terpischorean heights: "*Siou-oux City Sue-ue*" — *atapatapatap*.

I made my way out to the *benjo* on this cold wintry night, humming sadly: "*There's no business like show business . . . .*"

At the plant I struck up a friendship with Newfie, a wild colorful Newfoundlander who had avoided being sent out to work since we'd arrived. No halfway measures — he faked madness, knowing his captors had a superstitious horror of insanity. It was total nonconformity, something that boggled the rigid Japanese mind. When they came to force him to work he bounced and leaped from bed to bed, shrieking and babbling till they retreated in fright. This came up once a month. Finally Reid, fed up with his antics, kicked him out of the barracks.

But very little changed. Newfie charmed and bedazzled his *hancho* into letting him sleep all day in a hidden corner; he was awakened for lunch and at day's end. "That'll be the day they git any work outta me," he told me. He clowned with me, screwing up his battered boxer's face, bowing over my hand. "May I kiss yer dainty hand, me darlin'? Oh please! please! A tender word, a little peck?" He was much in awe of my erudition. "You shouldn't oughta be here," he said. "It's a shame. This place is fer no-good bums like me." We talked of "after it's over," that persistent dream. He said: "I'll take all me back pay to New York, stay at the fanciest hotel, buy a top hat 'n tails, blow it all — women, booze — king fer a week! Then I'll be a bum again, where I belong." He had a violent tick that jerked his jaw away from his bull neck, caused, he said, by "fallin' out of a window and landin' on me head" as an infant. He became a brilliant black-marketeer and con man, swinging magical deals at the plant with great zest. And, true to his word, he never did a stitch of work.

I was getting the hang of this existence, but it was slow going. Little skills eluded me. Like blowing your nose on the march. With noses running and no handkerchiefs, you just blew. I watched Bob shoot a jet out like a bullet — it looked so easy. I would lean out at the right angle, aim with one finger on one nostril and let fly exactly the same way. Then find the snot all over my chest. Hopeless . . . .

A small supplement to our diet came from the peels of tangerines dropped on the roadside. We used to gather them, wash them under a tap behind the paint shop and chew on them for a bit of much-needed Vitamin C. Too much of this would induce diarrhea, so we couldn't overdo it. The chewiest, most enjoyable ones were those that had been hardened by time and the stamp of many feet — I liked to think of grapes pressed by peasants' feet and aged into fine wines. It filled a little corner of emptiness and, with a faint flavor still present, brought the illusion of eating.

When the weather was fair I often walked along the waterfront toward the waiting scaffolding, munching away at my goodies in a mood of pleasant euphoria. With a little push of the imagination I would become a carefree prince in disguise strolling on a vast stage singing: "*A wandering minstrel I, a thing of shreds and patches . . . .*" After all, I was in Japan, surrounded by passing citizenry — not dressed-up actors, either, but the real thing, with a real Japanese sky and sea and busy shipyards, not a painted backdrop, heightening the illusion and carrying me away for a few precious moments. "No one can deny, *die Gedanken sind frei.*"

These periodic excursions were becoming my fix, and I indulged at every spare moment. Once in the hot, cavernous bowels of a freighter under construction, I sat down to rest on a plank that was covered in wires and hoses — it was the middle of bedlam, with planks above and below me and the deafening thunder of riveting guns amplified in the confined shell of the freighter's hold. A ship was being born in this inferno, in the clamor and din and clutter and clatter and roar. Sparks from welders' torches came showering down around me in the dim light like exploding fireworks. Bodies climbed around and over me with the dense stink of sweaty split-toed rubber-soled shoes. In the shattering noise and blinding flashes, one could feel madness descending. Sound and darkness gradually faded as I crept into my silvery chrysalis and let it close about me . . . . Drifting . . . drifting lazily down a quiet stream in a rowboat . . . let the oars rest . . . let the gentle waves take me where they pleased . . . . A summer's day with the blue of the sky clear, deep, translucent, reflected in the water in layer after layer of deeper, cooler, pristine blues . . . . Silence covering the planet, broken only by the tinkling hum of crickets, frogs scraping away at their violins . . . . A soft breeze, of course, to caress my cheeks and cause the leaves from an overhanging branch to flutter like joyous flags celebrating my passage as I floated by. The sun warmed my closed eyelids, creating abstract shapes of vivid golden artifacts for my indolent pleasure. My bare feet dangled in the soft healing waters, my unblemished skin carried a clean scent of fresh soap to mingle with the faint perfume of flowers on the river bank . . . . Belly full after a succulent eight-course meal . . . clothes new, light, spotless . . . . Peace had rolled across the world, closing down all welding torches and riveters' guns, leaving only the universal melodies of bird song to color the silence.

When we worked behind the large shipyard's kitchens we noticed that now and then the cooks dumped coagulated noodles into the garbage cans behind the back doors. These were half-raw lumps of dough that hadn't cooked properly and had gone solid. To score on some of that meant overcoming many ifs. One could sneak over to the cans *if* the *hancho* wasn't watching, *if* no guard was in the offing, *if* no cooks noticed, *if* the noodles had an off morning. Often when we did get to the cans, we found them empty or the cooks ran out and drove us off with hoses. If on rare occasions we did manage to nab a lump of noodles, we had to hide it and scurry off to a nearby *benjo* to wolf it down. Usually the *hancho* worked with us, and there was no chance of getting near the tantalizing cans.

One day a group of us were tarring the undercarriage of a railway car when an order came through for a priority job elsewhere. The *hancho* left me behind to finish up and went off with the others. Great — no supervision, no guards in sight, a chance to check out the garbage cans. It was one of those days gamblers know about when everything feels right. I double-checked for guards: none. Kitchen doors closed. I knew it. Good! I scuttled over to the cans, hastily raised the lids and — joy of joys — jackpot! Heaps of steaming lumps of coagulated noodles! I wanted to whoop — this was my day! I threw a quick glance over my shoulder toward the kitchen doors, then dove in, scooping up huge gooey gobs of hot noodles, cramming them feverishly under my shirt, wet and sloppy against my chest. *One . . . another . . . another . . . enough.* Then I dashed away, hugging my precious cargo under my jacket, making for the *benjo* to hide.

Now these war-time *benjos* were a unique phenomenon. They had to be seen to be believed. With the manpower shortage they received lowest priority, and no one ever cleaned or emptied them. There was no plumbing system. The pits under the floor holes had been filled to the brim long ago and the turds rose high above the holes like miniature mountains, evil and festering. They rose so high it was dangerous to squat. You had to straddle the mound and empty your bowels half standing, adding your contribution to the height. There were several enclosed cubicles, each with its gruesome floor-hole. But these mounds were not dead. Months of rotting neglected feces had produced a horde of white maggots that covered the floors and walls, crawling and squirming upwards inexorably like an invading army. It was the type of den Dante would have reserved for his more vicious sinners.

I darted into the first narrow cubicle and locked the door. The stench was thick enough to drive nails into. I kept a lookout for guards through a tiny shoulder-high window as I straddled the magic mountain and leaned against the moving wall of worms, squishing them underfoot. Then out came the lumps of half-raw noodles. I joyfully gobbled and gurgled my ravenous way toward the ultimate, the prisoner's Nirvana: *a stomach full to bursting!* "O *de King of Babylon Balshazaar! Sat dere feastin' on his golden piazzer!*"

Well, not exactly a golden piazza. But certainly enjoyed more than the most sumptuous feast of Babylon.

Chapter Thirteen

THE HIGHLIGHT OF THE YEAR was the arrival of Red Cross parcels. We were being sent one parcel per week, but we received, on average, only one a year. Even that, when it arrived, was a heaven-sent miracle, a radiant dream image that sat before us, shimmering, new, unbelievable, threatening at any moment to vanish as we gazed. No pirate ever unlocked a casket of jewels with greater awe, surprise and reverent joy. Number one on the hit parade was the large thick bar of chocolate, scored in small squares, each of which dissolved lingeringly in the mouth, coating the insides with its thick patina of creaminess as the maddening aroma rose like a snake-charmer's hypnotic flute music, filling our heads.

There was a huge tin of powdered milk, which could be stirred into thick cream. There were tins of meat and vegetable soup — known as M&V — jam, cheese, butter, in gleaming new cans with spotless labels beckoning happily like expectant lovers; there were packs of fat, smooth American cigarettes — gold on the black market! There was the unfamiliar sound of laughter, giggles of astonished delight, hoots and yelps of unclouded ecstasy rising to the startled rafters.

Surreal recipes, concoctions, combinations were invented. I saw one man cut a clove of black-market garlic into fine pieces to be stirred into a plate of chocolate shavings. The orgy continued into the wee hours, sleep was forgotten. Snatches of song echoed strangely, spontaneously through the hut: *"O-o-oh Nelly putcher belly close t' mine, an' wiggle yer bum!"*

All next day at the plant, conversation buzzed with spirited accounts of inspired scoffs and the myriad ways of doctoring rice. That night the trading started. The center aisle was crammed with emaciated bodies shouting trades, offering deals, the air ringing like a stock exchange in crisis:

"Butter fer jam, anybody?"

"M&V fer chocolate!"

"Har-har!"

"Two decks of Chesterfields for chocolate!"

"Up yours!"

"Two decks fer jam!"

"Cheese for butter!"

"Butter for M&V, anybody?"

"Rice and soup for five fags!"

"Beans in the morning — five fags!"

"Six chocolate squares for butter!"

Dooley, a lisping, camel-eyed, toothless Grenadier, leaned against my aisle railing, shouting out a foolishly desperate and outlandish offer far above market value:

"Cheese and two decks fer jam!"

It was snapped up in a jiffy. "That's a crazy price, Dooley," I said. He nodded, fingering his tin of jam dolefully and in tones of angry resignation muttered: "My fuckin' thweet tooth."

The trading increased after supper with only twenty minutes to lights-out, the offers more bizarre, the clamor rising to a crescendo of mass hysteria. A madness was taking over the hut, exhilarating, comic, appalling. I hadn't realized till now how close we were to the brink, how easily we could become unhinged.

As the days wore on, the food disappeared and trading took on a quieter, more intense and desperate quality. I began to notice new things around me. We *were* going balmy, come to think of it. It had crept up on us gradually but it was there. Look at Berry and Caruso, two Grenadiers in our section, partners, another unity of opposites. Berry, a tall, blond Norwegian; Caruso, a short, dark Italian. Berry was sensitive, intelligent and high-strung. He studied Russian vocabulary with me as a mental exercise and taught me how to say grace in Norwegian. Dominique Caruso was a miner from Sudbury, a natural comic, simple, warm. I called him "my bambino." We spurred each other on to flights of comedy.

Berry and Caruso planned to open a restaurant after the war. This was no vague dream; this was detailed, with elaborate diagrams drawn up of the restaurant layout. Berry had been an assistant pastry chef, and the memories of those hundreds of creamy delicacies, known and handled so intimately, was obviously maddening. To plan to spend his life immersed in these mind-bending stacks of goodies was ultimate paradise. The plan legitimized his right to wallow in it to his heart's content, and no one could sneer. Lists of menus were agreed on, costs revised, after many serious conferences. I was shown the plans — the sink here, chairs and tables here, fridge here, counters there — plans made by men hovering at death's door. I nodded sagely. They were not kidding. "Good position, yes. I see — window here, sign above it, looks good."

Later a dispute broke out. Berry couldn't see the sink on the left, it had to be moved. Caruso refused. Tempers flared. They finally made it up and the restaurant was back in business. Then one day Berry refused to be the cook. He was a trained, skilled pastry chef, and he was damned if he would be diverted to the job of chief cook. To hell with that — they'd hire someone. "We can't afford it," Caruso argued. "You'll have to do it for the first year."

"In a pig's arse I will — *you'll* do it!"

"Me? Are you nuts? I have to serve and run the goddam place!"

Tempers again. They nearly came to blows. We watched, following the argument closely. What was unsettling about this was that not only were *they* going bonkers but *we* considered their antics quite normal.

It was an infection, an insidious virus. Yet it was also a canny shield, built by the mind for protection. How else could one accept this hellish state without illusion? We could hope, laugh, clown, play out our games and shut out the reality about us. If we had chosen to see clearly, to react to all this hopeless, dehumanizing ugliness in a direct and healthy way, we'd have been at each other's throats, tearing each other apart or taking our own lives. No, this was better, necessary. And invisible.

I was unaware of my own infection. I thought *I* was very sane. I lay on my matting in the darkness, kept awake by the hundreds of sand flies biting my stomach, edging me closer to madness. I was thinking too much, scheming. There was a jungle mentality growing around me. Blacky was away in hospital at Shinagawa — I was on my own. It was dog-eat-dog here, every man for himself. Would I survive it? What were my weaknesses, my strengths? I was an idea man, wasn't I? I must use my creativity as a weapon, yes, but how?

I evolved a plan, a survival plan. Every act, every decision, would be based on its relation to survival, no matter the cost. I would apply this principle to my parcel. How could I use it to aid my survival? If I ate it, like the others, it would be gone in a week. A flash of ecstasy, then . . . gone, a lovely memory, nothing else . . . and back to the meager rice and beans. No closer to getting home. But if I didn't eat it — what then? Foolish amounts of rice and beans were being swapped for small, tantalizing treats.

As an experiment I traded a quarter-pound tin of butter for three rations of rice and beans. As time went on, the ante would rise. I began trading some of my parcel for butter. It would keep, it was small, easy to store. A week passed and I was offered six rations of rice for a tin of butter. I ate my chocolate, stretching it out with a miserly two squares a night, kept some powdered milk and, with a herculean effort, traded *everything* off for butter. It was my sacrifice, my price for survival. I clung to that. There was important protein in the beans — that would build strength, health, bring me home.

Soon I was getting twelve rations of beans for my butter. Twelve days of going off to work with a solid breakfast under my belt, with no mid-morning shakes. In a few weeks I was getting twelve half-rations of rice and twelve rations of beans and I was regaining weight, conquering hunger. My competitiveness, my self-satisfaction increased. I was fighting the world and winning! But I was not conscious of my growing obsession with my brilliant plan, my lofty sacrifice, unaware that it was consuming me, clogging my brain with calculations, darkening my thoughts, destroying my inner light. I was turning myself into a hard, cold, mean survival machine running on a narrow, steely track. Syd Varcoe had once recited a poem to me at North Point, describing himself in his hobo days: "I'm a lean dog, a mean dog, baying at the moon . . . . " Now that was me . . . but that too was part of the price.

It was like the classic tale of the poor tailor who sang all day long, driving his neighbor frantic. Finally the neighbor gave him a bag of gold. The tailor was rich: he hid the gold, worrying about it being stolen, and fretted so much that his singing stopped and the neighbor lived in peace thereafter. I had been that tailor — now my song had stopped.

A let-down, a depression set in once the parcels were finished off. Life seemed more unbearable after we had "drunk the milk of paradise." We had been offered a reminder, excruciatingly brief, a teasing return to a former life, but it was snatched away again and we were flung back into the pit. A little trading was still being done on a small, cautious scale, with suspicion and distrust. I locked my butter away in Caruso's small strongbox (for a small fee). The image of these small tins hovered before me, warming me throughout the day. I went to sleep thinking of them — my hoard, my gold, my stake in survival. I was winning the battle. Ah, but losing the war. The loss, the erosion of spirit, was insidious.

My loyalties toward everything once cherished were withdrawn. Ideals, morality, ethics were soft indulgences that had lost meaning. Now I looked back at that way of life in the harsh cold light of my new realism. Old belief systems had collapsed. Philosophy — hah! I smiled grimly in the dark, thinking of that. I had once been the mountaintop philosopher, above the fray, surveying the follies of man from my lofty perch. A stupid game . . . . And at North Point, was that me? Bringing sweetness and light to suffering souls? Bringing library books, the joys of learning to rouse sleeping brains, debates, lectures, art classes — the bloody Florence Nightingale of the netherworld, holding back the tides of darkness. I had reveled in my newfound virtue, swimming in a warm pool of narcissistic glory. But it was all games, illusions, reflections on the wall of Plato's cave. Plato understood that only the tins of butter were real. They were truth. They would deliver me.

I savored this new cold, crystal-clear realism whose vinegar taste shrank the inside of my mouth. I'd sought and found truth at last. I could never have found it in my North Point evangelical zeal — to hell with all that. I thought of the rapturous romantic glow through which I had gazed at the Hawaiian Isles. What an infant. What a stranger. This bitter shaven-headed, cynical, flea-bitten old man had nothing in common with him. I understood my mother more now and why she had wept so mystifyingly that summer day . . . . In the park after a rainshower I had found a large round raindrop, a magical transparent globe sitting in a curled leaf, gleaming with its own uncanny beauty. Reverently I had detached the leaf and, stepping softly, walked home with it and brought it intact to show my mother. She had gazed at it and at my seventeen-year-old face, transported with joy, and burst into tears. I was perplexed, and asked for an explanation. "To think," she said, "that once I saw and felt exactly like that."

Now I knew. I was there, and beyond. Gone was the optimism, the humor, the clowning. Bye-bye to the songs of innocence. My face (Bob later told me) had changed radically. The expression was angry, grim, mean. Everyone was my enemy, even God. I had traveled through aeons of time to reach this austere plateau, this barren wasteland where nothing green grew and earth was hidden by cinders. All adornment, all mists stripped away. Only clarity left, only butter. Truth was butter, butter truth. I'd found it at a terrible price, or so I imagined. All I'd really found was another, more destructive illusion.

Winter was back . . . with its murderous winds, driving in from the ocean, attacking the miserable, cowering creatures crawling over the earth's surface. It whistled through the huts whose poorly built rafters strained and creaked overhead. With winter, the spirit went into hibernation. Fear and brooding took over. Pneumonia returned. Even speech grew spare as though opening one's mouth let in the cold. Hope dried up like dead leaves.

With great fuel shortages for the people, there was no question of any for the *furyos*. I would slide, shivering, under my thin blankets, pull them over my head, then open my mouth to blow my warm breath down around me, slowly heating the air, and hoping to fall asleep before the sand fleas started biting. I'd forgotten them during the summer. I could feel them rising through the matting to reach my body warmth . . . hundreds . . . . I didn't have much to offer but whatever I had, they wanted. They loved me and my sensitive skin. Blacky never felt them, nor did the others. I pictured them assembling for their nightly attack, organizing, squeaking orders in subliminal sounds, converging on my undefended carcass. If the itching started early, sleep was hopeless, and I would squirm and scratch and twist on their rack for hours, then finally drop into a stupor of unconsciousness toward morning and rise to face the day on three hours' sleep. My belly was always covered with a red rash of bites. At last I found an answer in mothballs. I found a man who had a few large mothballs. When and how he got them or why he kept them I never learned, but he sold me one for a half-ration of rice. I shaved it into a powder and spread it inside my underwear against my skin. It did the trick. It burned my skin but drove them off, and I slept the sleep of the blessed.

Out at work, I shivered for hours at a stretch. There was no getting warm. The stove in the paint shop was a haven of bliss, but our chance at it was all too brief. There was no washing. Lice flourished. The pores of my skin were gray and clogged with dirt. The ogre of cold pursued us all day, all night, pervasive, all-powerful, laughing sadistically at our feeble attempts to elude it. It was there all winter. Beside us, within us, attached, like some hateful Siamese twin.

Then on a *yasumi* day, a miracle happened. A shipment of coal arrived. Coal! Real coal! As though we'd issued a collective prayer so intense, so far-reaching that even God and Nippon Kokan could not ignore it.

Hot water was prepared and the two cement tubs in the washroom were filled, one for washing off the dirt, Japanese style, one for soaking. Since the coal was limited, the same water would have to do for all five hundred men. We were in ten sections of fifty and went in by sections, meaning fifty men went together into a tub built for a dozen. Fifty men, nose to nose, arse to arse, jammed into one tub. The first section would get the clean, boiling water, the last section the dirty, tepid guck. But we were happy for a bath on any terms.

It was an all-day carnival. Our section was near the front so we would get the hot stuff — hot being a euphemism for hell's fire. We stripped quickly in the cold air, washed (with whatever slivers of soap we owned) in lukewarm water, then stepped into the hot one . . . and yelled! Not with joy but with pain. This was impossible — madness! What did they think we were? The problem was that to stay hot all day it had to be very, *very* hot at first. Our skeleton carcasses were crammed together in this boiling vat, mouths agape and gasping, eyes bulging.

"Holy Jesus!"

"I'm scalded!"

"Ha-a-alp!"

"Are they crazy?!"

"Goddam cannibals — preparing us for supper!"

We sat or squatted in water up to our necks. I felt scalding brands gripping my entire body. To move increased the pain. Was this what lobsters felt? I looked around at the fifty heads floating like the tops of totem poles on this glossy surface, haggard features twisted in shock, turning livid. If it's heat we craved, it's heat we were getting! Suddenly someone giggled wildly, shouting: "I feel like Sam McGee!" Others joined in. We all took it up. Giggles turned to laughs, laughs to guffaws, guffaws to roars, and soon the room was bursting with sound — fifty hollow-cheeked, red-faced, bug-eyed, apoplectic totem heads reached a howling crescendo in an explosive outpouring of hysteria.

We were fifty Sam McGees reveling in our own cremation.

It was 3:00 a.m. as I stood in a small dark room beside a long coffin. It was my turn on fire-guard duty. The huts were silent, full of exhausted bodies escaping to their havens of unshackled dreams. Lyle Ellis, our section leader, lay in the coffin, another victim of pneumonia. The two of us now shared this lonely vigil. I had stopped here to say my own goodbye and fell into a reverie. I was groggy with lack of sleep and felt reality slipping away in the darkness. The hundreds of dreams filling the air close by distorted my thoughts.

Only two weeks ago this man was busy, vital, cheerfully pursuing his extra duties. Now he didn't exist. Or did he? In my mind and memory he was vividly alive. The dead continue, after all. I saw him as he was at North Point, a tall, lean, clean-cut, young staff sergeant from San Jose, California, keen-eyed, adventurous, quick-witted, efficient. A natural leader, he took charge of Brigade to fill the vacuum Matthews had created. His example reminded us that we were still soldiers. He was always closely shaven, his battle dress immaculate as he brought the rice or buns from the kitchen and dished it out with occasional calm, humorous quips. He joined our little coterie of pundits from time to time to enjoy a little wit and share some good talk. It was whispered that he looked too well fed and that some of the food disappeared between kitchen and hut, but there was no proof and we gave him the benefit of the doubt.

I could see him again on the *Tatuta Maru*, lugging the rations to our group, bravely keeping up appearances to hide the collective fear reflected in all our eyes. Then his tireless morale-boosting leadership here in 3D, where the endless rules, details, fussing, kept him on the go at high speed, draining his last resources and finally his life. There were few extras here to sustain his large frame, and toward the end a certain meanness had crept into his spirit as it did in many of us — but we wouldn't speak ill of the dead. Now he was "well out of it," the ubiquitous requiem when a prisoner died. After all, our turn might come soon but only after more months or years of suffering — wouldn't it be better *now*?

I reached forward and touched the rough wood. No air in there, but then, like a womb, he didn't need any, didn't need *anything*, he was totally free. Was death so bad? It no longer seemed so clearly limned in black and white: it was a shimmering gray. What happy arcana was he hiding in there? No hunger, no longing for home, no exhaustion, no insults, no beatings. Peace. If happiness was the absence of misery, then he was a lucky man . . . . Then why, I wondered, didn't we all kill ourselves? Spite, I supposed. Contrariness. Too many trying to do us in. We accepted their simple logic: if they wanted us dead so badly, then that itself was reason enough to stay alive. Or was it just plain instinct?

The long box stood before me, dim in its outlines as though floating in the darkness, gently drawing out my thoughts. Goodbye, Lyle . . . this isn't much of a funeral, is it? We don't grieve for you. What do we feel? A little envy? Relief that the Grim Reaper passed us by? But somewhere back in San Jose someone will mourn you properly. We just can't, you see. We block you out, as you did us. We must leave no room for sorrow, a luxury we can't afford. If we didn't, we'd die of it, dissolve from stone into a soggy lump of tears. We're enclosed in separate coffins of our own. Even sympathy must be hoarded. We breathe the pure, thin air of survival. Outside, out there somewhere, the air is human, maudlin, civilized, forbidden, fatal . . . we must keep that out.

So many deaths, now so routine . . . the earlier ones were the hardest. I thought of Lavoix, the MP who died in North Point. He had been the spirit of laughter on the train across Canada, joke after joke in his hoarse, rasping voice and heavy accent that had us all convulsed:

"But boss, I don' water de grass now, it's raining outside."

"Well, don' be stoopid, use umbrella!"

He took two weeks to die — and he knew he was dying. Like a man on Death Row awaiting the inevitable, he wept shamelessly with no inhibition.

"I don' wan' to die," he moaned, and his hollow, pockmarked face, wet with tears, was contorted in fright . . . .

And Hope, once the tall, broad-shouldered, lantern-jawed MP, reduced to a bent heap of pain, a portrait of sorrow, sitting on the floor of Agony Row, rubbing his "electric feet," rocking to and fro, eyes mad and distant as though discerning the face of the Angel of Death, invisible to us. Death in those days was an unfamiliar visitor, always drawing shocked response.

My thoughts wandered back to my first intimate encounter with death. At eighteen, four years ago — four centuries. Brina, a close friend, a tragic suicide . . . how it shook me to the core. In winter I wandered in the graveyard all day, freezing, weeping, talking to her, babbling my grief.

Lyle seemed to be listening quietly, intently . . . the walls of the room were invisible in the darkness. The air was crowded with phantoms as the years passed before me. How full my grief was then, I thought, how soft, raw and open my heart. Hank's death had brought it all back. And now? The same heart was encrusted with scar tissue, tough as a walnut shell, like all the others . . . . Feelings? Yes, I had those, but unhealthy ones for the most part — hate, anger, longing. Laughter? Song? True, I still did that, but wasn't that too part of survival — escape, revolt? And would we really survive, even if we lived? Would there be anything left worth saving? Weren't we being subtly murdered now, by inches? We were not just standing still, marking time as we imagined. We were being invisibly destroyed day by day from within. Death was a tricky customer. He was not only inside this coffin, relaxed, fulfilled, cozying up to Lyle Ellis, he was everywhere, relentlessly, patiently dogging our footsteps, sitting beside us as we worked, ate, slept, stealing our humanity. Was there any defense against him? Only time would tell.

The greatest symbol of our revolt, our escape mechanism, was Paddy Keenan, our regimental sergeant major, a thin, gnarled, red-faced veteran of the British Army of World War I. Twice a day the hut lined up for *tenko* (roll call), conducted in Japanese with the commandant, interpreter, NCOs and guards inspecting. At the shout "*Keirei* [parade]!" we scuttled into position before our bunks.

Each of the ten section leaders in the hut reported the number present and sick. *"Ki-o-tsuki* [attention]!*"* and *"Bango* [number off]!*"* We numbered off in Japanese. Any mistake was rewarded with a wallop.

Paddy led the inspecting party, bellowing *"Tenko!* Look lively, lads!" in his best parade-square voice. His tunic and shorts were pressed and spotless, his brass insignia shone lustily, his polished boots gleamed defiantly, his puttees were perfection.

One of our subtle but less uplifting forms of revolt was the carefully deployed art of farting. Since there was no regulation against it, we indulged in it with increasing intensity. Men saved all their gas for *tenko* and timed it to cut loose as the camp commandant passed with his coterie. It had begun to reach the point of a triumphant fanfare following the inspecting party as it moved down the center aisle. The intent was not lost on the commandant.

One day, after roaring *"Tenko!"* in his hoarse Cockney foghorn voice, Paddy cleared his throat for an historic announcement that went echoing through the hut:

"It 'as been brought to the hattention of the authorities that certain practices of the prisoners 'ave been found to be hoffensive to the hexistin' powers! Heffective as of this date, *all forced fahr-ting will be strictly pro-hibited!"*

Yes, Paddy Keenan did things in style. He moved in an enchanted aura of untouchable certainty — "I am the very model of a modern major general." When he strutted proudly down the aisle exuding his special brand of defiant confidence, the dingy barn with its bare rafters faded from sight and a broad, immaculately tended, sun-kissed parade square unfolded before our eyes. Japan, the guards, the hunger, the dirt vanished. We stood at attention in our spanking fresh uniforms, rifles correctly sloped, muscles bulging, bellies full. He was magic; he was home; he was freedom and derring-do. The present became a triviality — tough, but only a brief passing phase in the swashbuckling life of a soldier, and we would soon be reminiscing about it all over a bottle of beer. Escapist? Completely. But who the hell wanted reality? No actor ever offered a more meaningful daily performance than our Paddy Keenan.

In our incessant discussions Bob and I rehashed and relived the many movies and scenes we recalled, comic, passionate or tragic, till we knew some of the lines better than the actors. He had worked as a movie usher and watched everything that came by, without boredom, as often as sixteen times. I would revert constantly to the high point of movie going — French cinema — and, of course, the number-one genius of all time, Harry Baur, who could be the most vicious, violent Rasputin, with his craggy, mangled face, and turn that same face, as Beethoven, into a stoic, gnarled mountain out of which oozed near-invisible rivulets of the tenderest, most exquisite sorrows. I described the memorable scene in which he played the *Moonlight Sonata* with his lover beside him, telling him their love was dead and she would be leaving him now to go off with another, never to see him again. As she spoke he played softly, with no sign of listening except for the tears that coursed steadily down the rough lined cheeks. The sonata was the sound of his wounded soul. What I didn't mention was the special niche this music had carved in my own heart. It fed all the romantic yearnings of my youth for great tragic experience, rich dramatic sorrows. Sadly, this desire was fulfilled too swiftly by the suicide of Brina and, at eighteen, I had a bigger helping of tragedy than I'd bargained for. The *Moonlight Sonata* became the vehicle for that pain and they became enmeshed.

Each evening as I dashed off to rehearsals at the Y, I had stopped at my friend Phyllis's house for our brief ritual. She would turn the lights low, light a candle and sit down to play the sonata. Very slowly, very softly. I'd light a cigarette and with a curiously delicious, sensual sadness drift back to the wintry graveyard where Brina lay and let the music sink me deeper and deeper in the icy earth. All the Romantic poets of the ages seemed to join in this weeping.

Tombstones rose about me, joining the chorus of sound . . . the uncanny joy of dead souls swaying to the rhythm, singing that the secret of life was tragedy. The music rose higher, lifting like the wind fanning snows . . . the ghost faces, like Brina's, suffused with sadness, serenity, knowledge withheld . . . .

The piano notes ended. I would butt my cigarette, thank her, kiss her gratefully, absently (poor payment for what she had offered), and hurry off, replete. My fix. I sensed that the process of sorrowing was an instrument of healing. Generous Beethoven, a vessel, a medium, always offered me that.

Now suddenly the news came through that the commandant had let Reid out to buy some records, and he had a copy of Beethoven's Fifth! Oo-ee! Would we get to hear it? Yes, an evening was scheduled one *yasumi* day for anyone interested!

Bob and Blacky and I went off to the Hong Kong Ballroom, our tiny barren bathhouse, unused in winter, where the gramophone had been set up. We brought tiny footstools to sit on, hard on the bony backsides but better than the cement floor. A couple of dozen prisoners converged quietly like a gathering of scarecrows at a witches' sabbath.

We sat reverently, waiting for the music to begin. I imagined a symphonic orchestra in tuxedos or tails, tuning their instruments as I leaned back in my red-and-gold-cushioned seat. The fat, bored bourgeois audience, with paunches full of steaks and wine, couldn't listen as we would. What a crew we were. Gray skin marked with dried-up pus sores, pores clogged with dirt, bodies humped forward, bony knees high and sharp, faces gaunt, eyes curious, burning, eager, uneasy. Some had never heard classical music but had come along for the ride. It was certainly the strangest audience Beethoven had ever been played to and the most humbly attentive.

The music began, not softly, not gradually, but loudly, defiantly — a challenge to the gods, to the fates. Beethoven linking hands with this little band of lost souls, united in a symphony of survival . . . . One voice — his, ours, mine — from our deepest core, sending all our anger charging to the surface: *tn-tn-tn-TOMMM! tn-tn-tn-TOMMM!* Shouting, "I-will-not-DIE! I-will-not DIE!"

We joined in his leonine roar: "I-will-not-DIE! — I-will-not-DIE! — I-will-not-DIE!" Smite me, Lord! Strike me deaf, curse me, corrode my spirit, my life, Beethoven snarled, but my soul will not bow! It'll shake itself free — leap forth, become thunder, crashing out of darkness, raging through the heavens to the edge of dawn! . . . where he paused, to rest, to linger . . . to transform himself into new energy. Then, in his new voice: "Hear me as I stand now astride mountains: I sing out greeting to distant planets and wait for an answering voice . . . . "It creeps in faintly, asserting the presence of life . . . then a *roar* and swift crescendo of exalted trumpeting, a singing to the universe that there is more, there is more, there will always be more, more joy, more beauty, more rage, more everything!

I listened, gazing about me at the grimy, flimsy walls, blasted out of sight by the music. No, Beethoven didn't die, he was very much alive here on the other side of the planet — even death couldn't beat the bugger down. And well he might be defiant. He knew. His genius was victory itself. He walked arm in arm with God, with me, with all of these rapt listeners. No goddam prison of deafness, no miseries could confine this furious celebration of freedom! He had come to the right place.

The concert ended. We returned to our bunks in silence — removed white tie and tails — retired to our spacious, luxurious bedchambers . . . and so to sleep.

Chapter Fourteen

A S TIME PASSED THE CAMP took on the character of a giant
bathhouse in which there were no longer any secrets,
only here it was the soul that was naked for all to see.
No protective societal posturing was attempted. Each
man felt himself pitted against a hostile universe in a struggle to
survive: there was no extra energy wasted on pretext. To combat
the isolation, one took a partner with whom one shared all. Every
act was known to all and remembered. It was a static society,
congealed in a timeless continuum. The guards became an organic
part of our lives for better or worse. Bad luck had brought us
Corporal Yamanaka, in charge of the guards, mad, colorful,
vicious. I was in his bad books and, once there, my status was
frozen. He was not leaving. I was not leaving. And there we
remained.

The word was that Yamanaka was dying of TB or syphilis and
hated the rest of mankind for being healthy. One of his many sides
was his vision of himself as a brilliant sleuth. He indulged this
fantasy to the point of fitting himself out in outlandish disguises to
conduct his extracurricular spying activities, all based on the
prerequisite of our being congenital idiots. His pet disguise was his
wounded, crippled-soldier routine, in which he swathed himself in
bandages from head to toe, with a huge turban-like bandage across
his face and a splotch of red paint for a realistic touch. He would
come limping along, leaning heavily on a cane, planning to look
inconspicuous among the shipyard workers as he sidled up to us.
He was as inconspicuous as a Santa Claus parade.

"Uh-oh, look what's comin'."

"What?"

"Detective Yamanaka of Scotland Yard on the prowl."

"Which outfit?"

"The wounded-soldier number."

"Christ, that's worn to death."

There was the one with the long white beard. There was the derelict in patches. There was the civilian with panama hat and sunglasses. We would look busy at our work, bent over the anchor chains, pretending not to notice his approach. He would come limping along, drawing slowly nearer while we waited till he was standing beside us. Then, as one man, we would whirl around to face him, come smartly and respectfully to attention, and whip off a spirited salute, shouting: "*Ohayo Yamanaka-san!*" Furiously he would return the salute and stalk off in a high dudgeon like the frustrated villain in an old melodrama who snarls: "Curses! Foiled again!"

My own showdown with Yamanaka came when the radio station in Tokyo devised the idea of broadcasting propaganda messages overseas via shows made in prison camps. When they came to 3D, Captain Reid asked me to work up a concert and emcee the show. This was fine for us, since we could send lists of prisoners still alive and messages to families. We took for granted that our governments would delete any propaganda and forward the names to our loved ones.

In my script I referred to 3D as Camp Carefree, knowing this would please the censors while the sarcasm, laid on with a trowel, would be understood at home. I thought of trying the handy gimmick used by the Americans that went: "We are being well treated here and the food is great. Please tell this to all my friends in the army and navy and, above all, *tell it to the marines*" — counting on the censors not recognizing the current slang for "baloney."

On *yasumi* day a flurry of technicians descended on the camp to set up for the broadcast. The atmosphere became completely transformed. These were all civilians with no sign of army protocol, and we were the stars, to be accorded full, respectful attention. Since I was the emcee, they showed me special deference, consulting me at every turn. I was getting carried away with my new-found powers, unaware of being closely watched by Yamanaka in the background; he had orders to steer clear. The well-known Japanese dictum, "The nail that sticks out gets hammered," applied perfectly to my situation. Yamanaka was seething. Imagine a stinking *furyo* putting on such airs! Ordering Japanese people around! Who does that dog think he is? *Bakayaro*

. . . . Just wait till this is over and I get my hands on him — I'll show scum what scum is — give him something to remember!

The broadcast took several hours and went well. I read off long lists of names and messages between songs. Actually the broadcasts were hushed up by our governments, but ham operators on the U.S. West Coast did pick them up and relayed them to my family and many others. But I was to pay a heavy price for my day in the sun. I had offended the "proper place" protocol, a terrible insult, something that would have prompted a samurai to lop off a commoner's head. Yamanaka bided his time.

The stress of the broadcast and the lack of sleep brought on another bout of malaria. I reported sick, but Captain Reid had to send me out to work. He gave me a few Atabrine pills that made me slightly deaf as I marched out to the plant. I wore all my clothing but still shivered, aching in all my joints. We had just been issued a few good warm Red Cross hats with earflaps, and I was one of the lucky recipients. I pulled the earflaps down for more warmth.

Yamanaka took a dim view of prisoners getting good hats to wear — those filthy *furyos* were being shamefully coddled. Then he spied me, not only sporting one of the new hats but pulling the earflaps down over my ears *without permission* — how dare I! He bellowed at me from a distance in Japanese. No one understood him. For my part, I didn't even hear him, being slightly deaf from the pills — a double crime. He had me.

He fell on me like a thunderclap, shouting questions I couldn't make out. I didn't know what I'd done. When I gave the wrong answers, he ripped my hat off and started whipping my face with it. There was a buckle on the end that made a painful weapon. I tried desperately to appease him by answering "*Hai* [yes]!" — which roused his anger, then "*Nai* [no]!" — which was worse. He was working himself into a fury. He threw down the hat and seized his rifle. He started clubbing me over the head with the butt as he fired questions, demanding answers. The blows added to my dizziness and the shooting pain soon took over, blocking out my malarial aches and fever. The blows still didn't appease him but only seemed to spur him on till he seemed to luxuriate in his rage, conducting it like a maestro in an ever-ascendant spiral toward some sexual sadistic climax. I felt myself spinning and whirling through a horrible nightmare of pain, enveloped by crashing blows and crazed shrieking. Was there no end to this? He drove me before him into the lunchroom, ordering all the prisoners inside to watch the punishment.

Grant was called up to interpret. With all 400 men listening, Yamanaka began firing a new series of questions. "Why didn't you answer when I called?"

"I didn't hear." *Whack*!

Every answer was met with a shriek and a blow. Nothing I could say was right. Only now he was using the steel barrel of his rifle, smashing it across my bare skull. My scalp was cut and blood ran down my face. I felt enclosed in a box, being knocked to and fro against its flaming sides, which sent out scorching pain. The obvious unfairness of the questions, his vicious, power-crazed hatred, the blast of stunning blows had an electrifying effect on me — I was nearly overwhelmed by the lust to kill this man. I felt possessed. Hate sent jets of flame through my veins, driving everything before it — all pain, all fever, all caution. I felt like a mad dog straining to leap at his throat and sink my teeth in it. He wanted humility, fear, and saw clearly the naked fury in my face. We were two men locked in a mortal embrace, with one tied hand and foot. He drew his sword from its scabbard, fired a question at me then turned to Grant and jerked his head at me in a contemptuous gesture that meant "Tell the scum!"

Grant said, "He wants to know how you'd like it if he cut your head off."

I stared at the blade. The fear I'd held at bay returned at the sight — this man was crazy. *He could do it*. Bloodthirsty bastards . . . they chopped heads off like apples. In *hara-kiri* they cut their own guts out, then a pal lops the head off. Instinct gave me vision: he must be reminded that his duty was to see that we worked, not to kill us. The company owned us — he'd have to explain his actions. I turned to Grant:

"Tell him my boss doesn't want his men working without their heads." I jerked my head at Yamanaka, imitating his insulting gesture.

"I can't tell him that," Grant hissed. "He'll blow his stack!"

"Tell him anything," I said, beyond caring, beyond sanity.

Grant invented an apologetic answer that brought another blow, but apparently the flow of blood down my face appeased him at last. He turned to harangue the silent prisoners and stalked out.

It was over.

I walked to my lunch table, weak, trembling and sick, the numbness receding, the pain advancing with the returning fever. Be tough . . . . In the wake of a typhoon that had passed at last, leaving my scalp torn, my body loose and rudderless, I was afloat in a sea of pain but . . . *still afloat!* The knowledge carried an odd exhilaration. I wasn't exactly a portrait of victory but in a peculiar way I had won. It was his intent to see me grovel and I had not. Anger had, thankfully, sustained me. Once again I felt deep stirrings of new powers, a sense of invulnerability that left me quietly exultant.

I moved into my place beside Buddy Dicks. The glances at my bloodied face were sympathetic, embarrassed. I knew their thoughts, guilty relief that it wasn't them, anger because in a way it was them.

I tried to put away the ugly memory of the beating. It was over — bad luck, and that was that. But it was not over — just beginning, in fact. That night and for many succeeding nights and days, Yamanaka crowded in on all my waking thoughts. I had never hated like this before. The rage roared in me, unrequited, straining to explode the dikes of brain and body. My hate spread outward with a feral blood lust. I craved blind revenge on all, every man, woman and child in this accursed land, every home, flower, brick, stick, garden, temple — all. Kill, destroy, wipe this blight, this vast cesspool from the face of the earth! Till now my anger had burned at a low flame, a smoldering abstraction. Now it had become personal, taken shape, entering my soul. I was sick with it. He — all of them — wanted my death, my pride ground to dust, wanted me to quake with fear at their power. Well, someday, somehow I'd return the favor, dance on their goddam graves! Drop by drop the poison seeped into my marrow, turning healthy tissue into something foul, resistant, irrational.

I knew revenge was not possible and the frustration ate at me. It was a fever in the bones. I craved a ritual killing each night to quench my thirst for blood. I fell into vivid reveries, in which Yamanaka and I were locked in a small empty room . . . . "Now," I told him, "it's just you and me, baby, you and me. No bayonet, no rifle, just our bare hands — you hear that, you bastard? And only one of us gets out of here alive." Then I knocked him crashing against the wall. I proceeded to beat him to a pulp in long, lingering detail. It was partially satisfying, soothing. It became my ersatz reality, which would have to do.

It took weeks for the anger to fade. When it did, I thought it was gone for good. He was, after all, just one sick man belonging to one sick army. But it had eaten deep into my being. The streams of the unconscious are not so easily dried up, as I was to learn in the next forty years.

As we began to fit in, becoming part of the social fabric, workers and prisoners forming more and more permanent ties, a black market gradually came into being. Some indulged on a small scale, but a few managed to become big entrepreneurs.

Erny West was the most active. A former used-car salesman, he lived and breathed deals. Small featured, with an engaging chubby-faced smile and a thick hide, he had made contacts with civilians and *fu*-men, trading anything, risking punishment. He was humble, nervous, hyper, tireless. Nothing daunted him — slurs and insults rolled away, ridicule or sarcasm passed him by. Even his throat was high-geared; it gave off a rhythmic, snapping, half-gagging sound between phrases as though his body motor could not slow down to wait on his words. He would sidle up to me, blinking and twitching.

"Anything to trade, Ally?" *Clack-clack-clack* . . . .

"Not a thing, Westy."

"You sure?" *Clack-clack-clack* . . . .

Top man in the field was Charley Clarke. He was a staff sergeant in the Postal Corps, a decorated veteran of World War I, bright, fearless and enterprising. He seemed to watch the doings of his fellow man with an ever-present, sapient, sardonic smile. His job as rations supervisor put him in the company of guards and *fu*-men all day long, with ample time to wheel and deal. He was short and stocky and never lost weight. He had a good face for a portrait, which I did once — strong jaw, heavily lined face and strong knobby nose. During the fighting he had shown himself cool, daring and resourceful. We were in awe of his powers. He had the *fu*-men eating out of his hand — or, to be more accurate, *he* was eating out of *their* hands: a variety of exotic extras that at times included roast chicken. A measure of his status was the spectacle of the all-powerful cooks humbly bringing him hot bricks to warm his bed on cold nights. Now *that* was power.

One day, at mid-morning *yasumi*, we slipped behind the huge wooden blocks that supported the freighter to sneak a forbidden smoke. It was a dark spot, crowded and fairly safe — but not today. A slick little *fu*-man appeared out of nowhere and nabbed us in the act. He unbuckled his belt and lined each of us up for a belting. We recognized him as one of Charley Clarke's biggest black-market suppliers. What luck! The others collected three or four thwacks across the face but I played it smart. When my turn came, I smiled my most winning smile.

"*Watakushi tomodachi* Charrey Croku [me friend Charley Clarke]," I said, offering him a broad, intimate, conspiratorial wink.

His face went rigid and he flew into a towering rage — *thwack!* The belt came whistling through the air. How dare I accuse him of any dishonesty. *Thwack!*

"No — wait — wait" — he must have misunderstood — *thwack!* "Me — friendo Charrey Croku!" This repetition drove him to a frenzy. "Wait — you! Croku — friends!" *Thwack!* "No — *friends!* Get it?" *Thwack!* "*Tomodachi!* Croku!" *Thwack!*

The more I insisted, the more he lashed out. I went on babbling and he went on flailing till one of the painters shouted some worthwhile advice: "Shut yer stoopid mouth!"

I did, at last. But not before I'd collected about three times as many blows as the others for my brilliant strategy.

On a morning in March, I was carrying a fifty-kilo sack of cement up the steep gangplank of a freighter — shrouded in gloom, putting one foot in front of the other, as I had all winter, day in, day out. Thinking of rice. Of sleep. Of getting warm. Of mothballs. Of the wind. Of the scaffolding. Of Ellis and Emo and the others who had died.

Bob told me how he had put Jimmy Emo into the coffin. He was on duty that night, with the huts deep in sleep. He and Paddy Keenan tried to lay Jimmy in the coffin, but it was fully a foot too short. They doubled the legs up at the knees and shoved hard, but the head rose like a live thing as they pressed. Bob had been very fond of Jimmy, recalling the little things: in the tropical heat and thirst on the *Awatea*, for instance, when we were allotted one glass of beer per man, Bob had stood outside the sergeants' mess while Jimmy, typically, passed glass after glass out to his men through a window. No one else did. Now as he lay folded grotesquely in the fetal position, the horror of handling his dead body was too much. The head *must* be forced down to close the lid. Paddy balked. Bob had to seize the skull and press it with all his strength till the neck seemed to snap and the limp head slid down. It was like killing, making him die twice. They closed the lid, but the trauma was never closed down.

Was my turn coming up? How? One of my fevers could turn to pneumonia, then *pfftt!* And into the box.

One foot in front of the other . . . how long, O Lord? The weight of the cement felt like a bag of stones. I reached the deck and piled it with the other sacks.

It was too early for the shakes and I could still feel my breakfast with me — the better time of day. I paused at the ship's rail to rest and gazed out to sea. The sun had broken through a cloud cover and was dramatizing all the objects on deck with its magic of light and shadow. It struck the waves that were rippled by the breeze, turning them into thousands of flashing, twinkling stars that dazzled the eye. I watched the festival of light out there, so full of gaiety, as it grew into a vast sprightly silvery-costumed dance ensemble, twirling in unison right out to the distant horizon. There was something strange, something new . . . the breeze brushed my cheek tenuously . . . it was no longer wind. It was *warm*, and so was the sun! Spring? The realization came flooding over me, announcing itself, unfolding me like the sun in this new comforting warmth. Spring was coming.

The endless winter with its pitiless cruelty, its soul-destroying hopelessness, its relentless death toll, was withdrawing, being politely eased out in the softest, gentlest way by stronger forces — *life* forces. Little shoots of grass were lifting their heads all around the world — the buds of trillions of leaves were swelling irresistibly, flowers germinating, life awakening. My God, there was more bloody power in their happy little yelps of infantile joy than in all that dark corrosive pall of evil! It was beaten, conquered

— God Almighty, I'd made it!

I leaned over the rail staring at the shimmering waters, eyes half closed, opening my pores to let the joyous astonishment, the relief, the victory take hold. The myriad flashing wavelets were converging, singing, hooting, waving to me, celebrating their arrival — a marvelous bloody fiesta of life was going on out there! I was swimming in its blinding light, swept up in it as it reached inside me. A fierce surge of reviving power, of invincibility gripped me — and with it a new irrational optimism. I was part of that undeniable life force. Its victory was mine — *we were one* — my whole being was filling up with one loud primordial roar, a great Olympian *yes*. I was suddenly certain I'd live! *I knew it.* And the thought brought a burst of laughter up from my depths, laughing in the face of the gods. They just couldn't kill me! They tried and they tried and they failed. I was superman and nothing could touch me now! Go ahead — beat me, starve me, send down your fevers, your hot feet, your electric feet, your marauding fleas, your stinkin' plagues, I've had 'em all! Do your damnedest — it doesn't matter, goddamit, I'll *live* — I'll *survive!*

Chapter Fifteen

MOST DEATHS HAD OCCURRED in winter. Farther north it had been worse. Jenkins, coming in a later draft, ended up in Niigata, a northern camp that caught the cruel Manchurian wind. They did longshoremen's labor, unloading barges of pig iron, manganese ore, soybeans. Arriving in winter from tropical Hong Kong, they succumbed to pneumonia in droves. Of the three hundred sent there, more than a hundred perished from illness or maltreatment; eighty died in the first three months.

Although illness among us had decreased with the brown rice, there was still plenty of sickness around. Some feet and nerves were damaged beyond repair, and a permanent sick squad called *romokyu* was kept in camp. They were given sitting jobs, picking out and separating nuts and bolts for future use. Though more peaceful, the life of the *romokyu* or *nutsu-borutsu* was bleak and dreary, with no glimpse of the outside world, no contact with real life, no break in the monotony. We envied and pitied them.

One of our part-time interpreters was a small, sprightly soul called Koyanagi. He was a middle-aged civilian who had worked in Windsor, Ontario, for eleven years, then in Detroit for nine. He had a sardonic sense of humor and a familiarity with street slang that delighted us. Behind tiny twinkling eyes that seemed to seek out the humor in any situation shone a certain softness, a guarded sympathy that we sensed. Although he was cautious, there was none of the "space" we usually felt established subtly around even the friendliest civilian.

One day Erny West was caught trading; he was sent up to a Tokyo jail for several months, living under grueling conditions. He returned thin, pale, subdued, and was greeted by Koyanagi with a cheery: "Herro, Westy! How you like in a Big House?" But under his brusque, morale-raising chiding lay a heart full of genuine pain, shame at the sight of our suffering and stark living conditions. Few

knew that he was bringing large quantities of medical supplies
—Atabrine, aspirins, sulfa drugs — to Captain Reid, at his own
expense and risking the wrath of the military. When I reported sick
with malaria fever, it was Koyanagi's Atabrine pills that Reid gave
me to keep me going as I worked. Forty years later his widow told
me how he used to come back depressed from his duties at our
camp and describe his upsetting experiences.

Again this marked the moral differences between civilian and
military thinking, differences we could see, sense, yet somehow not
grasp. It may have been the Japanese youth, imbued with the
Bushido spirit, that helped mislead us.

I was dogged by the memory of the elderly three-bander who
had hidden me away to rest when my fever was high. There was a
similar incident with the *furyo* who slept behind me. He heated
rivets all day, every day, a maddeningly dull job. One day an
elderly *hancho* stopped him and motioned him to follow. He placed
a small sack over the *furyo's* shoulders so he would look busy and
led him away. They strolled around the shipyards in a leisurely
sightseeing tour for several hours, a psychological boon and relief
from the monotony. He had nothing much to offer, only this small,
giving gesture, but I was struck by the compassion and wisdom it
revealed.

Walter Jenkins described an incident in Niigata in which he and
a friend were unloading charcoal in the rain, their cadaverous faces
lined with coal dust. They wore bulging Japanese raincapes. Two
young children emerged from a flimsy shack to watch these six-
foot-four monsters with their black-lined Kabuki faces, looking like
creatures risen out of the deep. The boys had long thin loaves of
bread in their hands. Was there a woman in the shack who had sent
them? Walter eyed the loaves hungrily. The older one, about
eleven, approached cautiously, fearfully. He broke off half his bread
and handed it up to Walter. The monster growled his thanks, broke
it in two and handed half to his friend. They wolfed it down in a
flash as the boys watched. Then the smaller one, about six, edged
forward, gazed up at this great mountainous dinosaur with its
strange blue eyes and beak nose outlined in black, its bleached hair
and elongated head, and offered his entire loaf.

Often, on the two-mile march to and from the shipyards, I would
let my thoughts wander down the side streets as we passed.

Houses, huts . . . where families lived. How? Pleasantly? Happily? Peacefully? There were no trees, nothing growing at any season on this cindery surface, but there must be plants in pots, a spot of green on a windowsill, a flash of color. People passed, some coming from work, some in kimonos and sandals with towels, heading for the communal bath, some in groups in the morning doing their exercises . . . . I felt a familiar curiosity, a strange longing, as one does gazing up at a lighted window. A wanting, a selfish possessiveness. I needed to bridge that impossible space between us. To break out of line, walk away from the gloomy column, shaken free, alone, to wander where I pleased, at a leisurely pace, down this street or that, wherever fancy led. I imagined following that man home: entering his orderly little kingdom, removing my shoes, squatting on the mat with his children, speaking with his wife in Japanese. I'd speak with the old parents, ask about their history, smoke with them. I wanted to ask the children about school, their teacher, their studies, to examine their books and the drawings in them, to see what they ate, to listen to the conversation . . . .

But this was war, and war was more than injustice; it was grotesque illegality, legislated hate. It decreed enemies, friends.

Yet here and there, the categories were pierced, spaces bridged. Jan Solecki, our choir leader at Sham Shui Po, was working with other *furyos*, unloading railway cars under an elderly Japanese *hancho*. The boss could see they were weak from hunger and straining at the heavy labor. At one point he motioned them to follow him and led them to a distant railway car. It was locked. He forced the lock and broke into the car, which was stacked with potatoes. Stealing food in Japan carried a two-year jail sentence for civilians, to say nothing of the punishment a guard could mete out on the spot. They watched in astonishment as he liberated a whole sackful, enough to feed the dozen men. He brought them to a place where he set a small fire alight in a grate and had them place all the potatoes in a pail of water to boil. Then they returned to work. When the potatoes were done he poured off the water and told them to eat them all. He wanted none for himself and said he was not hungry and didn't care for potatoes . . . . He was an average, innocuous-looking family man. Yet he had overcome the normal Japanese repugnance for stealing, ingrained since childhood, and quietly risked his job, his security and years in prison for a group of strangers, aliens, enemies. No doubt this produced a huddle of very confused potato-gobbling *furyos*.

Yasumi day. *Yasumi* . . . probably the loveliest word in the Japanese language to our ears. Whether it came at mid-morning or late in the day, it always brought rest, relief, a halt to labor. And if we could manage to forget for a few brief minutes, that is, block off the labor ahead, then we could sit down, lean back, stretch our sick, tired limbs, and wallow in the sensuous abandon of the Now. How much more so to attain a whole day of *yasumi*. Heaven-sent. Rest and peace were synonymous. And the Lord said: on the fourteenth day let there be *yasumi* for those ugly forsaken *furyos* — so they might remember . . . what? That they were still human, made in the shape of God, not workhorses. Let them rest, sleep, laugh, dream . . . and hope.

I washed my mess tins, folded my blankets, then — my ritual. I drew out my diary and my sheaf of letters, carefully arranged over the years. I lay back and stretched my bones and muscles luxuriously. No rushing, no crowding, no bustle . . . a Sunday calm. The six letters read last *yasumi* day were at the bottom. Six nice "new" ones awaited me. I hadn't seen them for three months — surely I'd find details I'd forgotten.

Hmm . . . August 1942 . . . brother Harry saying: "So much has happened since you left . . . " in less than a year. My God, how much must have happened in *three* years? No letter from Evelyn, not a one, leaving room for endless speculation . . . . Had she fallen for someone else and decided to spare me the extra pain? That may be better for her — God knows what shape I'll be in if I survive. And if I don't? Yes, this way was better . . . . Good that we gave each other total freedom. Or maybe her letters got lost — many did. Some took a year and a half to arrive . . . .

I took out the photos: proof, living proof that I had a family. No fantasy, they proclaimed their undeniable existence: sisters, nieces, brothers, parents, standing there gazing out at me with unclouded smiles expanding like flowers out of unblemished minds, reinforced by good food in their bellies, clean clothes, a cozy backyard . . . and love, alive and pulsing in their hearts, in their eyes, spreading protectively outward to fill and enclose my bed space. I could feel it, smell it, like the sweet pungent scent of new-mown hay, shutting out this festering cesspool.

Pop, grinning, balding . . . sending out his vibrations of comfort, stolid in his unchanging cocoon. He was clinging hopelessly, blindly, to a horse business as it went down the drain, refusing to acknowledge the auto and the motor. How could life go on without horses? How could things change so? Faith, confidence slipping away . . . . Mom, the fount, the center, gradually taking over the reins . . . . I gazed and gazed till at last I achieved total immersion. I was *there*, free . . . we were together at long last, pressing bodies close, clinging . . . . Tears of joy, of unbearable longing suddenly gushed forth and I swung my arm over my face, feigning sleep. This was not the place for tears. They were inadmissible, dangerous, a weakness where the weak did not survive . . . .

I opened my eyes and stared at the barren rafters and the hollow-eyed faces passing. *This* was the real, these skeletons were the ugly truth — those soft, round, happy creatures were a dream. They had no substance. I became aware of the distance, of the vast yawning gulf crowded with death and agonies that lay between, with no bridge long enough to allow passage. We were as separate as the dead from the living. How could we ever be joined again? It was too perfect, too beautiful to hope for. And with this came desolation in waves as I sank under an ocean of despair . . . lower, lower, dropping into bottomless darkness. I'll never see them again . . . I'll die here . . . soundlessly, invisibly. And it won't matter a damn. This ugly barn had such a permanence, a totality, that it closed out all effort, all struggle, all imagination. The here and now was here and forever . . . .

Did others feel this horror? What went on in each man's inner world was kept there under lock and key. All winter I had watched Jimmy Mitchell, who slept opposite me, crawl into his blankets and draw them over his head. The tough Sudbury miner . . . . From the inside came the muffled murmur of his voice praying. That must be nice, talking to God at such close quarters. I envied that. I'd tell Him a thing or two. What was he saying, I wondered? Lord, I don't deserve this punishment, what the hell have I ever done to you? Bugger-all. Doncha know a damn thing about justice? Aincha gonna kiss me? I like to be kissed when I'm bein' screwed — ha, ha, sorry Lord. Look, I'll forgive and forget. I won't tell anyone what you done, as long as you promise to get me the hell outta here, okay? A deal? . . . And what would the Lord answer? "Jesus, fella, I'm sorry," or "Tough titty, I move in mysterious ways."

Outside the blankets, Jimmy was a model prisoner, strong, long suffering, independent. Well, weren't we all? We could grouse, like good soldiers, but we knew our limits, our unwritten code.

What strange denizens we were in our *fundoshi*, our awkward clogs clanking by, our shaven heads like plucked chickens, our protruding bones, bones, bones. We had our foibles, our rivalries, our gossip, our frayed nerves that erupted in quarrels. There was anger, blind and shapeless, that found outlets in mean little acts of petty spite — like pausing to deliver a long foul fart beside a man eating slowly and blissfully after one's own rice was finished. And there were noises that grated — something I was hypersensitive to: Westy with his cluck-clucking throat, Robby with his loose phlegm, Fortune with his wet snoring. But this must all be shut out now. This was *yasumi* day, the sabbath reserved for my inner world.

I opened my diary to make my entry. In it I wrote: "Hey — sister Sally's birthday coming up. Happy birthday, Sally Susan! Sorry I can't be there in person or send a card. I'm sort of tied up at the moment. A little patience is in order — *sukoshi mada*, as we say here — wait a little. I should have that tattooed on my arm. It's the answer I always get when I ask a worker how long the war will last — *sukoshi mada*. If *yasumi* is the loveliest word, certainly *sukoshi mada* is the most maddening. I'm sending off these immortal words as a birthday greeting via telepathic airwaves:

> When next this day we celebrate
> You'll see me scoff, dear Susan,
> From early morn till evening late
> and 'twon't be rice I'm usin'.

I rose and strolled slowly down the aisle toward the *benjo*. Some men slept, some sewed patches, darned socks, scrubbed clothes in cold water without soap, or unrolled butts, then patted the tobacco into brown paper and rolled new cigarettes. The sun sent cheerful morning beams through the windows, and even the guards patrolled at a slower, lazier pace, pausing to stare curiously or chat.

It brought to mind the delicious Sunday quiet of Montreal, the main streets deserted, clean, spacious, asleep in the spring sun, free of auto noise and clanging streetcars . . . . The few pedestrians strolling, unhurried, going nowhere. Tree-lined streets, fragrant and still, piano notes drifting through an open window, bittersweet Chopin, trembling in the soft air . . . .

Gramophone music grew louder as I drew near to it. The camp had one old scratchy phonograph that passed from section to section each *yasumi* day. We knew every note of the few worn records by heart. I listened nostalgically to Paul Robeson's voice — or its garbled remains — singing of a mighty mountain and river. Something of his power did manage to force a way past all obstacles to roll majestically across the planet to Kawasaki and reach a few empty souls starved for these heartening sounds. Soon I would start rounding up our own musical talents to throw together our compulsory concert but, *sukoshi mada*, for the moment I was at leisure, savoring the easy, unstructured atmosphere of the hut. It was a collective unwinding, a holy renewal.

I stopped to gather the latest rumors from Charley Clarke. Twenty-two hundred Red Cross parcels sitting in Shinagawa — for us. Yes, I'd heard that. But was it true? More than two per man? Last year we got two-fifths. Charley swore they were there — and were counted. Great . . . . Any news of Europe? The Russians had 'em on the run. Everyone advancing. Things were certainly not standing still. Powerful forces were at work, in motion; we were inching closer to freedom. I couldn't see it, true, but the knowledge was there and that too was part of the truth, something to grasp at. In fact it was all turning in our favor, wasn't it? *We* were winning the war. Now wasn't that heartening? Well, yes, but where did it leave us? That's not the point, we must take the long view — *sukoshi mada*. We could be free by Christmas '44! Gloomy Overton challenged that. Any bets? Yes, optimistic Allister took him on. A deal: ten bucks' worth of tasty delicatessen meats. We licked out chops over the details.

Talking so sanely, so normally with intelligent people did fine things to the psyche, lent shape and meaning to events "out there." A surge of optimism raised me to the skies. It was so *logical* that it should all end, and end soon, and we would return to live happily ever after. Well, why not? Suddenly all the months and years fell away as though they had never existed, and the feel and taste of freedom came pumping through my veins like strong whiskey. Strange how in the course of one day I could take these wild swings from the depths to the peaks. I kept forgetting that anything was possible — after all, the letters and photos were real, they couldn't be denied. Nor could the news from Europe. Damn it, weren't the Russians storming their way hell for leather toward Germany? Wasn't Robeson's voice here, now, to carry me off over mighty mountains and rivers to ethereal heights? It could end — it *had to* end sometime. Any day now — four months, six months could do the trick! A breeze! O God — give me all your fleas, your miseries, hunger, malaria — who cares? Anything's worth it when it's that close! Free!

Ah, but the games of the gods were far from over. In fact our death warrants had already been signed, sealed and delivered. And the nearer we came to the war's end, the nearer we were coming to our own end. Extermination had been decreed for all POWs. It was written, in fact, in unmistakable black and white, that we were all to be put to death in the event of an American landing on Japan. All the camp commandants had standing orders from on high, in detail, even to the point of how to save on ammunition by substituting assorted methods of extermination that covered beheading, hanging, poisoning and other such jolly blandishments. It's all on record, found among the official files, a charming military fun program that included the following:

> The P.W.s will be concentrated and confined in their present location and under heavy guard as the preparation for the final disposition will be made.
> (a) Whether they are destroyed individually or in groups, or however it is done, with mass bombing, poisonous smoke, poisons, drowning, decapitation, or what, dispose of them as the situation dictates.
> (b) In any case, it is the aim not to allow the escape of a single one, to annihilate them all and not leave any traces.
> AUGUST 1944

And then the bombing raids began.

When a siren went off in the shipyards, we were herded into the lunchroom. How the creaky old wooden roof would protect us was a mystery. It was probably to keep us out of mischief. There were no bombs at first, just reconnaissance by the dreaded B-*nijukus* — B-29s that flew at such luxuriously majestic heights that no ack-ack or fighter planes could hope to reach them. We paused at our lowly labors and gazed up at these supernal beings, so high they seemed motionless: tiny silvery-white fish, mere specks glinting in the sun, pure, luminous, remote. And yet so near. To think that there were men up there — only a mile away — clean, well-fed, smooth-faced, confident, superior men who belonged to *our* side. It was hard to hide our satisfaction. Let 'er rip! was our first thought. Give it to the bastards — they've had it their way long enough. Killing, murdering, torturing, enslaving — now it's *their* goddam turn. Vengeance? Yes, indeed. Our long-stored anger craved it — immoral, inexorable, honey-sweet vengeance — call it retribution or justice, if it eases the conscience, it's that too of course, and if the innocent must suffer with the guilty, well, that's what war is all about. They started it — and we'll bloody well finish it!

But what if the bombs hit *us*? Naaah — impossible. It was all for *them*. By 1944 each hollow-eyed surviving *furyo* had an iron gut and bones of steel. Anyone who'd lived this long must be immortal. We'd already been hit, many times, consigned to the flames only to keep rising renewed, like a phoenix.

The war news was filtering in. Charley Clarke was getting copies of *Mainichi*, the Japanese English daily that was, of course, full of blarney but did give the position of the combatants. And he had hidden maps to follow the progress. No one had to tell us it was going badly for Japan. The workers' rations were poor. There was little meat or fish. They had a few pickled vegetables with rice in their lunch boxes. Some told us that rice was scarce at home, sometimes non-existent. And of course when rations grew tight, the *furyos* were the first to feel it.

Actually we had more in common with the workers than with our well-fed countrymen up there. We worked together, suffered the U.S. blockade together, went hungry together, feared the military together, dodged bombs together. But the inside of the head — ah, that was different. And as the war progressed, the gulf between "us" and "them" often widened, depending on events. As hope entered and flowered inside our shaven skulls, gloom entered theirs. Naturally their propaganda would never admit to any loss or defeat, perish the thought. But they knew. They were getting the picture when, as a precautionary measure, we and they began digging bomb shelters all over the place — no danger, of course, but . . . well, once in a while some lucky bomber might slip through, you never know. So we'd better start drawing up evacuation plans, just in case . . . .

Our own position, our role as enemies began taking on new meaning as conditions deteriorated. We may not be exactly to blame, not logically speaking, but still . . . we were part of *them*, the evil, lazy, fat, vile, affluent enemy, the international conspiracy of Jews like Roosevelt, né Rosenfeld, and Churchill, whose mother was Jewish, using all their stolen wealth to attack peace-loving Japan. They would be defeated in the end, of course, justice would be done by Japan's superior fighting forces, but in the meantime, patriotic sacrifices must be made . . . . As for this hated enemy, we had always been an abstract thing — in newsreels and newspapers, not entirely real. Till the bombs came.

Those dreaded B-*nijukus* were very real. They could kill, burn, destroy. And they came from the brothers, cousins, friends, countrymen of these tall, gangling, freakish prisoners. We felt a new helplessness, a sickening vulnerability, and bore the growing hostility as one more cross on our scarred backs.

One sign of the changing situation was the new respect shown us by the commandant. Whatever the psychological reason, the bombing was working in our favor. It may well have been pity — after receiving the liquidation order, he may have succumbed to respect for the condemned. But now he allowed us a small library. Lieutenant Quinn and Captain Reid were allowed out to select books from various stores. Quinn, a middle-aged U.S. naval officer recently arrived, was housed in a little cubicle at one end of the new hut into which we had been moved. It was built with upper and lower decks to house both Rifles and Grenadiers under one roof for easier control. Quinn was a dour, humorless, pudgy-faced type with hanging bloodhound jowls, black bushy eyebrows and an impressive officer's cap, which he must have worn to bed, since it was never removed. Shiny, braided, bulging with authority, it seemed to endow him with magical powers.

We came to his room and opened the sliding door. It was clean, simple, ascetic, with a small table and chair, the bed matting a raised platform like ours, Japanese style. On one wall were two shelves, *packed with books*. My heart leaped at the sight. Books — God Almighty. They looked so distant, so foreign. I felt, in my shabby unwashed clothes, like a barbarian, a Stone Age man, standing on the threshold of civilization, peering in at something I had no right to touch. I felt I'd not seen nor even held a book for ages.

Now as I gazed at these shelves of books I felt a hunger, a craving only a starved man could feel. I wanted to devour all of them in one great greedy gulp. I picked one up and stroked the surface, holding it like the hand of a lover. I thought of the author, the months or years involved in its gestation, in shaping these thoughts, the places he'd lived in while writing this, the warm intimate friendship he was offering me and I was accepting. Did he know he would be reaching me, confiding in me, in a distant prison camp in Kawasaki? Did he know he would be warming my bleak, winter evenings? Did he know he might be saving my life?

I seized half a dozen, hastily, before they vanished.

"One book per month," Quinn informed me sourly with his droopy-cupie lips, as though reluctant to allow pleasure to get out of hand.

Painfully, I replaced five of them. Bob selected one. We returned to our bunks, left our clogs at the foot of the ladder and climbed up to our bed spaces, which lay alongside the main aisle. The image of Quinn's face followed me like an irritating odor. One a month? Whose rules were they? Who the hell did he think he was? Bloody bureaucratic parasite, feeding off our labor.

To hell with him. We settled back on our mats for a good read. I opened the book ceremoniously, tenderly, examined the design of the type, the dedication, and dove into a new kind of feast. My soul was smiling.

The story, the characters, joined me now at work. I would sway on the scaffolding, mind far away in a distant land, following the fortunes of colorful characters who entered more and more into my existence. On the two-mile march to and from the shipyards, Bob and I discussed their fates, their choices, their conflicts. We could hardly wait to reach camp and dig them out. Sometimes we read passages to each other. Twenty minutes to lights-out was too brief, so I took to reading and eating. Bob considered this sacrilegious, an insult to the rice, arguing that I was missing the full enjoyment of my food. I held that each enhanced the other by association.

We devoured the books all too soon, my appetite hardly appeased. Then I hit on the idea of getting non-reading friends to take out more books. I grew greedier and greedier, sending more friends to a suspicious Quinn, asking for names they couldn't pronounce. I piled them high on my shelf. My treasure trove. I felt secure, comforted by their proximity. This was my link to civilization.

One day I was on my belly, happily absorbed in a book with my head close to the top of the ladder. Suddenly a face appeared beside me. The head seemed severed at the neck by the edge of my upper bunk. Sleepy eyes, bloodhound jowls, topped by the official braided naval hat. *Yecch*!

"Well!" I said, trying an old gag that seemed apt. "Who ordered John the Baptist?"

The face remained stony. The eyes roamed to my shelf, settling on the huge stack of books. The jowls quivered to control his outrage. Hell with him — I was going by *his* stupid rules.

"To what do I owe this friendly call?" I asked brightly.

There was a pause in which I gathered he was selecting words. "I thought I told you," he rumbled, "one book a month."

"Right."

"Then what are you doing with all those?"

"Oh — *that*," I waved airly. "They were taken out by others. They like to keep 'em on my shelf."

"I want them back where they belong!"

"Of course! As soon as they're through. They have a month, I think." Gotcha.

There was a pregnant pause. I have never heard teeth gnash, but there must have been a lot of that going on inside his mouth.

"Let's understand each other, Allister," he growled. "The camp library is in *my room. Not on your shelf.*"

"Sure thing."

There was one last helpless baleful glare then, like a submarine, the head sank slowly out of sight.

That was pleasant. Chalk up one more loss for the U.S. Navy.

I turned to my shelf to feast my eyes on my loot. There they sat, so quiet and self-contained. But what a wallop they packed in their tiny space, what a concentration of imaginative thought and energy. Fat and wise in repose, serene as Buddhas. My smiling accomplices, my support system. Bless them! They would sustain me through the winter months, warm companions come to guide me, soaring with me, out and beyond the confines of this cold, dreary prison to faraway islands and bygone days. By selecting them I had renewed them, given them new life. Now they were returning the favor.

The greatest honor accorded us by Nippon Kokan was the construction of an old-fashioned sit-up outhouse, built right in the middle of the shipyards like a Western shrine. A grand international gesture, a recognition of our existence, definitely a frivolous luxury. A one-seater, true, no bigger than a phone booth, but a marvelous status symbol. An end to years of squatting. Squatting on your haunches was all right if you were not constipated. But many were. I was. I would squat till my muscles ached and stiffened. And since few *benjos* were cleaned, the cow-pies often rose so high under you that it was impossible to squat in safety.

The greatest blessing of all was the privacy. For prisoners who were never alone, who lived collectively in one great wide-open barn, one's life was always a public affair. Except for the semi-darkness you were always visible to five hundred sets of eyes. At the shipyards you were surrounded by bodies, under the vigilant eyes of guards and *fu*-men. Now, at last, you could walk away from all that and retire to the delicious, if not fragrant, privacy of a Western *benjo*. It was a marvel. The Rolls-Royce of crappers. You could sit, rest, relax and revel in the sweet solitude of this fecal haven.

I would sit there, drifting back to my childhood in Manitoba, where I once sat in a similar dim interior . . . enfolded in innocence, free of care, listening to the ringing buzz of crickets, the murmur of warm prairie winds, as time slowed, lazily, to a standstill . . . .

Small wonder there was a line-up outside, awaiting a beautiful experience.

Cold winds were driving in from the sea. They had a bite to them. The first cold breath meant hunkering down for the next battle looming. Was I ready for another winter? How many would go down this time?

And winter came. A bad winter. More deaths. I recalled a drawing, a vision of death I had seen once as a child and found imprinted on my mind. A long bridge with thousands of tiny figures crossing it, symbolizing the journey of life. At intervals a trapdoor opened suddenly and a figure went hurtling down into space. As humankind reached the last half of the bridge, more and more trapdoors opened, more figures dropped through. There was something so inexorable, so unjust, so accidental, so silent, so sudden, so menacing in the spectacle that it had filled me with horror. Now I was trudging along that bridge with trapdoors flying open all around me.

Chapter Sixteen

B
Y MARCH 1945 THE BOMBINGS had become a daily way of life,
so much so that work at the plant slowed to a crawl. When
the sirens blew, the familiar clatter, roar and din petered out
and an eerie hush drifted ominously across the shipyards
like a wind of evil. Then in the silence the tiny silvery-white fish
appeared, twinkling high in the blue. The dreaded B-*nijukus*. The
stillness was the stillness of death. We moved past the buildings
that stood waiting helplessly, humble and subdued.

We were herded quickly together in the lunchroom, made to
crouch under the tables for a restful interim, then sent back to 3D at
a trot on our beri-beri legs. There we were hurried into the covered
trenches we had dug out behind the hut. This was repeated almost
daily, till finally it was decided to break up the camp.

We knew nothing of the Japanese plans, only that fifty men were
given orders to pack for a move. I was on the list. We prepared in a
state of anxious dread. After all, this had been a sort of home for
two years. These men had surrounded me since we'd left Canada.
Now it was all to change drastically. George Grant was the only
other signalman going. Where were we to be sent? There was no
information and the void was filled by morbid speculation and
rumor. Repatriation? Oh, sure. We'd been there too often. Germ
experiments? That was too horrible. We'd heard vague, half-
formed hints of a camp in Manchuria where prisoners were used
for experimentation. No one knew where this had come from —
could be from Shinagawa, the Tokyo hospital, where someone may
have picked up some gossip from the top doctors. I ignored it.
Actually there *was* such a place, we learned after the war. The
scientific and chemical experiments on thousands of Chinese and
Russian prisoners were so grisly they made Mengele look like a
pussycat. In this case our ignorance was a blessing.

Wherever we were to go, there would be a search. My precious
diary might be found. I left Bob most of it, thinking he would

remain, and kept the rest.

On the last night, Bob and I lay under our pooled blankets in silence, hearts full, minds racing. Would we ever see each other again? Parting was always an exquisite army punishment not found in the training manuals. Barracks life produced an intimacy missing in a daily job. You *lived* together, as only a family lived. Friendships were formed swiftly, made strong and deepened by the unspoken awareness that a life-and-death gamble shadowed every word and act. Then, abruptly, you were moved. And all friendship, all warmth, all sentiment, was savagely chopped off and you were parted from men you would never see again. It happened in training camps at Huntington, at Kingston, at Debert, at Sham Shui Po and now it was here again — this, the most painful of all, after the longest, most intense span of shared experience, indelible in heart and mind.

My fellow inmates, bound to me by our common fates: Caruso, we had clowned together . . . . Berry, we had studied together . . . . Leo Berard, we had talked so much, studied vitamins together . . . . Charron, tap-dancing, planning programs with me at North Point . . . . Bruno with his wrestling act . . . . Tommy Marsh, with his bitterness, cynicism, his hidden purity . . . . Robby with his hot rumors, Clarke with his deals, West with his clucking throat, bringing me rice on my birthday . . . . Speller wielding his rice ladle . . . . Blacky, sharing all, becoming a blood brother over the years . . . . Bob, with his supersensitive perception, his laughter, his understanding, his life permanently interwoven with mine . . . . What would happen to them all? Would they live or die? At one level it didn't matter, they would all be dead to me. I would be cut away again, set adrift on a menacing sea. I would have to dig up all my strength tomorrow — shake hands and walk away. No *au revoir*, *auf Wiedersehen*, be seein' ya — this was *adieu*, goodbye, and that was it.

Bob stirred beside me and for the last time said, "'Night."

I sighed. "'Night."

And so to sleep.

The order came to leave.

We said our goodbyes as I had foreseen, with little emotion, hardened by this time, inside and out. The soft, vulnerable areas had been driven deep underground, guarded by a superstructure of steel.

We were loaded into two open trucks where we sat on our kits, waiting to leave 3D. I looked back at the flimsy wooden hut, its air soaked with the memory of two long years packed with hope and dreams, with incredibly high moments, with endless miseries, with intense longing and bleak despair, with raucous laughter and hidden tears. I gazed back at the cindered yard where we'd strolled, round and round, talking. Of home, of movies, trying to remember the names of film stars . . . . Where we'd lined up for work each morning wondering what the day held, and lined up at day's end, eagerly anticipating the bowl of supper rice . . . . Goodbye to 3D. I should have been grateful to leave it all behind, but it somehow symbolized a kind of security, stability — in all its ugliness, at least we *knew* what to expect. But now, what lay in wait out there was the unknown, the undefined, a huge invisible presence bulging with menace. Where was the old adventurous spirit? Dead and gone. It was just peace I craved, one day of forgetting, one day free of gnawing anxiety.

The trucks pulled away and went clattering down the dirt roads, past dismal shacks, warehouses, small streets — it felt odd, passing it all so swiftly after using only my legs for locomotion for two years. What a powerful miraculous affair a motor was: no one pulling or pushing it, carrying so many people without effort. Life had suddenly speeded up — time itself was flying past. The others were caught up in a sort of uneasy euphoria, an odd holiday mood. Who knows — it might be a *good* move: better conditions, better grub . . . anything was possible. Anyway, why worry about tomorrow, it's *today* that counts! And this was something — zooming along so free and easy, seeing new streets, new people, waving mockingly at the curious faces. And we may be getting away from those damn bombs — *that* was good. Those B-29s were getting too close for comfort.

The bleak terrain, factories, warehouses remained the same as we sped by, the main difference being the number of bombed-out areas. They were really puttin' it to 'em around here. It was getting worse and worse. We stared around uneasily. What the hell were we getting into?

By the time we reached Tokyo, the picture was unfolding. The devastation was complete. Nothing but a few charred sections of low walls had been left standing. We were appalled at the sight before us. Amazing! Rubble as far as the eye could see. Charred rubble. Ashes . . . as after some great sacrifice — which it was. It all seemed pulverized by some gargantuan sledgehammer wielded by a furious god. It *must* be the wrath of God — how could this great Armageddon be the work of man?

We had no idea we were in a city. There were no streets. These were fields — vast fields of scorched metal, bricks, tangled debris, scattered litter. The wheels of the truck went bumping along as though rolling over thousands of bodies. What *was* this? We could be riding across a phantasmagoric landscape of hell or some strange planet over whose entire surface a twisted metallic fungus grew — food for herds of iron dinosaurs.

We fell silent and stared in awe. No sign of life, no buildings, no trees . . . . Did they still believe they were winning the war? We drove on and on, with no sign of change, no end to this . . . one great continuum of death. Only later did we realize we had driven through one of the world's largest cities.

At last we stopped at our new home: Sumidagawa, decrepit, small, uninviting, in a coal yard on the outskirts of Tokyo beside a rail ramp. This was a rail and canal junction; long rail platforms ran parallel to canals, where beans, rice, coal and pig iron were loaded from rail car to barge. In the coal yard trains brought coal to be unloaded and shoveled into trucks. Since most civilians had been evacuated because of the bombs, prisoners — expendable — were brought in to replace them.

The hut was a small, run-down, two-tier affair, half the size of 3D, with a tiny square in front and a narrow space on one side. It sat squeezed between dark mountains of coal. It housed 250 *furyos*. I gazed at it warily. It looked wizened, shabby, giving off the depressing air of a neglected invalid, shut away somewhere to die. It was made up of mixed nationalities: Yanks, Brits, Scots and now Dutch, Indonesians and Canadians.

We were numbered and searched, then led into the hut, exchanging cautious, anxious glances with the residents. They wore odd shirts and exotic headgear, from naval hats to tam-o-shanters. They were bearded and long-haired, very unmilitary, with an unsettling air of disorder and laxity. The first heartening sign was their weight. They looked bulky, muscular, almost to my eyes, *fat!* I poked George Grant. Looks good, looks good. George and I sat on our kits in the center aisle, waiting to be assigned bed spaces.

The locals, distant and unsmiling, eyed us coolly. They had been here a long time and considered us green, potential trouble; later on, they would judge us to be a bloody menace.

Jerry was an exception. He was short, broad shouldered, with a dashing sea captain's hat and rugged, handsome good looks. He squatted down beside Grant and me, very friendly and full of chatter. A little too friendly? What was his game? Grant began on a slightly less than esoteric note.

"How's the grub?"

"Stinkin'."

"Then why's everyone so bloody fat?"

"Stealing," he said. "We stole copra."

"What's that?"

"Coconut — we were unloading it all winter."

"Terrific!"

"It's all gone now."

Our faces fell. But they did work on beans and rice, he said. Stealing was tricky, and they were tough here in punishments. But he'd be glad to show us the ropes. He produced some roasted soybeans and gave us a generous handful each. My warning bells clanged. After years of struggling to survive, one just didn't *give* that readily. Very pally, very helpful, very warm. He introduced himself and held out his hand. So formal? We each shook it, and he held on a shade too long . . . clinging? Sex? Oh, yeah — *that.* Of course. I remembered how, after one day of good eating in 3D, our conversation quickly turned to girls. Here, after eating well all winter and no women — well, it would be a whole new ballgame.

We were led to our bunks by a tall, cheerful Japanese sergeant-major who carried a long pole. He used it to underline an order by cracking it playfully across our skulls if we were slow to understand.

"That's One-Eye," Jerry told us. "He runs the joint for the Turkey. He laughs a lot, but don't let that fool you — he's a fuckin' menace. Loves to beat up on you."

"Who's the Turkey?"

"The CC. He never shows up much. Battier than a bedbug. He screams a lot but he won't bother you. The guy to watch for is Piston Fists. The worst. Crazy

Paid an American boxer to teach him how to punch. He's murder. When you get crunched by Piston Fists, you know about it."

The rattan pallets were the same — thirty-seven inches wide, seven feet long, in a row of seven, divided by the same thin stripping. The same shelf stretching from aisle to wall. The pallets were soiled and full of fleas and bedbugs. Lice were plentiful. Grant and I were on an upper platform.

These new Canadians, One-Eye decided, must be knocked into shape, and he lost no time starting. Herb Fortune, a tall dark Grenadier, was caught taking a drag outside the hut. One-Eye stood him to attention and slowly removed his white cotton gloves. These loose gloves were a sign of high rank or class. One wall-eye was far out of line and seemed to stare sightlessly to the side. In his tall, shiny riding boots he cut quite an impressive figure and seemed to know it. His height probably won him his high rank. He did a lot of strutting and, I imagine, spent plenty of time in front of a mirror. But when the white gloves started coming off, finger by finger, we learned it was time to brace ourselves. The gloves were not to be soiled on grungy *furyos*. Bare knuckles could be easily washed. He had a bright, cheery way of going about the business of punishment. He started walloping Fortune, who was pretty tough. But this went on and on. He could punch with the closed fist, a new bit of Americana for us. The blows continued, staggering Fortune, who was dizzied and struggling to stay on his feet. It was a weird beating to us, with none of the usual anger, no shouts, no mounting rage. One-Eye seemed to be doing some kind of enervating exercise, almost a sport.

"Fall down, ye bleedin' ijit!" a Limey yelled.

Fall down? In 3D, if you fell down, you'd had it. You could get your head stomped or ribs kicked in. But here the mores were topsy-turvy. At last One-Eye stopped, exhausted. He seemed miffed — as though we were not entering into the spirit of the thing. He slid his gloves on and walked off, muttering in tones that sounded disappointed and mildly irritated.

"All you have to do is fall down," Jerry explained later. "The sooner the better. That means he's got a dynamite punch. That's all he wants. Then he puts on his Mickey Mouse gloves and fucks off, happy as a pig in shit."

I learned what he meant a little later when he lined up a Yank for a beating. "Watch a pro," Jerry said.

Off came the bulky white cotton gloves, with lots of friendly talking and grinning. His shiny riding boots were planted wide apart as he swung a roundhouse punch at the Yank's head. The man's entire frame seemed to jolt as though struck by a truck, his arms flew outward from the impact, and his head jerked backward. His legs went limp and slid from under him as he dropped to the ground, flinging out an arm to arrest his fall in a perfect Hollywood stuntman's drop. He lay half conscious, groggily shaking his head.

One-Eye let out a yelp of delight and voiced his satisfaction as he stepped back to enjoy the sight. Then he slipped his gloves back on and walked off, both he and his victim completely satisfied.

"A nice little arrangement," Jerry said. "You'll get the hang of it."

The rice ration was about as meager as at 3D, but we were heartened by the prospect of getting into the rice and beans on the loading platforms. At first we thought it was bad luck when we found ourselves assigned to the coal platforms, as we were day after day. Orders would come each day with the number of men needed in each platform. A middle-aged American straw boss was in charge of selecting men, and it finally dawned on us that we were being shafted. All the good territories had been staked out, and they had no intention of sharing the spoils with any of these skinny, hungry greenhorns. There were fifty Dutch and Javanese who came after us, equally gaunt and hungry looking. They, too, found themselves on the coal pile.

You couldn't eat or steal coal, and it was the hardest and dirtiest work. None of the work was easy. On the rice and bean platform each man had a quota of sixteen tons to carry per day. On the coal we had to push the railway carriages, the *kashas*, up the track, heaving and straining, till they were in place above the coal pile. Then we had to let down the doors and shovel the contents onto the pile. Each man had to shovel down a thirty-ton quota. When trucks were to be filled, our quota was sixteen tons per man, shoveling upward. This made our labor at 3D seem a picnic. And on these rations the situation looked grim.

Our only relief came when more men were needed on the food platforms. When this chance came, we had to steal as much as possible. Twice a day we were searched on entering camp, and the search was thorough: every man was checked — legs, arms, bodies, hats. The regulars brought in their rice in their shoes, a little each day, playing it safe. We needed more and ran extra risks, hiding rice in shoes, hats, sleeves, socks, kettles. This was resented by the regulars, because it could expose their hiding places and lead to trouble. We were warned to stop it, as were the Dutch, but they too were desperate and took dangerous risks. We told the regulars to go fly a kite. Antagonism was rising.

There was plenty of cooked rice to be had for a few cigarettes. Many of the regulars had hot plates, homemade electric grills for boiling cans of rice. The Yanks outproduced everyone. Under a bed space they had constructed a giant stove that cooked thirty cans at a time. The enormous cloud of steam was a problem that they solved by ingenious timing. When the hut was emptied in the morning for roll call in the yard, all the guards were outside. At a signal, the bed was raised by sick men, and the steam poured up into the rafters. By the time everyone returned, the steam was dissipated; the smell of rice cooking could be from the kitchen. Where all this rice came from was a mystery to me. It was not till months later that I found out.

Grant and I became partners — "muckers," the Limeys called it. In 3D Jack Rose had been his mucker, Bob had been mine. Fate seemed to have tossed us together during the battle in '41 and back together now in '45. Since we'd always liked each other, it was a good union. It meant splitting everything, sharing all good and bad fortune. It was a marriage without sex, a nuclear-family idea, a way to share, belong and close ranks against a hostile world.

Grant set about collecting materials for a hot plate. Patiently he gathered bits of coil and wired them together. He found a brick and dug away at it, carving grooves in concentric circles. It took weeks of laborious effort. He fitted the rusty coils into the grooves. He collected wire and made a long line, attached to the hot plate at one end. The wire was cunningly hidden behind beams and, under cover of darkness, run up to the ceiling and connected to the main electric wire that ran along the center of the hut. We finally had our very own hot plate that could boil two tin cans. In these we put a handful of stolen rice kernels and water. Delicious. We were eating extras at last!

Others did the same, and soon there was so much juice being tapped from the main line that it could short. This would create a crisis: a Japanese electrician would be brought in to investigate, and all lines would have to be hastily, painstakingly removed. It would take many days to get it all hooked up again.

To avoid this anarchic situation, it was agreed to allot time slots to each section for use of the line. A voice would shout: "Number 8, 9 and 10 coming on! Number 5, 6, 7 — get off the bloody line!"

"Roger! Over!"

But all this competition didn't sit well with the Yanks who ran the thirty-can operation. They had to sell at lower and lower prices — the bottom was dropping out of the market. Often their extra rice sold for as little as one cigarette per can. They were called the Barons, our own version of OPEC, and the Barons were losing power and privilege.

One day on the coal pile we heard that a Japanese electrician was coming to check the wiring. Panic! Grant and I could hardly wait to finish work. We went charging back to camp, tore up the ladder to our bunks and started unfastening our complex system of hidden wiring: under the shelf . . . along the vertical posts . . . climbing up to the other beams in broad daylight and following it to the center line. It took long, intensive effort. Then we hid the wire and waited, relieved that we had got there in time. All through the hut, wires were being hastily dismantled and hidden.

The Japanese electrician didn't come that day. He didn't come the next day, or the next. But he *could* come at any time, the rumor said. In the meantime there was no hot plate, no rice, and we were hungry. When we went to buy rice for a cigarette, we found the price raised to five. We couldn't afford it, but others could. The stock-exchange prices were rising each day. The demand was there: hunger. And the Barons just happened to be there with the supply. Why hadn't they taken theirs down? They refused to be intimidated and were willing to take their chances. Brave men. They could afford to be, since they had originated the rumor. And now they were restored to what they considered their rightful position, in control of the market.

Slowly the hot plates came back into use and prices nosed downward. At intervals there was a sighting of the phantom electrician, followed by the same mad scramble. It might be a bluff, but who could afford to risk it? The punishments in this place were no child's play. So production flourished in the Barons' corner, and they continued to rule the roost.

On the coal we worked stripped to our *fundoshis*, faces and skins coated in coal dust as we stood knee-deep in the open railway car. It was perched on a high ramp as we shoveled the coal. The hardest work was pushing the *kashas* uphill on the track before unloading. A dozen men heaved and strained against the bulky iron and wooden back of the car to nudge the great stubborn beast forward over the rusty rails. At the end of a hungry day we would gather, exhausted, in the coal shack for our rice ball, an extra for filling our quota. This was the highlight of the day. Unlike the reddish "Korean" rice, this was gleaming white and hot, and we held it in our coal-stained hands like a rare pearl. It had its own subtly rich aroma and taste, and our starved palates were attuned to all the nuances of its flavor.

On our return to camp we took our thin towels and went off to the washhouse at the side of the hut, where we doused each other with cold water and scrubbed the coal dust off our hides. Our hair was growing back now and we were gaining some weight. In fact, as we clumped down the center aisle, near naked in our *fundoshis* on the way to wash up, we passed the dour-faced Yank straw boss who smiled, patted our butts appreciatively and winked. I was flattered. At least it meant we didn't look like zombies any longer. That brought a new hazard. The slightest physical attribute that could be seen as feminine was noted and inflated by the imagination to satisfy a sex-starved appetite. It didn't take much. Newfie, with his street smarts, sized up the camp very quickly. He was wheeling and dealing with verve, adjusting easily. "This place is aful, aful," he told me. "I does me deals with me fuckin' back t' the wall."

One of the reasons the Yanks didn't want us or the Dutch on the rice platform was that we slowed them down. We were weak and unskilled, but they were old hands, having built up their carrying muscles over time; they could empty a railway car of rice into a barge with smooth efficiency. Three men with hooks would swing the fifty-kilo sack onto the shoulder of a waiting *furyo*, who trotted off with bent knees, like the Hong Kong coolies, then stepped onto a plank that stretched across the hold of a waiting canal barge and flipped it down to a pile below. We were awkward, puffing and straining under the weight, rubbing our shoulders raw and wobbling along on beri-beri legs. And we were always sneaking off to get into a sack of rice we'd broken open, inviting reprisals. The Dutchmen were even bolder.

On the bean platforms there were Brits and Yanks. The bean sacks were much heavier than rice. The rackets were well organized here, and even the *fu*-men were in on it. We were astonished to find an American roasting huge amounts of beans on a large open stove in full view of the guards. It was his job. Beans for everyone. At the end of the day he filled each *fu*-man's pouch with beans for his hungry family. Evans, a baby-faced Yank, was in charge. The face was misleading. He ran a tight ship. His face was smooth, expressionless, totally peaceful. No detail escaped him. His type of confidence was so much a part of his being that it was hard to imagine fear or hesitation in any situation. Men twice his age and strength accepted his authority without question. Everything here was under control. It was such a well-oiled arrangement that the Yanks began treating the *fu*-men with a certain disdain. At one point I saw a long, lean, unshaven Texan reclining in otiose regality on a pile of sacks, taking a *yasumi*. The *fu*-man brought a broom and asked him to sweep the beans off the platform. The Texan glanced at the outstretched broom contemptuously and said: "Up yo Oriental ayuss." The *fu*-man withdrew.

What kind of place *was* this?

I lay back on my lice-infested rattan matting at the end of a day to think, or try. I lit a fag and automatically waved my hand slowly to and fro as I smoked to avoid a smoke spiral that could catch a guard's eye. No *yasumi* day here, no time to really relax the brain, regain perspective on what was happening, where I was the in world. The brain was all clogged up with scheming, planning, shooting angles, racing, racing to keep ahead of the game, get more food, like . . . vultures, scavengers, tigers — obsessed, hunting, foraging for survival. Wasn't I a part of planet life, the animal kingdom, doing what comes naturally? Then why didn't it *feel* natural? Why did it seem so wrong, twisted, grotesque? Because I was more than animal. I was given a brain, a beautiful instrument, meant for more than hunting and foraging. But people at home lived this way too. Wasn't this a microcosm of our own society? The same greed, the same running, jockeying, struggling for more, the competitiveness, the hedonism, the Barons. No, this was a sad caricature of it, a travesty — how could this be normal?

I missed 3D. Not home — that was too distant. I missed Bob, with his probing insights, dissecting nuances — he understood. I couldn't dig into this with Grant. He was all right in his way. I clung to his gutsy honesty, his stable, healthy presence. He was a part of 3D. There had been a structure there, a groove in which I fitted comfortably. I wanted it back as a dog wants a former cruel master back. I used to think them all mad, didn't I? They were, but it was all relative. Compared with this they were bedrock solid. This place was . . . sinister. Yes, I was gaining weight, eating better, looking better, but this, was really an insane asylum and I was being caught up in it. All my patterns were being jolted, up-ended: beatings without anger, fists instead of palms, prisoners fat instead of cadaverous, One-Eye tall instead of short, men changing to women. Food all around me . . . punishments ferocious . . . fear and anxiety gnawing at my jangled nerves day and night. What would time do to us all?

So far the rest of the Canadians were retaining their identity in the middle of this Sodom and Gomorrah, with a kind of simple, rustic balance. That took some doing. They suffered for their quiet, sober realism — a subconscious choice that needed a special kind of courage. They weren't for playing any artificial roles. True, they were not as quick, as colorful, as charming, witty or inventive as the Limeys, Scots and Yanks. They were dull, slow, resigned . . . but they were stronger. They were still sane, they were not *lost* . . . that was the difference. The denizens of this netherworld had sold away their souls. They were dancing ghosts, become totally one with this environment — happy, adjusted, their imaginations could not stray beyond the confines of these walls. I thought of the handsome young Limey who stopped me on the rice platform. He was sparkling clean, clothes spotless, fresh smelling and laundered, shirt white and crisp, complexion soft and pink. Now here was a man who took a pride in his appearance, I thought, and wondered how he could afford to look so well. I found out.

"Would ye like to 'ave me tonight?" he asked breezily.

"Pardon?"

"Piece of arse — three rations o' rice. Like to 'ave a go?"

"Oh! Uh — no thanks." Nothing like getting down to it. No place for candlelight and wine.

"Why? Don't you fancy me?"

"Oh sure! You're, uh, very nice. But I can't afford it, sorry."

"Pay me later if ye' like." He could have been peddling apples.

"Uh — sorry, mate. I prefer rice."

He looked at me in surprise, as though I were queer, then shrugged and turned away. Time was money. Jeez . . . a high-class whore. As wholesome and guiltless as a Boy Scout. What went on inside that boyish head, I wondered? In all their heads? Would the Canadians soon fall into line? This place had a devilish power. It throbbed with vitality, energy. In the middle of all this death and desolation, it flourished luxuriantly like a poisonous plant, feeding on itself.

I thought of the men around me — Herb Fortune, Newfie, Pat Metalluc — no, they wouldn't change. Pat was a former boxer, an Indian with a battered face, square jaw and broken nose. He spoke quietly, sparsely, and exuded power. He was modest with a gentle spirit and a shrewd, droll eye for man's folly. His was the kind of confidence I envied; knowing his own ability to chop a man down to size, he didn't have to prove himself to anyone. He looked at the shenanigans around him with a patient smile. They played games like "crunchers," where a man who farted had to say "no crunchers." If someone said "crunchers" first he could punch the offender on the arm, often leaving a bruise. Mettaluc's words were pithy. "They're like little kids," he said tolerantly and remained aloof.

Even Captain Martin, our commanding officer, was strange. He lived in a cubicle at the front of the hut and seldom emerged. He was a sickly looking, emaciated Texan whose eyes were shifty and restless, his face scarred, his body tortured by some twitching nervous disorder. He seemed to behave like a scared rabbit —

shades of Matthews. Jerry told us his story.

"That skinny, nervous li'l guy was once a big husky Texan, believe it or not. He was in an officers' camp, and the order came through for them to work or get a working-over — and out they went. All but Martin. He told 'em to go to hell, he knew his rights. Wouldn't move. So one fine day they took him out on the parade ground in front of all the others and a whole gang went to work on him. They busted every bone in his body and mangled him good — left him for dead. But he didn't die. Ended up in hospital and it took three months before he could stand. But he was a fuckin' wreck — nerves all smashed to hell. He was never the same. Then as a sign of respect they sent him here — put him in charge, where he don't have to work. That's our Captain Martin, an okay guy, gutsy sonofabitch. The Turkey likes him and they get along good. Whenever we wanna chase down a rumor, he asks the Turkey and gets it straight from the horse's ass, yes or no."

Chalk up one more lost soul.

Day after day the coal pile used up precious energy, increasing the hunger. The proximity of so much rice was tantalizing. A few daring souls partly solved the problem by sneaking off across the tracks to the closest rice platform for a "score." Bing Maher, a hungry, fearless loner, took his chances nearly every day. He was a tall Westerner with a deep bass voice and a slow, monotonous drawl. He had a long head, even features and turned-up nose that reminded me of Demant. He seldom smiled. He liked to speak in long rhetorical sentences made more solemn by a deep basso and a deadpan expression — words of sly sarcasm, delivered slowly with obvious relish. A play-acting style, but his stealing was very real. He wandered across the tracks with the same slow, deliberate pace he used in talking. That took nerve.

But nerve is what everyone seemed to have. There was no room for anything else if one was to survive. The penalties were fierce, but they were accepted like the weather. Smitty, a young Dutchman, was probably the bravest man I ever met. He befriended us on the coal pile and we were instantly won by his sunny disposition. Unlike the other Dutchmen from Indonesia who were older men, sober and distant, Smitty looked about seventeen, a babe in arms, with blond hair and a round, pink, apple face.

Everything produced laughter as though life were a lark. He gossiped and beamed, radiating joy and warmth. With clothes clean and scrubbed, he always looked like a kid dropping over from a swim at a holiday camp, making coal and hunger unreal. Usually he had just dropped in from a nearby rice platform. He knew what gangs worked where, how many guards were around and which platforms were deserted and available for stealing. He had boundless energy and optimism and *enjoyed* his escapades. Sometimes I hated him for his high spirits and fearlessness. That's not courage, I told myself enviously, he's too bloody dumb to know better. But he was not dumb; he was bright, quick, even brilliant. Still, didn't courage mean overcoming fear? And if you had no fear, what could you call it? An enviably happy state of being.

One unlucky day Bing asked Grant and me if we cared to come along. It was a hungry day. I looked at George, and at that wide exposed road, the series of tracks, railway cars. Why not? Others were doing it and getting away with it — getting a good feed out of it. But I was no Bing, no Smitty.

I was Chicken Willy. Still, it seemed so easy . . . just keep your eyes peeled: if there was a work party, the guards stayed close to them, so give 'em a wide berth. And if we were caught? A crunching. Well, it wouldn't kill us. Our rice stock had been empty for a while and it was coal, coal, coal, every goddam day . . . hell, let's take a chance.

We slipped away from the coal yard and followed Bing down the open road. God, we were visible from any distance . . . . My heart was racing, the adrenaline flowing. We hurried across the tracks to the shelter of some rail cars. Using them as a screen, we covered the quarter-mile distance to the rice platforms. This looked easier than I'd thought. Bing reconnoitered and spotted a British gang loading rice on an adjoining platform. We kept out of their view and found a stack of rice sacks. Grant hastily pulled out his long trusty stocking and Bing started filling his. We were absorbed in our task when there was a sudden shout:

"Nanda!"

We whirled to find ourselves facing — Piston Fists! Jesus! Not a guard or civilian but Piston Fists, vicious, sadistic, the worst, the very worst of them all. The one sonofabitch everyone tried to avoid. *Caught* — dead to rights — trapped. Shit! The bastard had come smelling around, searching this far away, *hoping* to catch someone. And he had.

He recognized Grant instantly, having often used him as interpreter. Grant detested him and he knew it. Piston Fists was a clean-cut, nattily dressed corporal who had bought the best clothes the prisoners owned from parcels received over the years — new shirts, socks, belts, underwear. He was shrewd enough to know they came from a wealthy land where the best of materials were in abundance. All this only intensified his unhealthy envy and nationalistic fervor. He was too clever, too perceptive not to know Japan was losing the war. He had a grudging respect for George, sensing that he was one *furyo* who would not be humbled. So now it was time he had a good lesson, this cursed interpreter — thinking himself so superior. George was the white man, the hated enemy who flew over Tokyo at will, high and untouchable, and rained terror from the skies. Well! Now I have one, helpless, trapped, at my mercy, and we'll see who's superior!

"Ki-o-tsuki!"

We came to attention, staring straight ahead as he circled us, talking, describing our crime, licking his chops. We'd made his day. He stopped in front of Grant, staring at him, then barked in Japanese:

"Who is going to win the war?"

The answer had to be Japan. George kept his face blank and said: *"Wakaranai* [I don't know]."

"Wakaranai — bakayaro!" He slapped Grant's face viciously. What did this have to do with stealing, anyhow?

He resumed his cat-and-mouse pacing. He was bored with ordinary beatings. Brutality should be given more meaning — raised to the level of an art form. This would have to be something special, something to savor, something psychological . . . . At last he had it.

He called a guard who led us toward the British working party. He stood us to attention and ordered them to load sacks of rice on our shoulders. Then he gleefully told Grant that he would beat only *one* of us — the first one who dropped his sack. Grant translated.

Piston Fists walked away, pleased at his originality. He had the white scum competing against one another, struggling out of fear to beat one another — it was perfect! He settled himself at a distance to enjoy a pleasing spectacle.

The minutes passed . . . . We began to sweat. It *was* clever, devilishly clever. Grant stood in the middle. The fifty-kilo sack was heavy enough at the best of times, when you could spread your legs apart to take the weight. But now, with feet together, it was a double struggle to keep it from slipping and keep the weight on the backbone. It grew heavier and heavier . . . . My weak beri-beri legs began to quiver . . . . Would I be first? My shoulders and neck were in pain. Five more minutes of this and I was done for . . . . But a beating by the dreaded Piston Fists? Did I want George to drop his first? Would I feel relieved that it wasn't me, at the expense of my buddy? Bastard — this was just what he wanted. But the pain, the pain — it was growing more intense. My trembling legs could buckle at any moment, but I can't drop it!

The Brits were passing, loading rice, watching. Their view of us was usually one of affectionate disdain. But now this was a common enemy. A passing voice said: "Drop it all together, mates."

That was an idea — make *him* choose.

"Whaddaya say, George, shall we?" I gasped.

"Okay," he panted.

"Bing?"

"Yup."

"Okay — at the count of three. One . . . two . . . *three*."

We leaned forward and sent the bags crashing down on the cement platform.

There was a constricted cry of rage from Piston Fists. How dare we! We'd pay for this insult — all three! He came charging down on us, aiming a running punch at George's throat. George, who had a little boxing training, saw the direction of the blow and tucked in his chin to protect his throat. The fist struck his jaw and he staggered. Then Piston Fists went to work on him, proving his well-earned reputation for murderous punishment. I flinched at the sound of each blow. George was gasping and grunting with pain.

When it was over at last, it was my turn. I waited, heart pounding, bracing myself. He walked back a few yards, then came at me on the run, with the same flying punch aimed at my throat. But I had no boxing experience. I only knew that boxers protected their chins, to avoid being knocked unconscious. So I made the mistake of pulling my chin up and taking it on the throat. Crack! The pain was blinding. I felt I'd been guillotined. The rest of the beating blurred behind the choking pain of my throat. When my ordeal was over, he turned on Bing and repeated it.

Pain passes, scars heal. But my throat remained painful and would not heal. For months I had trouble swallowing, as though a potato were lodged in my gullet. I cursed the Yank boxer who had taught Piston Fists. But he hadn't taught him that sick, venomous hate that had grown over the years and produced the force behind these lethal fists. War, or nationalism, or human nature — whatever the causes, I knew I was paying for somebody else's sins with every gulp I took.

We were also used as cleanup squads, an easier job but depressing. We were brought to the bombed-out areas where the friable city had once stood. Roads and streets were being cleared of rubble. People did manage to go on living in all this, in hovels, in basements, in roofless shells of buildings, scratching out a living somehow. Life, if it could be called that, went on again. If people make a city, this was still a city and the spirit could not be crushed. Amazing people — they accepted disaster fatalistically, as their soldiers accepted dying. They were trained to endure, in the samurai tradition, and they did.

In a way the Japanese civilians were worse off than us. They ate less now. They could not steal, some because of their sense of honor, others because of fear of punishment. There was a two-year prison sentence for stealing. We, by contrast, had no honor left to lose. And we were already in prison. What else could they do to us? They could beat us, which they did, but that is no deterrent to a hungry man. So we stole, and ate and grew huskier than the civilians.

We were gathered in one place in the middle of all the chaos to hear the commandant make a speech. He was a tiny, wizened officer who had lost all his marbles long ago. Hard up for personnel, they must have dug him out of mothballs. He stood on a box above us, hopping and shrieking in a high quavering voice. An interpreter translated. We were to gather all metals into neat piles. Then he lost himself and swung into a patriotic speech, exhorting us to work hard for the love of Japan, to show duty, loyalty and self-sacrifice. Why he thought this would galvanize us I don't know. I could only suspect that he couldn't remember where he was and thought he was addressing his own troops going into battle.

Then we set to work. We moved among the ruins like phantoms after the world had ended, picking up pieces of torn scrap iron and metal and gathering them into small piles.

There was half a wall here, a window there. Doors, leading to nothing, stood staring, swathed in memories. There were pots and pans, utensils, parts of stoves and tantalizing hints of former homes, former lives, as intriguing and disconnected as scattered jigsaw puzzles. I felt, as I scavenged, like a detective at the scene of a crime, trying to put the jigsaw pieces together, to see it as it was. There were houses here once, trees, little flower gardens, even *birds* . . . streets, neighbors, shops, signs, prints and scrolls for sale, grocers, bakeries, ladies in kimonos with gay umbrellas, children with schoolbooks, tall buildings with offices full of bustling energy, talk, laughter . . . . I raised it all back up before me, and over it came the shadow, the heavy gathering darkness, the raucous voice of Tojo I'd often heard blaring over loudspeakers, urging greater sacrifice, promising glory. The Tojos, Hitlers, Duces of the earth were busily preparing the world for all this — the carnage, the massive funeral pyres. This is how it all ended up . . . with ghostly me, surrounded by other homeless, ghostly millions, picking our way among the embers, wandering over the Plains of Death.

Chapter Seventeen

EVERYONE ON THE RICE AND bean platforms prospered. But we Canadians were seldom lucky enough to get there. Nor were the Dutch and Indonesians, who lived as one "Dutch" unit. When we did get that assignment, we tried smuggling some supplies for the hungry days ahead. This was rocking the boat, not playing the game, and infuriated the regulars.

Just as butt hunting had been a reflex action at 3D, here we were always on the alert to any possibility of theft. Stealing was literally a way of life. The twice-daily searches became a challenge. We invented new hiding places. We were allowed to bring kettles of tea to work to satisfy our thirst, so we fitted some with false bottoms, the upper quarter holding tea, the rest packed with rice. I cut a one-inch hole at the center of the lining of my Red Cross hat. When the hat was turned upside down, I could pour rice into it, pinch it closed, turn it right side up and shake it till the rice was evenly packed around the inside. In this way when the search order came to lift our hats and shake them, I could do it without spilling any rice, if I shook it gently. The blue sweater that I wore under my work jacket was tied at the wrists and rice was packed inside the sleeves. During a search we would open our jackets to let the soldier tap our ribs and waist, but he would tap our arms only on the outside of the jacket; the sweater sleeves inside were not touched.

The Dutchmen, tall, emaciated, hungry, took greater and greater risks, as we did. One hiding place after another was discovered. Beatings increased. But there was no stopping us. We worked hard, needed food. As for beatings, that, like death, would always happen to the next man, not you. Not if you were clever.

The regulars fumed. We were the spoilers, the greedy, useless scum, tossing clinkers into well-oiled machinery. Our own sense of outrage increased. Those bastards were hogging the food platforms — if we got a fair chance at them, we wouldn't have to risk our hides and suffer these ferocious beatings. Everything was out of whack, everything going too far. Thievery became epidemic.

At last One-Eye had had enough. Too much was too much, and he would end this once and for all. The decree came down that the next prisoner caught stealing would be stood at attention in front of the guardhouse for twelve hours. He would get no food or water. He would be beaten by the guards every hour. The second man caught would receive double: twenty-four hours of it. The next, double again: forty-eight hours. And so on till it stopped. He thought the threat itself should do the trick.

It didn't. It did increase our caution for a while. But not for long — the temptation was too great. Besides, the alternative, hunger, was stronger, more immediate. Now the stakes were higher and we were playing a deadly game. The searches became more thorough, more extended.

And then it happened. Sure enough, a man was caught: Leduc, a Métis, one of ours. He was tough, silent, impassive.

"Ki-o-tsuki!"

We watched him stand to attention, heels together, waiting. The beating began. We walked away across the small parade yard into the hut, leaving a part of us back there with him. It could easily have been one of us. Twelve hours of *that?* All night, with no food or water? Could he take it? Could anyone?

As the hours crawled by, we strolled out to check his condition. A still, lonely figure, he stood erect, feet together, a lifeless monument encapsulated in silence. His face was lumpy and swollen. His eyes gazed dully, unblinkingly into space. Nine more hours, nine more beatings to go.

Grant, as interpreter, was called out to the guardhouse. One-Eye was lecturing Leduc as the guards beat him. George returned, looking nauseated and pale. He hated his role as interpreter, watching it all close up. He was sorry he had ever learned the language.

"Bad?" I asked.

He nodded, and lay down beside me.

I didn't want the details.

We went to sleep, thinking of that lonely vigil in the darkness. A sobering thought. How wonderful to be free to go to bed like this. It was better not to think of that man out there. Could that be me?

It was unimaginable, weakening. Would I stop stealing now? No . . . it wouldn't happen to me. He was stupid, I was smart.

A week later, George and I were assigned to the rice platform — our chance to score. One precious day. We took a long stocking, too worn out to wear any longer; cut off and sewn at the base, it made a good receptacle for rice. The image of Leduc had faded by now. So, sad to say, had our caution. What was past was past, a bad dream. Hunger filled the present.

We fell into line, waiting our turn to carry the fifty-kilo rice sacks. Three loaders stood inside the railway car and swung the sack high, thumping it down on our neck and shoulders like a blow. The regulars carried it easily, while we struggled under the weight. The planks above the waiting barge shook as we clumped across with quivering legs. The guards strolled by, vigilant at first, till they grew bored and lax as the day wore on. At an opportune moment, George and I slipped behind the rice sacks and ripped one open. Great! I kept a lookout while he quickly filled the stocking to the brim, and we hastily stashed it between the sacks. We would load up in the *benjo* at the end of the day. It was too tricky to work with rice in our shoes and hat and sweater.

Our tension mounted as the day progressed. At last we completed our quota of sixteen tons per man and hurried off to the nearby *benjo* before the march back. Here, in the dim light and close confines of a stall meant for one, we hastily removed our shoes and filled them to the brim. Grant had high Red Cross boots that carried a good amount. My shoes were low oxfords I had received in my one and only clothes parcel in 1943. By now they were worn out, with holes in the toes. I filled them quickly and forced my feet into them. Then I up-ended my lined Red Cross hat with the center hole cut out in the lining and poured the rice in till it was heavily packed. I patted the rice evenly around the inside lining, then turned the hat over and placed it on my head. A poor fit, sitting high in the air. It felt heavy and unstable, and I found I had to hold my head straight to keep it from sliding off.

There was no time for second thoughts. I hurriedly tied the sleeves of my blue sweater and poured rice down the inside forearms. All this twisting and squirming took time and we heard the guards shouting at us to get into line. We were the last to emerge into the bright light. A Yank glanced at me and stopped aghast. My hat sat perched atop my head. The rice in my shoes was clearly visible.

"Are you crazy?" he snarled.

The others looked at me angrily.

"What's wrong?" I asked.

"What's wrong! Any half-wit can see you're loaded to the gills!"

My heart sank. "Looks bad?"

"Looks *terrible!* Where's your goddam head? Get rid of it fast!"

Grant agreed. I turned to rush back to the *benjo* but my path was blocked by a guard — oh God! He drove me back with his rifle butt. I was herded into line at the end of the column.

And the march began. It was only a mile back to camp but easily the longest mile I ever walked. Everything went awry. My shoes leaked rice disastrously. At every step rice kernels shot out of my toes onto the dirt road — *clearly visible*. Guards walked in front, beside us and behind. The ones behind were sure to see them. The men around me saw them — the word passed swiftly up the line. Crisis! The regulars shouted for me to work my way forward to let the men behind me kick and scatter the rice into the dirt before the rear guards set eyes on it. George and I hurried forward till we neared the front of the line. My stomach was churning.

"You stoopid sonofabitch," the leader hissed. I looked back. The column of a hundred men behind me had been galvanized into some surrealist dance — a kicking, stumbling, scuffling, jerking shuffle-off-to-Buffalo as we moved down the road. Curses and threats erupted all the way down the line:

"Hope yuh get the shit kicked outta yuh!"

"You'll ge' a proper crunchin' f' this lot!"

Fear charged through me like a forest fire. Then I glanced down at my shoes in horror — there was so much rice packed into them that it was clearly visible on both sides of each foot. Grant's face was white. He felt responsible, frantic, helpless. My head seemed light and airy, giddy with a paralyzing terror. We shared the same thought: this was it. The next one would get *twenty-four hours of it* — twenty-four beatings, no food or water, standing at attention — that solitary, tragic figure standing in darkness all night and then all day. And more: I noticed my sleeves — was I hallucinating? — *they were leaking!* They were so threadbare by now they couldn't handle the extra weight of packed rice and were leaking the shiny kernels with every swing of my arms! I raised my forearms, pressed them to my sides — it was too much. I felt disaster descending, enveloping me. I had the wild urge to bolt — I pictured my hat falling up-ended, spewing up a volcanic spray of rice over all. I stiffened my neck, held my head steady, rigid as I marched. Good God, was I dreaming all this?

Arms tight, head stiff, shoes spitting jets of rice, pursued by a long jigging, wriggling procession whose amplified sounds of scuffling and cursing echoed in my ears — *kick-stamp-shuffle-shuffle-shove-hobble* — didn't the guards notice? What did they think it was, some crazy Western rite? Surely they must be wondering why this column of mad *furyos* were angrily jitterbugging their way to camp! I couldn't worry about that, or the collective venom: I saw only Leduc — the lone figure, the swollen face, the dark night, the blows — electric shocks of fear jolted me forward, and the terror drained my body of all strength as we neared the gates.

The cursing died out as we entered the yard and lined up before the guardhouse in a throbbing silence. I stared down at the ground: *black* — I had forgotten — full of coal dust and cinders against which the rice would stand out like lights!

The familiar ritual began inexorably. We formed up in three rows facing the guardhouse. I was in the middle one. I listened as in a nightmare to the long Japanese command ringing out like my own sentence of doom, ordering us to open ranks for inspection.

The search began. I unbuttoned my jacket slowly with trembling fingers. I spread my jacket wide and glanced down at my shoes: Christ, the rice was plainly visible! Hurriedly I loosened my belt and lowered my pants to hide it. I closed the belt, which was wound about my hips. The guard was drawing nearer . . . . *Pat, pat, tap, tap* . . . . To secure my leaking sleeves I kept my arms folded upward, unlike the rest, gripping the edges of my jacket. The hush in the yard was ethereal. The guard was searching the man next to me . . . my head was quivering with the effort to stay rigid. It seemed swollen, bloated, trying to pry itself loose from my neck . . . . The others stood at attention, eyes turned in my direction.

Now . . . I stared in front of me and nearly shrieked when the guard's hands touched my upper arms. I tried to control my trembling — would he feel it? *Pat, pat, pat* . . . his palms traveled down my arms like deadly snakes, pressing the outside, unable to reach the inner arms, poking at the sleeves, my head ready to explode . . . . Passing on down the legs . . . *tap, tap, tap* . . . closer to the rice. Inside legs . . . outside legs . . . . He stood up as I spread my jacket wide, tapping the ribs with everything quivering uncontrollably, even my teeth which I clamped tight — couldn't he sense anything? Couldn't he hear my heart thundering and crashing against my ribs?

Pat, pat, pat . . . . Were the shoes hidden? Hat straight? *Tap, tap —* a pause, tapping ceased. *Why?* He moved on . . . had I done it? No, it was not over yet. I didn't dare lower my arms. As an excuse to keep them up I pretended to be fiddling with my jacket buttons, taking a long time to button up. The order came to raise our hats and shake them. I did this gingerly. The search ended.

The command came to close ranks. All stood at attention, awaiting dismissal with arms at their sides. I delayed lowering my arms, still adjusting my buttons, unaware that the guard corporal in the guardhouse was watching me in mounting anger. Who was that stupid *furyo* holding things up? Suddenly he came tearing out of the guardhouse, dashed through the front rank and struck me across the face, and my hat slid off over my ear. I grabbed it before it fell! I lowered my arms slowly.

When we were dismissed I still had to cross the yard with rice spraying from my shoes over the black surface. The others gathered in a surly knot around me, resuming their shuffling dance routine as we moved slowly forward in an unwelcome show of togetherness till we reached the door of the hut. Once inside, Grant and I fell on each other's necks and giggled in nervous hysterical relief. *Made it, bejesus!* We ignored the curses singeing the air around us and hurried off to our bunks to unload our haul and stash it away.

Since the foraging for food here was rewarding and there were no outlets for the excess energies, sex seemed to dominate thought and action. Stan, one of the Brits working on the coal pile, used to sit among us in the small coal shed at the end of a day's work, penis in hand, coaxing it lovingly into an erection. Masturbation was a flourishing industry. The many synonyms I'd collected — creamin' yer puddin', pullin' yer wire, floggin' yer duff, beatin' your little brother, lopin' your mule, gleanin' yer lizard, jockeying your joystick, etc. — testified to its important cultural position.

Stan was heavy set, apelike, slovenly, always dull and slumberous from lack of sleep and overeating. He took on other men's stints of fire-guard duty during the night for a ration of rice, staying up half the night and earning two or three extra rations. He was very basic, his interests limited to stomach and penis. Alf, his sidekick, was his opposite. He was tiny, nervous, easily excitable, with a caustic tongue that rattled away perpetually in staccato machine-gun bursts, railing at everything in sight. He feared no one, despised everyone. He wouldn't shut up, even on parade, talking incessantly through the Japanese commands. As we lined up to get our orders for the day from the Japanese foreman, his rumbling could be heard:

"All right, let's 'ave ye, sick ol' cow . . . . Blow i' out yer arse! Four-eyed bastard . . . . Speak up, ye creepin' sod!"

And when the orders were over:

"An' the same t' you, mate! On yer way — noice 'avin ye! Toodle-oo 'n tweet-tweet!"

He saved his finest tirades for Stan, the main butt of his wit and venom. He was jealous of Stan's bulk and hated his cow-like equanimity, lassitude and stupidity. It all rolled off Stan, who would grin sleepily with heavy-lidded eyes. It wasn't food or sex, so it didn't matter.

One day Stan sat proudly stroking his tool and held it pointed skyward in full flower. Alf had had a bad day and was in a dark mood.

"Pu' that ugly thing away!" he ordered furiously. "Ye look like a fuckin' bull in 'eat!"

It was particularly big that day and Stan was particularly proud. He leered at Alf and said slowly: "Fine bloody size, i'n it? Lookit that now. Pity wastin' it."

Bing nodded. "The torch be yours to hold it high."

A sheet of white flame seemed to flash in Alf's eyes. "I'll bloody give i' somethin' t' do!" he snapped, lunging forward and seizing the proud rocket. "Come on then!"

"Eeah! Leave off!" Stan yelled, roused at last.

But Alf yanked, Stan leaped to his feet and Alf pulled him out through the door into the coal yard. "We're off for a bi' of a spin!"

he yelled viciously. "Come on!"

"*Aaoo-o-o-ow!*"

Alf broke into a run, gripping the poor pecker at his side as he ran with Stan pounding along, yowling pitiably, belly and pelvis thrust forward, trying desperately to keep up the pace. They went roaring and shrieking around the coal pile, making a full circle of the entire coal yard like antic figures in a film cartoon leaping along the horizon, before finally returning to base. The great organ was a limp and sorry sight.

Ah, Ozymandias, lo how the mighty have fallen.

A not-so-funny offshoot to this sexual climate came in the form of a guard who took a shine to me. He must have absorbed the insidious vibes of the camp. He had a soft, smooth, girlish look, with limpid brown eyes that settled on my face and stayed. During searches his hands lingered and did a lot of unnecessary patting and stroking. He found excuses to pick on me and badger me. He was bad news. He didn't know how to give vent to his own confused emotions, so he feigned anger and kept poking me at every opportunity. I remember throwing snowballs at a girl I was attracted to in high-school, trying to hurt her, in something of the same spirit. But this wasn't high-school stuff, it was heavy-duty, and I didn't need it. I steered clear of him, not wanting to stir up this witch's brew. When I saw him from afar, I ducked behind doors and other bodies and gave him plenty of distance.

Then one warm night I was on my way to the *benjo* at 2:00 a.m., stumbling sleepily along in the semi-darkness, naked save for my little cotton *fundoshi*, when as luck would have it I ran smack into him. He was patrolling inside the hut. He blinked in surprise and delight and barred my way. He started prodding me, firing questions, growing excited and faking anger. I sensed that he didn't know what to do with me or with himself. He had me where he wanted me and didn't want to let go. Then he grabbed my arm and pulled me over to the light. The hut had a hanging bulb at each end beside the doors. He pushed me under the light, then placed his bayonet point at my throat, pressing my chin up to force my face into the light. I felt he was loony and I was frightened; he was enjoying the fear in my face. I didn't know where this was going or how it would end. It was taking on a nightmare quality, with the knife at my throat and his voice talking in a half-menacing, half-caressing tone. Then by a stroke of luck, Evans, the Yank leader on the bean platform, came by on his way to the *benjo* and stopped at the sight of the startling tableau — face under the light, bayonet at the throat. He was swift, resourceful, fearless and heaven-sent. He came right over.

"What's goin' on? What've you done?"

"Nothing. This guy's having his jollies."

"*Nanda?*" Evans demanded. The guard waved him away. Evans boldly took the guard's arm and said: "*Hanashi gunso* [speak to the sergeant] — come on. *Gunso, gunso* — okay?" It was just the right word. The thought of explaining to the sergeant was frightening and brought him back to reality. The bayonet came away from my throat. He turned, shook off Evans's hand and hurried away. Evans went on his way.

"Whew! Thanks!" I said to Evans's retreating back. He raised his arm in a casual wave and turned the corner. The right man at the right time in the right place. Lucky escape — or had I been praying under that light, I wondered.

Chapter Eighteen

T HE NEWS WAS CONFIRMED. It was coming in from gang after gang working in different areas. No doubt about it. "Germany's *kaisanged* [finished]!" I sat down to record the date in my diary, and my thoughts. At long last! How did I feel? Ecstatic? Victorious? Not exactly. I had looked forward to this for years, sweating it out, month after month, rumor after rumor, picking up the war's progress in exciting driblets. And yet . . . why did I feel so let down? So strangely depressed?

I knew why. It was the awareness that out there, all over the world, cheering mobs were celebrating, going wild, getting drunk, kissing, hugging, dancing in the goddam streets! How could they? How dare they? As though the war were over, as though we didn't exist . . . . I gazed about me: nothing had changed. The same louse-ridden mat, the same ugly barn, the same coal pile, the same fatigue, the same food, sneaking a smoke furtively on my bunk as usual, waving my hand slowly as I smoked to avoid any funnel of smoke to catch a guard's eye. The same everything. We were on an island cut off from the world, a world that went happily on without us, leaving us behind in a different, static time frame. There, time moved on, event followed event. Hitler killed, Roosevelt dead, Russians in Berlin, Europe at peace, fascism dead and gone, everyone going home . . . . But — hey, wait a minute: wasn't there some little pocket of resistance holding out? Oh yeah, Japan, way off there in a far corner of the globe, a mere bagatelle. Weren't there some prisoners there — been there for a long time? Can't remember now, can you? No, forget it — war's over. Pass the champagne!

We continued to steal, and the "crunchings" grew harsher. One-Eye made more surprise inspections. He would suddenly climb up the ladder to inspect our bunk; he usually found our kit improperly squared off and used his long bamboo pole to knock all our gear off the shelves and cheerfully wallop us over the head with it. We would watch our few precious possessions strewn over the bed mats in as big a shambles as he could create, then he'd climb down. He and all the guards were growing meaner. Was it the war? The bombing? The hunger? We couldn't guess, but they seemed intent on making life more intolerable than ever.

I was just relaxing after a bruising day on coal when I heard the warning alert: "Flag up!"

Trouble. We jumped up to check our shelves, our hidden wiring. A guard was coming down the aisle. They usually stayed outside, patrolling past the windows. He stopped at our bay.

My heart raced as he looked up at our bunk and made for our ladder. He mounted it, step after step, rifle, bayonet and all. He stood at the top, gazing at us with eyes that seemed to glare angrily behind heavy lenses. They lit on the number sewn on the breast of my jacket.

"*San-hiaku-ni-ju-go-ka* [325]?"

My stomach began churning. What now? I nodded.

"*Hai.*"

He blinked at me for a few moments. He laid his rifle, topped by the long, murderous-looking bayonet knife, down on my small pillow and pointed to me, making motions of drawing with his finger. It was my turn to blink.

"*Atisuto-ka?*"

"Oh! Artist? Yes, *hai!*"

He bowed. "*Watakushi-atisuto onaji.*"

"Ah! You're an artist too? Whew! Good God — really?" The eyes I took to be glaring were really soft and excited. His face, now that I looked, was gentle. He pointed to my kit.

"*Doko desu ka?*"

"Where? Right here — yes." I hurriedly took out my sketchbook, and he sat down on my bed matting to examine it curiously. He nodded approval. I watched his slender fingers turn the pages gingerly, as though handling an ancient scroll. Then he spoke in Japanese, saying things I didn't understand.

"He wants to exchange work," George said. I nodded. Then he opened a kit he carried and produced a small inkstone, brush and water and settled down to paint a quick scene on a blank card. I watched his deft strokes gliding over the paper, the brush poised vertically as though floating above the surface as a riverbank took shape under my eyes. Trees appeared . . . a boat and boatman, drifting along in some distant, unattainable dream world, where birds sang freely and the pure air smelled of moist greenery . . . peace and beauty lay unchallenged over all, proclaiming this The Way . . . .

When he had finished, he handed it to me as a *purezento*.

"*Arigato*," I said feelingly. "*Takusan arigato* [many thanks]."

I sat down to do a quick pencil sketch and offered it to him. His face lit up. "George, tell him I'm sorry I have only a pencil sketch to offer." George did.

He smiled and said gently, "Sō-ka," nodding his understanding. He sighed as though not wanting to leave our ugly lair, then folded up his paint kit and rose. He lifted his rifle and gleaming bayonet, paused and bowed. I returned the bow. He turned and bowed to George and the others, who bowed hastily in astonishment. Then we exchanged another bow before he turned and climbed down the ladder. I watched him march off, a soldier, a guard, an enemy, a visitation . . . he may, I thought, have dropped from heaven. Wherever he came from, he had shown me a faint glimmer in the darkness, a vision of the possible, so painfully brief, so tantalizing — before we both sank back into the slime.

We went out on a "garden party" — not tea and crumpets and flowery ladies' dresses, but a gang to plant spuds. A space had been cleared and potatoes taken along to be planted in the unfriendly soil. It would be a very sad crop; the good earth would have very little chance to prove its worth, since most of the potatoes would be gobbled up before they reached the ground.

But this day was unique for us in that it brought us Gallo, a young flier, just arrived, shot down nine months ago — meaning he had lived, laughed, eaten, sung in the free world for the last four years! We gathered around him, staring, examining, questioning, with the fascination of scientists discovering rocks on the moon. More accurately, he was an astronaut, from out of the future, landing in a time machine, bringing the culture of another planet.

He was an astonishing twenty-one, a dark, slender young American, with a soft, narrow, sallow face, boyish and still unformed. Twenty-one! He would have been seventeen when we were captured. His clean, well-cut officer's uniform made him even stranger. He answered everything with a patient smile, like a seasoned politician beset by avid reporters.

He told us of new developments that had taken place: rationing, women in men's jobs on the production lines. Hey — the songs! Tell us the songs — what are the latest hit tunes?

Well, there was "Rosy the Riveter," very big in the States. Rosy — a riveter! Was a lady riveter a normal part of life now? Yeah, lots of women doin' that. Men are at the front. It was a woman's world! What changes! A goddam Amazon society!

And there was "Pistol Packin' Mama." How did that go? He obliged, singing out in a pleasant baritone. Some were feverishly scribbling the precious words, some hummed the melody, trying to commit it to memory with a pathological desperation.

"And Crosby has a big hit called 'White Christmas'." His voice dropped to a soft, crooning imitation.

I closed my eyes as he sang. What a gloomy song, full of sadness, nostalgia — thick snowflakes drifting silently down on snow-covered steps, porches, trees . . . houses full of warm lights and healthy round-faced children. I was transported back to the places and times entwined in the songs and dreamy tones of *"der Bingle*," "Sweet Leilani," as we sailed away from Hawaii at sunset . . . . "All the Things you are," strolling down 42nd Street off Broadway . . . . "Blue Moon," sitting in the park on a summer night, letting hopes, dreams, ambitions soar across the dark heavens.

Suddenly all the clichés and corny, gooey sentiments were invalid, swollen by a transcendent emotion, by years of inhuman craving. They were all transformed now — no longer pop songs but made part of the world's stark realism by millions of suffering souls.

Gallo told of many events, many people who had died, filling in the blank years with an endless calendar of continuing life. Roosevelt dead — we knew that. Hitler nearly assassinated. Really? Ah, why did the stupid bastards goof on that! The Germans, like Napoleon, were trapped and destroyed by the Russian winter — wonderful. The German Sixth Army was surrounded and captured — great.

"Any new pin-up gals?"

"The same, you know — Rita Hayworth."

"Rita who?"

"Jesus — Rita Hayworth."

"Who's she?"

"Whew. You guys . . . . Lemme see — Lana Turner, Jane Russell . . . and Grable — Betty Grable?" He looked around inquiringly. We all shook our heads.

"Never heard of them."

"Boy — how long've you been here?"

"Too damn long — 1943."

"Nineteen forty-one," I said, gloomily asserting seniority.

It was all immensely satisfying and strangely shocking. For some reason we had expected life to stand still, to remain as we knew it. Our mental pictures were clear and remarkably solid, carved in a pre-war mold. That was the least they could do for us. But what was emerging here was deeply disturbing. The strong foundation of our world was dissolving under our feet as we listened. The people, the places, the way of life had been in motion for years. And the speed of motion had itself changed, accelerated. It hinted at a new pace I was not accustomed to. Would I feel like Rip Van Winkle? Even ideas, attitudes and thoughts were different. Things sounded crazy, childish, out of kilter, as though people had lost track of the basics. The world was unbalanced, coming apart. Why had I been foolish enough to believe the war would affect only me and leave the rest of the world intact? I thought of the last war and the lost generation that followed. Would that be us? Would we fit in when we returned — *if* we returned? All the things I'd daydreamed — had they all been swept away?

Would we, the men from Hong Kong, be the legion of forgotten men? Think of all the great battles that followed, gobbling up the headlines and broadcasts. Think of the millions bombed and slain around the globe. Think of the women in men's garb on the production lines, making bombs . . . Rosy the riveter. It had all moved on past us. History had run over us like a steamroller, leaving us behind, squashed in the muck.

It didn't really matter . . . nothing mattered but freedom. Just turn me loose, end it, and I'll worry about it then. Whatever the changes, it'll still be heaven. A different one maybe, but heaven nonetheless. Give me Rosy the Riveter. Give me Pistol Packin' Mama. I too am Dreaming of a White Christmas. I'll take it. What was that doggerel I wrote at Christmas '44? "And so, by Xmas '45/Let's hope to hell we're still alive."

Hard to believe I was well into my fourth prison year. But my legs knew, and at last the day came when they said, "Enough." Swollen with wet beri-beri, they finally balked at bending or holding steady under the heavy sacks. What do you do with an old horse that can no longer pull its weight? I was valueless. At least you could shoot a real horse and sell it for horsemeat. An old Eskimo co-operates and goes off to die. This was a working camp with no room for deadweight. It was not the relatively lax 3D, where invalid *romokyus* sat and leisurely separated nuts and bolts. Here it was sink or swim. You had a few days to get well; then, well or not, out to work you went, bound to whatever albatross the fates had chosen. There were no rations for unproductive bodies, and food must come out of the healthy man's plate. In happier circumstances this is called sharing. Here the sick were ugly parasites sucking the blood of their own kind. Not a pleasant prospect. I chose to go out and try to play along.

Razelski, head of the rice platform, saw my knees buckling as I struggled under the heavy weights. He may have felt a pity he couldn't admit to, knowing it had no place in the scheme of things. But a natural leader, as he was, is resourceful, and he quickly turned negative to positive with a little creative legerdemain. A deal was struck. He persuaded the doctor to keep me in camp indefinitely as long as I could create pin-up girls for the delectation of the citizenry — feeding the camp's spiritual needs, so to speak. Materials? I could leave that to him. He led the Barons, I recalled, and they commanded undefined power sources, always swathed in a mysterious cloak of intrigue. He brought a four-foot sheet of thick cardboard, gleaming white, and a set of children's crayons.

In the days following I set to work bringing a shapely hula-hula dancer into this dingy gloom, the exaggerated hips undulating under a swaying palm. The breasts, too ample to stand up on their own in the harsh light of truth, stood up anyway, in full flower, since this was the stuff of wet dreams. I was artist-in-residence. The hut was almost empty as I worked, surrounded by an eerie stillness, the air void of sound and life. It was always so crammed with bodies, shouts, noise, fast footsteps clattering by, energies bouncing and clashing, that the contrast was unnerving, as though some great cataclysm had swallowed up all living things and made me doubt my own presence. Wonderful, this solitude, a heavenly peace with the absence of evil, and I savored it as I scratched away at my silent dancer.

I heard a sound of wheels outside and low voices: that would be the sick men bringing pig feed on the cart. It was that and a lot more. This was the day that was to reveal the source of the Barons' boundless supply of rice, their secret power conundrum unraveled. No bank heist of millions could have been more ingeniously, meticulously planned.

I was roused by the unusual sound of pounding feet and glanced down at this apparition of a prisoner roaring down the center aisle in broad daylight toting a fifty-kilo sack of rice! A hallucination? I whirled in astonishment to spot the guard, who was passing the windows and only out of sight for thirty seconds. In that time the rice was seized by waiting hands and sent sailing up out of sight. But how in the world . . . ?

I learned how later. The sick men were sent out with cart and sacks to sweep up the rice from the loading platforms for the pigpen. A common sight. Here, the loading gang slipped them a pack of good rice, which they hid under their own sacks and brought in without a search. Split-second timing sent it from the pigpen through a window and into waiting hands.

I was stunned, admiring and angry. No wonder the bastards could cook thirty cans a night on their massive stove! No wonder they didn't need to risk their necks as we did. Calling *us* greedy — bloody hypocrites. But what an operation! American enterprise on a grand scale — "Barons" was the right name. They were robber barons with the same spirit that had carved out vast empires of wealth and power in the New World. Yes, the soul of J. Pierpont Morgan was here, alive and flourishing in Sumidagawa.

Now a new phase began. Somewhere in a distant U.S. Air Force HQ, Gen. Curtis LeMay decided that Tokyo had been neglected. There still remained some pockets of life that had missed his tender ministrations, and he proceeded to fix that. Waves of B-29 bombers increased until their visits became an almost nightly routine. These fire-bombing flights had a new quality, with the no-nonsense stamp of LeMay efficiency. They flew very low for better aim and saturation coverage — at high risk to crews, of course, but these were expendable, being wisely made up of many green youngsters. We must remember, after all, that there was a war on, and war was not for sissies.

No mollycoddling air-raid shelters here, we just stayed in our hut, exposed and waiting. With great conflagrations on all sides, we had ringside seats at the windows on our upper bunks, watching the nightly festivities — man at his destructive best, glorying in his carnival of mayhem, using all the powers of technology to murder and kill and burn his fellow creatures. Inspiring, how far we'd come. What had once taken years to devastate could now be eliminated in a few nights. And you didn't even have to get dirty doing it — all pushbutton squeaky-clean. The wonders of science!

We crouched by our windows watching these gargantuan forces locked in life-and-death combat that threatened to engulf us at any moment — an extra touch of spice that heightened our interest. Who were we for? Those sowers of fire and chaos who were us? Or the wailing, shrieking victims who too could soon be us? I was for both and neither. Part of me said a pox on all of you — tear yourself to bits, you goddam maniacs, just leave me out of it! But there was no rising above it. We were very much in the eye of the hurricane, with fear, hate, horror, vengeance, rampaging through our veins, colliding in hearts and minds.

There was a peculiar and terrifying quietness about the battle, as though we were watching a silent movie. A wave of about nine B-29s appeared overhead, gliding as if in slow motion, spaced evenly, in single file. Their naked whiteness was picked up by powerful beams that fastened on them remorselessly to hold them paralyzed, suspended in one place as ack-ack zeroed in on them, bursting all around their fragile bodies in a deadly fireworks display. I wanted to shout warnings — for chrissake, get out of the way! But there was no dodging, no changing course; orders were orders. The low pounding timpani of the ack-ack beat out their broken rhythms, a weird cosmic jazz. Then there would be a noiseless flash and a B-29 would explode into the black universe:

pilots, observer, gunners, operator, the whole crew — clean, tense, full-bodied, bellies lined with bacon, eggs, coffee, alive one second, non-existent the next. Enviable in a way — no pain, no fleas, no beatings — just *gone* . . . . Another hit — only this one was still visible, burning, trailing smoke and flame, wavering, plunging, out of control, a meteor sailing down, down, to oblivion.

Fires were getting perilously close. After another hit, two white puffs came sailing down toward us — parachutes! Almost directly overhead! Coming down so slowly, gaily, lightly, like free-coasting birds, two hated killers being delivered alive as a welcome sacrifice, a gift to their long-suffering victims. Crowds rose out of the earth on every side, racing to be first. What were these men thinking as they drifted closer and closer?

"Bloody fools," Grant muttered angrily. "Should've stayed with the plane."

"While there's life there's hope," Fortune said doubtfully. "Maybe the police'll get 'em in time."

Newfie snorted. "I'd blow me stoopid brains out before I'd go down into that."

Then the sound of a mob crazed with fury. It began as a distant hum, high and harsh as a wind through wires, then growing gradually to a low roar, a football crowd on its feet for the score, the kill, rising gradually to a crescendo as the parachutes drew near. The crowd converged on the target with all the pent-up rage of men who have watched their loved ones burned to cinders, their homes and possessions erased.

"Wolves," Newfie whispered. "Hungry wolves after a rabbit. Dey'll eat 'em alive."

Tension mounted as we watched. I was covered in gooseflesh, shivering, listening. I knew they were lost. But what a way to die. The screaming continued at high pitch. What were they doing to them? Smashing, clawing, tearing them to pieces with hands, nails, clubs, stones — fighting to get at them. Kill — *kill*, the theme song, the hackneyed chorus of war.

Night after night it went on. What a show. A dazzling performance, with musicians and singers pouring forth fire and death as they turned the space between earth and heaven into a huge tortured stage full of wondrous light and sound.

A hard act to follow. What could really top that? What the

producers needed now was a last act that would absolutely slay 'em . . . . Well, what about an atomic bomb? *That* would do it! Now there was an inspiration, perfect — the grand boffo finale they'd never forget. Unequaled in the whole history of man. Truly worthy of the crazed maestros who were busily orchestrating the demise of our planet.

And wasn't there a certain inevitability to the Bomb? Wasn't there a fitting idiocy in the truth of it, the final, terrifying, unacceptable Truth, that this was the best, the most humane surgery left to man to end his own agony? To establish peace on earth?

Chapter Nineteen

AUGUST 15, 1945

NORMAL DAY, HOT, BORING, clear, with the hope of an air raid. But there was something strange in the air. We had never, ever been sent back to camp at mid-morning with no air-raid alarm. Something wrong. Some change, something threatening. A move? Where to? Manchuria, some said, where we would be used for germ experiments . . . . Work parties arrived from various sectors bringing rumors of the war ending. Hah! We'd chewed at *that* old turkey often enough.

"No, but this *hancho* is a straight shooter — he's never slung any bull since we've known him. He said it!"

Just horseshit . . . . Another party arrived, saying it was in the papers! Another said it was on the radio. Impossible! The hut was filling up. No air raid. What the hell *was* going on?

More rumors . . . growing stronger. The air was becoming charged. No — I wouldn't let myself fall for that again; the letdown was always too painful. But word came down from the Barons. They had strong sources — a Yank had actually seen it in print. Could it be? For a moment my mind slipped out of equilibrium, and I was overtaken by a giddy floating sensation before I fought it down — I would not be sucked in again!

The Manchurian rumor grew stronger, but so did the other. Grant and I tracked down the Yank who'd said he'd seen it in the papers. He swore it was true. "I know it," he said. "This is it! It's all over! They've *kaisanged*."

"Was it a Japanese paper? You can't read Japanese."

"He read it to me — straight from the page. *Censo owari* — I shit you not!"

The giddiness returned. I stared at him. Liar? Dreamer? Nut? I'd seen it so-o-o often . . . the belief, the faith, the desire giving false shape, the rapturous illusion turning to vapor.

212

We walked away, moving from group to group, hearing hot debate that grew stronger and stronger. My head was swimming. This was crazy: had the chronic struggle for life, the indescribable longing, the endless variety of miseries, the soul-destroying years of non-life reached their finale? It was too enormous to grasp.

An hour passed. The fever intensified. Many were convinced, many were not. It became unbearable. *I had to know.* I decided on my own test. Kill or cure, I had to find out.

I walked outside the hut, sat down alone on a small bench and leaned against the hut wall. It was 2:00 p.m. I lit a cigarette, strictly forbidden, and waited for the guard, tense and fearful but impelled. A slight infraction would have brought a beating, a deliberate provocation such as this would be grim, but worth it. The guard came around the corner, pacing slowly, bayonet at his shoulder . . . I stared straight before me. He was coming closer . . . . I held the smoking cigarette to my lips, took a deep drag and blew it out slowly, gazing at him as I exhaled. He watched, blinked, hesitated and . . . *walked on.*

I knew!

I sat there, limp, weak, trying to encompass the mind-destroying knowledge, to pull it, push it, force it into some cohesive shape, and it would not respond. I had promised that when the great day came, I would climb to the highest peak of the camp roof and crow like a rooster. Belt it out to the whole wide world — cry freedom! Let the long years of suppressed life be blown sky-high! No question as to how I'd feel. But I felt nothing of that. I was not free, really, not physically, not legally. I was only enraptured by an idea, a concept no more palpable than a dream. How *could* I feel free? And did I really believe my own brain? My heart was in a state of siege. It refused to register the logic sent down from on high. It repelled barrage after barrage. Could it dare open the floodgates? Even when it should? I was unaware how completely it had sealed itself off.

I returned to the hut and lay back on my bunk, listening to the ongoing debate. Grant saw the expression on my face — blank, calm, distant. "You don't believe it," he concluded.

"I do believe it," I said, almost sorrowfully. "I think it's true."

He stared. "Then why the hell . . . ?"

I shrugged. "I dunno."

"I need real proof, not talk," he said. "I guess you do too."

I told him about the cigarette and the guard. He grimaced. "That could be anything. Those are new green kids in the guardhouse and he could've been confused. No, I want to hear it from the horse's mouth."

So did many others. We decided to get Captain Martin to tackle the camp commandant. This was the formula for putting all rumors to rest in the past. When a rumor persisted for days and became overpowering, it was Martin who could be counted on to nail it down. He would request an interview with the CC, then come to the front of the hut and shout in his strained, damaged, quavering voice: "At ease!" and the babble of voices would recede. Then he would shout with great effort:

"With regard to a certain rumor! It — is — not — so!"

Which put an end to all speculation. At 3:30 p.m., a group descended on the captain. He needed little prompting, since his own curiosity was rising. Maybe the CC did know. He was closeted with the CC for half an hour while we paced the aisle outside. Finally he emerged.

We scanned his thin scarred face. It was twitching, which was not unusual. Nor was the burning in his eyes. Otherwise he was expressionless, which was frustrating. He strode slowly to the front of the hut with something of what must have been his former swagger and shouted: "At ease!"

This time the hush was instantaneous, crackling. He stood in the center aisle, legs spread wide, arms akimbo and took a deep breath. Out came the familiar, quavering shout:

"With regard to a certain rumor!" And the taut, hollow face opened like a broken dike, letting through a rushing wave of joy for the first time, transforming it into a strange, scarred, radiant smile. "It — is — so!"

The hut exploded in a wild, exultant, Yankee-Limey-Scottish-Dutch-Indonesian-Canadian thunder of victory, of pent-up souls erupting, smashing the shackles of seemingly limitless defeat in a great triumphant jungle roar! Men charged down the aisle, whooping and bellowing, leaping and cheering. The sound spoke more of war than peace. The walls trembled with this new and strange onslaught of near fury that soared out into the summer skies and sent the camp staff racing for safety.

I tried to join the celebrative mood, laughing heartily with the rest, hugging, shaking hands, going through all the motions, wanting desperately to feel what they felt — eager to let the exultation pour over me. Then, God *damn* it — *why didn't it?* Why was I being cheated so sadistically at the last moment? Why could the others dive into the festive mood so easily?

But were they really celebrating? I stared into the eyes around me and caught the reflection of my own. Yes, the mouths were stretched wide with laughter, faces expanded in delight, but the eyes — the eyes were tortured and haunted, betraying the quiet fear, the doubting, the inner struggle of crippled souls. No, no . . . it was too much, too quick. We lepers couldn't shed our skins, try as we might.

No one revealed us to ourselves more than Newfie. His eccentricity had always bordered on the abnormal and now it had pushed across the edge. He climbed up to my bunk like a shivering animal seeking warmth, all his jaunty confidence gone. He had been peculiarly at home in this setting, and the enormity of the change was destroying him. Paranoia gripped him and he shook with fright. "You don't believe it, do you, Ally? Tell me de troot."

"It's true, Newf, it's over."

"Naaah — it's a trick, a trick dey're playin' on us, can't ye see?"

"No, no. It's really over."

"You know what I tink? Dey're sendin' us to Manchuria to dat germ place, and dis is how dey're suckin' us into it."

"They're not. They're not. Believe me. You heard the captain."

"He's lyin'. Dey're all lyin'."

I understood. Oh, how I understood. How close I was to the world of defeat, pessimism, shattered hope. How sane he sounded. Within a month he was locked away in a psychiatric ward.

And there was a very fine line dividing us. Looking back, I think I *had* slipped across the borders of sanity like Newfie, only unobserved. We were trying to swim in this sea of change, floundering, sinking, struggling for air. A strange new order prevailed. No work, no hours, no schedules for eating and sleeping . . . . No rules . . . . We were confined to the camp "for our own protection." Guards were still on duty to keep the people from attacking us. We had no contact with the outside world . . . .

Smoking was permitted anywhere, anytime. All the kitchen

stores were given out without stint — all the rice we could eat, all the vegetables. We brought blankets outdoors in the hot August nights to sleep on the cinders under the stars, free of our vermin-ridden bunks.

I developed a sudden mental block against rice, something I'd relished throughout the years in any form — white, brown, moldy, wormy. Now I grew nauseated at the sight of it. Some crevice of my brain had recognized freedom, accepting it before I could, a promising sign. I ate cucumbers instead. They were available in abundance. I craved them untouched, uncooked, uncut, pure, straight from the farm. I devoured one after another with an unappeased lust. I peeled them, salted them and crunched away at them greedily, counting seventeen before I stopped. My body was slowly reacting.

We gathered in groups, talking, wandering about the narrow confines of the camp. The regular camp staff had all escaped, rightly fearing our revenge. So many wanted Piston Fists's blood.

We staged an international concert in which I sang a Spanish duet with a Mexican-American. A Cockney sang a love song of his own making, in Japenglish, with lines like: "*Skies were gray . . . and she said abunai* [careful] . . . . " And there was a sprightly Scot singing, "*Yeu made me love yeu, Ah didna wanna do i'. . . .*"

We prodded ourselves to laughter, exchanged addresses, painted glowing pictures of things to come, acting, pretending, eager to capture some of the glow around us. We discussed the surrender and the details drifting into camp. The Emperor had made a surrender speech, we heard, couched in the most obscure terms, sounding at times more like a bland report to stockholders: "The war has gone not necessarily to our advantage." You can say *that* again! Yet they all understood. Game over, folks. Their turn now. We'd had ours.

There was one killer phrase about "endure the unendurable" that must have sent the nation spinning. It all sounded so impossible, knowing what we knew — how we were despised for choosing the ultimate shame of surrender rather than death with honor. What could be more despicable than a cowardly *furyo*, self-condemned, the lowest, the vilest, cursed to spend an afterlife of tragic degradation . . . . Now the whole bloody nation was being asked to do it! The holy Emperor himself — the god, so revered he could not be looked upon as he passed — *he* was surrendering! It really was unendurable, and unthinkable.

There were reports of great crowds massed, listening, weeping openly. Of the army having called for a hundred million suicides. Everything was standing on its head. What could such a trauma do to the national psyche, I wondered? Could they ever recover? What nation ever suffered so totally from defeat, the first in their history? Yet in their heart of hearts they must have felt relief. The killing, the bombs, the burning had stopped. Peace was what they craved. The Emperor gave them that and left them to work out the rest. But what about the army? How could *they* swallow it? All had solemnly pledged to die gloriously for the Emperor, never dreaming of such ignominy. It didn't make sense.

Actually there had been hell to pay with the younger officers, who staged a last-minute palace coup that succeeded for several hours the night before the surrender. They lopped off heads and searched wildly for the taped surrender speech (two copies were found and destroyed, the remaining one was already at the radio station). A minister of state escaped in a lady's dress: the army chief committed ritual *seppuku*, cutting out his bowels while his officers begged him to join the revolt. It was put down by a loyal group and the ringleaders committed suicide in the wee hours of the morning. Not a quiet night.

So this was peace. They, the defeated, were accepting it out there, picking up the pieces of their torn lives. It was *we*, the victors pacing the dingy prison yard, who could not handle it. We were struggling to achieve a massive expansion of perspective with minds so constricted by our narrow little cave-life that this sudden jolting exit into the blinding sun, with a view of vast rolling mountains, seas, skies, was too overwhelming. Hearts too were past repair. We were in the grip of a frightful numbness of spirit, unaware of our own state. The protective process that had taken place over the years had taken a terrible toll. Now we must struggle to *feel*. The palliatives for suffering had come to us like medieval physicians applying leeches to our flow of emotions, draining them dry, till at last we were totally purged, immune, devoid of all blood, the stuff of life. Jenkins described how, after weeks of care and nurturing, his best friend had died in his arms . . .

how he'd lain the body aside and gone out for a walk, feeling no more loss than a meal missed.

We wandered over the camp, letting feelings ooze back, drop by drop. We talked of home now, with a sense of growing reality, faint stirrings beginning to percolate below the surface, a tantalizing flash here and there — a bit more each day, like the tiny probing movements of a wild fawn. I was faintly aware of it as we moved about in a strange, dreamlike state, edging closer to freedom but still a good distance away. Home, loved ones, friends were faces painted on flat playing cards. We drifted to and fro, dazed, semi-conscious, like shell-shocked victims leaving a bombed house. Visual harmonies of future delight hummed in my head but came out sadly lacking in melody.

Even Smitty, eternal sunbeam, with his hardy, insensitive heart, wore a secretive grin as he approached; but his eyes were glazed over with a look of fixed, anxious surprise, as though questioning a universe that gave up no answers. I felt suspended somewhere between the ground to which I no longer belonged and all *that*, waiting out there, to which I was unable to connect.

When would they come for us? Nothing was happening. No work, no action, no appetite, no "real" food, no order. We had found the bluebird of happiness with wings of clay. I tried to sort it out in my diary. What would it be like out there? Released from the halls of the dead into the Future. But Future had always been remote, a misty loveliness, unreal, unlikely. Now it was about to become Present, and I would be plunked right in the middle of it. Was I ready? It would be a bit like meeting a lover known only by correspondence. I was intensely curious yet not eager, scarred by the chronic dread of disappointment.

Days passed. The Americans apparently knew nothing of our existence and couldn't find us. We saw occasional planes far off — American? Captain Martin had binoculars: yes, they were small fighter planes, circling, searching for prison camps. We took mirrors up on the roof to reflect the sun, hoping to catch the eye of a pilot. But they were too far away and saw nothing. Some planes began to take wider sweeps so we took bedsheets out, making huge banners, on the roof, in the yard, waving them to and fro. We felt like castaways on a desert island trying to signal ships. Each day they made wider circles, coming nearer. We could see *them* easily, damn them — why couldn't they see *us?*

At last, about August 21, a single plane circled closer. We dashed out to wave the sheets, flash glass, wave arms, hats, jackets. He circled nearer, spying something — a speck of white? A flash of light? Would he investigate? This way! A shout went up and everyone poured into the yard, redoubling our efforts — waving, shouting, twirling hats, jumping — would he see? Here! Here! We willed him toward us. His nose pointed in our direction — he must have seen — *he was heading straight for us!* A cheer went up!

We filled the small compound, waving, leaping, yelling at him. He was directly overhead and we could see the markings, details, crystal clear, no mirage. The motor's deep, powerful lion's roar was so unlike the tinnient, rattling Japanese sound — it was power, command, victory, release. Now we were all bellowing hoarsely, swept up in mass hysteria. He circled lower to be sure, and the din around me rose in volume. Then he dove at us, coming in low, barreling in over the tops of telephone wires, huge as life, with a head-splitting thunder. I couldn't hear myself shrieking at the top of my lungs — my entire being seemed to contract into a frenzied knot, one bomb of concentration, excruciating rapture detonating into the skies! As he came over us he dipped his wing in the most magnificent symbolic salute ever received. I was shrieking, waving, laughing, howling insane gibberish, freaking, weeping uncontrollably — the tears spurting up like an irrepressible orgasmic release. My dam had burst at last and out it all came, as though all the anguish of the planet had found me, and out of my bowels all the murders, tortures, all the Jews burning in Belsen, all the hellish years, had gathered in a million voices bursting all bounds.

Our faces were turned worshipfully heavenward to this god-plane that was now circling back to dive again, as though gripped by the concerted will below. He could not hear the bedlam, but he saw a yard crammed with leaping bodies waving hats, sheets, arms, and he was caught up in the fever. He seized the nearest object, a pack of cigarettes, scribbled a note, which he wrapped around it, and tossed it at us as he passed. We rushed to see it, and it was passed quickly from hand to hand.

The note was printed hastily in pencil. I stared down at the words: "Greetings to men of a brave and free world." Emotion bubbled up again in fresh waves of tears that poured down. There was a shock of newness, awareness that for the first time I could *feel* the total meaning of these words, feel them in my innermost being. Till now neither willing it nor thinking it could force its truth . . . . A few simple words . . . a cliché. But never had they carried greater power. How did he know? This bit of paper said it all, a summons dropped from the sky, proof, affirmation that it wasn't all a fevered dream. I could finger and touch its truth, flung instinctively by the hand of a free man only moments ago. I really *was* a man of a "brave and free world." The word *free* crackled like a flame before me, its glow spreading outward from this wrinkled paper, enfolding me in its radiance from head to toe.

It was the turning point, the total release from darkness. Birth. At last I understood.

It was over.

Chapter Twenty

THE QUALITY OF THE DAYS that followed changed radically in texture and meaning, though the feel of moving in a trancelike floating world that had slipped off its axis continued, even intensified. Planes came winging over, dropping notes asking what we needed. We painted "CHOW" on our roof in huge letters, a move we lived to regret. Large, specially equipped planes bombed us with half-ton drums of food that came whistling down in parachutes meant to carry a man one-fifth the weight. The result was disastrous. One drum went through the flimsy hut roof, the top bunk and the lower bunk and dug a hole in the ground. One hit a Japanese hut and killed a woman inside.

We were allowed out to find the drums. They were stocked with every blessing one could hope for: hundreds of Hershey bars, canned fruit, canned meat-and-vegetable stew, cheeses, cream, butter, milk, cookies, even rice pudding with raisins — four years of fantasies, craving, prayers, came to sudden life before our bulging eyes. All in a setting of filth, rags, deprivation. Is there any wonder our minds went askew?

Men ate as many as twenty chocolate bars and vomited. Cans of syrupy fruit were opened and tossed away after a few bites in the haste to get at the next taste thrill — and the next, and the next. Two mouthfuls of rice pudding made way for some beef stew — discarded for cheese, then chocolate. The waste, after years of miserly scrimping — and with people starving outside — was a shock to the psyche in itself.

Grant and I, bloated and nauseated, were wandering over a nearby field when we heard the familiar sound of bombers approaching and saw the drums sailing down. We started to run in one direction, looked up, saw the dreaded missiles overtaking us and doubled back, trying to gauge where they'd strike. It became so dangerous that a watch was set up to sound the alarm. There were several hits in our compound. The hut was unsafe. The only shelter was under the rail tracks set in a concrete ramp that ran beside the camp. As I waited underneath, a drum struck the rails and bent them in. Another landed beside me, sending a shower of cinders biting into my back. This lethal largesse was too much of a good thing. What a horrible irony, I thought, to be killed by food after the war was over. In desperation we painted "STOP" on the roof.

After the first spate of vomiting, diarrhea and illness, we made an effort at some kind of balance. Cravings were appeased, appetites tempered. Impatience now was the greatest enemy. The camp had suddenly become revolting in its ugliness and narrow confines, its vermin and ersatz freedom. We were free and not free. Now that we really could smell our freedom, we needed to see it, touch it. This was intolerable, a teasing appetizer without the meal. There seemed no plan for reaching us or getting us out. Each day with no news intensified the desire for action. We were confined to camp now to avoid trouble.

Smitty had an idea. "Let's sneak out of this place and find a brothel — have some fun."

We gathered in a little knot. "I could stand a little pussy," Fortune said. "Let's go."

"Do you know where this place is?" Grant asked.

"No, but it's worth a try."

"If we don't find it, we'll find *some* gash somewhere."

"Yeah, load up with chocolates."

"What if they don't come across?"

"We'll take it anyway," Fortune snapped. Grant raised an eyebrow. Silence. Fortune looked from face to face and his expression hardened. "They owe us," he growled.

No denying — years of brutal inhumanity had taken their toll. My diary at the time throbbed with outrage. No crime was too violent, it said, to repay this cursed nation or avenge those lost years.

A group of us removed our shoes, climbed over the sheds beside the fence and slipped silently into the coal yard, hopping gingerly over coals in our stocking feet till we reached a road and donned our shoes. We followed the road. No fence, no guards, no restraints! We fought a strange sense of guilt. Passing civilians stared in fear and astonishment. Afraid of us? Of course they were!

We were the victors — free men, lawless, predatory. The same *furyos*, ugly, ragged mongrels, yet totally transformed, mainly by the thoughts in our heads. There was an unexpressed but growing frenzy to taste everything, take everything — quickly — before it all vanished and new rules enslaved us again.

Smitty led us to a long narrow building where we might find women. It was not a brothel but some institution or workplace full of cubicles and rooms. We entered cautiously, and the young manager came to meet us. He was terrified, out of his depth and made a show of asking what we wanted.

"Girls," we told him bluntly. "*Doko desu ka* [where]?" He pretended not to understand our Japanese, but our aggressive air confirmed his fears. This was what defeat meant. He engaged us in conversation, struggling to establish a polite and friendly tone. Meanwhile the news of our intent swept through the building, and the women were clambering out of the windows. He talked on, stalling, explaining what the activity of this building consisted of — a sort of community center with instruction in various crafts. We tried to brush past him but he blocked the way, insisting on seeing some written permission. We said we were bringing gifts to the ladies and wanted to meet them, but he stood his ground, trembling, as though expecting decapitation.

"A very gutsy guy," Fortune commented. Finally he pushed him aside, saying, "Don't make me hurt you, Mac." We fanned out into the empty rooms in search of our prey, only to find the windows open and the women streaming across the fields . . . . Too damn late. We gazed ruefully after them.

"Oh well," Smitty shrugged. "This is not our day." There were some elderly women and a few children around, watching us curiously. We had seen so few children close up over the years that these tots with their doll-round faces and soft innocence, as yet undistorted by social strictures, were a phenomenon, something new and wondrous, belonging more to the world we had been denied and, in a way, symbols of the new life ahead. We offered them Hershey bars, which they refused, drawing back from these foreign giants in fright. We squatted before them, coaxing and smiling, giving bars to the elderly women, who readily accepted the *purezentos* with polite bows. At last the children gripped the bars unsmilingly but balked at eating them. They had never seen or tasted chocolate, or much of any other joys, for that matter, being as deprived as we were, part of the unseen casualties of war. We understood. We showed them how to eat it, watching their expression as they chewed. "*Maika* [good]?" "*Hai*," they nodded, joining us in the first taste of freedom.

We left at last, deciding to try another day. I was keenly disappointed. This was to be my dramatic deflowering. What form it would have taken I had no idea. It was all as vague and distorted as the mash of emotions chasing through me. I craved confirmation, sex, a meeting of souls, an instant love story in a capsule — everything was possible now, why not that? There was something uniquely fitting in beginning my sex life here. Hadn't I been robbed of my manhood here? This would have been the just and ironic completion of an equation. Fortune was right, they owed me. It was my turn to collect. But damn it, it was not to be.

I glanced back at the empty building and stopped. Hey . . . there were two floors to it. People couldn't jump from the upper-floor windows. We hadn't even looked there. Maybe . . . .

The others scoffed. The women could have gone downstairs first.

"I'll catch up," I told them. "I'm going back."

"Step it up," Grant said. "It's getting late."

I hurried back, entered the building and walked to the far end, seeking stairs. I climbed them to the second floor and saw a long corridor with a row of rooms. I slid each door open and peered in. The first two were empty. I opened the third and my heart bounced. I was right! There she sat: long, flowing, black hair cascading down over a sky-blue kimono, her back to me as she crouched over a low table. As though ordained, this was the moment toward which I'd been guided. This was the sweet fruit of victory, and the conquered knew the role they must play out. She would know. She would submit. I was a lawless, free-booting pirate boarding a galleon laden with jewels. No one alive was more entitled to this. I entered softly, sliding the door shut behind me. She turned at the sound. Beautiful! I knew it. Excitement left me breathless.

I advanced slowly . . . the fear in those eyes would fade, give way to gentle joy as she understood. They would grow soft and yielding under my tender caress as our spirits merged, victor and vanquished becoming one in our new sublime harmony. I had so much yearning and adoration to pour out over this girl that she would be swamped and gasping with rapture! It might be *her* first too. Adam and Eve. Before the apple of war.

She stared at my face and grew rigid. She rose with a swift rustling sweep of her kimono and gazed into my eyes, her own full of terror, yet piercing. There was a rare dignity and force to her rhythmic movements as, with no pause, she walked, or floated, toward me, eyes locked hypnotically in mine, more like a samurai swordsman straining to dominate an opponent. We were together — I had only to raise my arm to encircle her and she was mine! "You have the power — the right!" my voices screamed. "Use it — *use it!*"

She read the uncertainty, the brief hesitation — and tiptoed around me, gracefully, without haste, as though careful of waking a beast; then she slid open the door and vanished like a ghost.

I stood paralyzed, furious. "You miserable ninny!" my disgusted voices snarled. "The chance of a lifetime! After all those years — and you blew it! You are doomed, fool, to virginity for life!"

Gradually my tension drifted away and I was able to savor a sense of profound relief. "You knew," a truer voice said, "it could go no other way." I sighed and gazed sadly about me at the small spare cubicle.

I walked over to her table to see what she was working at, and stopped in dismay. Oh, my God, an art student. At work on a half-finished painting. Before it stood a vase and flowers. I stared enviously down at the oil paints, full tubes of fat juicy colors, lovely clean brushes, a palette of bright hues still shining and wet, all shouting up at me to touch them, use them, love them. My fingers itched to comply. I looked at her work and grimaced — rank amateur. Struggling timidly to master the rudiments of light and shadow, western style, with not even a hint of reflected light in the vase. Christ, she'd never get the roundness and volume with those flat, print-like daubs. And the flowers — no nuance in shading, no variation in shape or size — bloody awful. All it needs . . . .

I sat down on her stool, seized the brushes and set to work correcting her errors, establishing a bold reflection, grading the shadows, letting light steal in around the edge of the heaviest shadow .... Let's see now — she could fill this part in .... Soon I was happily lost in a world of vibrant color, light and shadow. What a wonderful give to the brushes, what a joy to bring a flower to life, let it dance and toss its head, raising its lips to the sun. Pleasant melodies of line and rhythm tinkled in my head as I worked. We were joined, this lovely girl and I, enmeshed in a spirit of sensual play, united in perception, in imagination, caressing each other. With this stroke, I thee wed. Our love was being consummated in a language of color, light and spirit.

At last I laid aside the brushes and surveyed the result. Good, good — that should do it. I smiled, envisioning her face. Surprise! Madame Butterfly, please accept this little love sonnet from over the ocean. So you see? We did make it after all, didn't we?

Liberation at last. The marines landed via canal in PT boats, arriving armed to the teeth. They came in crouching double, edging cautiously around the corners of the hut, guns pointed, trigger fingers poised. We stood in the center of the yard, beckoning and waving them forward.

"Come on, come on! It's okay!"

They stared suspiciously as though we were decoys; then, relieved and startled at so little resistance, they stood up uncertainly.

"Welcome to Sumidagawa. Point those damn things the other way!"

"No Japs?"

"Naw — they took off long ago!"

They returned our embraces gingerly, ill at ease, as we danced about them, drinking in the new sturdy uniforms, the short, businesslike guns, the smooth young faces. We circled them in awe and wonder, like spacemen discovering three-headed Martians. We needed to touch them, smell them, hear them, question them, confirm their reality — our first free men at close quarters, beings who had never known a day of slavery. We brought them into the hut, and they stared about in disbelief. I saw the dismal cramped quarters, the narrow bed mats through their eyes.

"You guys lived *here*?"

"Yup."

"Jeez."

They fanned out over the hut. We led one into our section and sat him down on a lower bunk so that we could fire questions and answers back and forth, probing. He seemed a teenager. His burnished face, made more youthful by the over-large helmet, looked to us like a well-polished stone, free of line or wrinkle, hard, solid, unblemished. His gaze was direct, unblinking, with no hint of our customary cunning or distrust.

His unit had fought its way up through the islands the hard way. "These Japs never give up. We hadda torch 'em outta caves, and they came out burning and fighting till they were gunned down." He told of the war's end, of dropping atomic bombs on Hiroshima and Nagasaki.

"What's an atomic bomb?"

"Somethin' new. Wipes out a whole city at one crack."

"Whew. No wonder they quit."

"A whole city? That's pretty gruesome."

"Tough titty. They started it. Hey, these bunks are pretty crummy — didn't you have bugs?"

"Sure they're loaded with them — lice, bedbugs . . . . " He leapt to his feet as though stung. "Take it easy, Mac, it's only bugs." His eyes showed genuine panic. Bullets must have seemed less threatening.

I stared at his gun — short, automatic, like a tommy gun. Loaded and oiled and gleaming and immensely comforting. After more news of war and affairs at home, he asked about souvenirs.

"Come on," I said. I wanted some too. He followed me to the guards' sleeping quarters. The guards who remained were teenage recruits, changed every month and unknown to any of us. They would have rifles and equipment to loot. I led him into a little dark cubicle. Three youngsters were lying on their mats in various stages of undress, their equipment hung up around the walls. They looked up anxiously as we entered and stood over them.

The marine's automatic weapon flew up into firing position and he flicked the safety catch in one swift motion. His face was blank, eyes suddenly burning with battle light. He swung the muzzle at them — the only good Japs were dead ones — and was about to open fire as he said: "So these are the bastards that gave you trouble!"

I grabbed his arm: "No — *no!* Don't! They're okay!" My heart was racing. He was ready to wipe them out with one burst. He paused, uncertain, as they crouched, cowering and trembling. "They're just kids! Not staff, not real guards — leave 'em alone!"

He lowered his weapon reluctantly. "You trust 'em?"

"Yes! Yes!"

I breathed easier. My God — what if he'd come in here alone? Three human beings wiped out with the flick of a finger. How many more had fallen before this instrument of death he carried? And he was under twenty.

We nosed around, gathering rifles, helmets and other equipment as they watched doe-eyed, without protest. Did they know how close they'd come?

"There are no staff left," I cautioned as we left, "so relax and put away that cannon."

I brought back my loot and stored it on my shelf: pouches, helmet, rifle. I gazed at the steel barrel, the kind Yamanaka had clubbed me with. Why did I want a souvenir of *that*? To remember. Would I ever forget?

I lay back on my bunk and thought of the trigger-happy marine . . . just a babe and he'd learned to kill so easily. Back in Idaho he'd hesitate to pick a fight, so easygoing, so wholesome. Yet here there was no doubt in his mind of his right to commit murder. That must be why men love war: the chance to play God. It doesn't come often. He accepted his role of judge, jury and executioner without a qualm. Amazing. War, the ultimate insanity, was the magic password. Once accepted, all values, norms, ethics could be stood on their heads and made to look very sensible. He defended his way of life by denying it. I had grabbed his arm and stopped death. For a moment I too shared the power of life and death — exhilarating and appalling. Maybe there was some poetic balance at play here. I had killed three men in the battle of Hong Kong; now I saved three from death. A strange equation . . . .

Now the fun was over and we could all go home. Back to sanity. Or was it? Could the world just flick a switch, sign a paper and return everything to its former state? Could the human brain go into reverse that easily? Could I? I'd find out soon enough.

At last our world, mired in cement, began to move. The pace soon accelerated to a dizzying speed, and we could only hang on for dear life. We packed hurriedly, were bundled into a PT boat and went bouncing and roaring out to a U.S. hospital ship to be scrubbed, fed, bedded, pampered. We were catapulted into a world where everything looked impossibly perfect. It shone, sparkled, throbbed with the incredible spirit of newness. Even the faces, the haircuts, the confident light in the eyes seemed inhuman artifacts produced by some super-efficient god-machine. The paint luxuriously covering the walls, the sturdy, unpatched, unsoiled new shirts and pants, the solid new shoes, the endless new rooms full of clean air and space galore, the new heavy bodies covered in layered meat and fat that had been increased ounce after ounce by feasting daily on meat and potatoes, cheeses, fruit, desserts — it was all turning my brain. I was jolted by the vision of a red-headed nurse, her hair flowing in waves around a lovely face, lips opened in a welcoming smile, maternal, sensual, ingenuous. Did they know what they were letting into their presence? Good God, we could contaminate the universe!

Before anything else, we were bustled off to be examined by medics. I stood naked while a doctor probed and checked. I saw him frown as he listened to my chest.

"What's wrong?" I asked uneasily. He ignored me. I was an interesting specimen.

He called over another doctor: "See this? It's what I've been telling you about."

The other squinted close. "Hmm . . . yeah! Right."

I was alarmed. Some rare Oriental disease? "What is it?" I demanded.

He removed a louse from my chest. "Lice," he said reverently, as though discovering moondust. I breathed easier.

"Oh, *that*," I said. "We've got plenty of those."

They handled me with gingerly fascination, an attitude that I was to become familiar with in the months ahead. Another whammy came when they measured my height.

"Five-seven and a half," he noted.

"Wait a minute," I corrected him. "I'm five-nine. Better check that, there's some mistake."

"'Fraid not," he said after rechecking.

"But that's impossible. I couldn't have shrunk that much, could I?"

"Anything's possible, although I haven't run across it."

"Ah so." The price. Silly to think I'd escaped scot-free. This was the first of the bills to come due over the following years.

Then the luxuries began. First the voluptuous showers, a large, even spout pouring steaming hot water in lavish abundance as I lathered and scrubbed with the foaming suds of a fat new bar of fragrant soap. Bliss! I lingered, considering the possibility of staying there forever. I dried with a thick, spanking white towel and slid into freshly laundered clothes, waiting for someone to shake me and say it was time to get up and out to the coal pile.

I shaved before a large mirror and examined the face before me: a stranger. That couldn't belong to me. It belied the creature inside. As though the Devil had selected a misleading mask, no lines, unmarred, soft tanned cheeks slightly puffed, hairless albino eyebrows, small effeminate mouth, pale-blue eyes: still young? Nothing of pain, anxiety, passions, terrors, sorrows — nothing visible on this bland surface? Would it appear all at once one day, like Dorian Gray?

We were shown to the crew's dining mess for breakfast, where bulky cooks dished up an endless array of food. What'll it be: fruit? bacon and eggs? sausages? toast? porridge? pancakes? fried spuds? Well . . . as a matter of fact we'd like it *all*. I mean, how could any of this be turned down? Unthinkable. We piled our plates high as the cooks stared quizzically. "Hell, you can't have everything, Mac!" Maybe not, but we could die trying.

They watched us swipe extra oranges and apples, hidden in pockets before they could vanish. "Hey, cut that crap," a cook snapped irritably. "The fruit's there all day and you can have all you want, doncha understand?"

The *furyos* replaced the fruit reluctantly and moved on in line. No, we didn't understand. It was a collision of two cultures with no communication.

I looked down at the thickly buttered toast in my hand and saw it in double vision. This was the same hand that had emptied dysentery pails of shit. Would it ever really be clean?

And when we'd plowed through all that food and learned we could have seconds, we gathered at the end of the line for a second round and a third. The staff were kept hopping all day, gawking at these weird creatures who kept forcing food into bottomless pits and refusing to leave.

"You can always come back tomorrow," one disgusted cook railed.

"Maybe," we said, our voices echoing down the long corridors of sad experience. "Maybe."

This confusion continued at many levels. I passed a *furyo* being questioned by a curious nurse about prison camp.

"How was the food there?"

"Oh, it was pretty *sukoshi*," came the calm response in our standard Japenglish.

"Pardon?"

He raised his voice a pitch. "I said pretty *sukoshi*."

"I don't understand."

Nor did he. Was she deaf or something? Why an intelligent lady couldn't understand plain English was baffling.

Yes, there would be much to learn and unlearn, even normal speech. I recalled the first time Captain Martin lined us up to number off in English — we stumbled and bumbled our way through it like raw recruits. Yet we could rattle off our numbers in Japanese with machine-gun speed.

At night I lay back on a billowy mattress between crisp, shockingly white sheets. A soft blanket, a clean-smelling fresh pillowcase under my head, a small radio beside me playing jazz tunes, my belly full of meat, potatoes, cake, coffee. I needed to laugh, sing, weep simultaneously to release the great gusts of emotion. And this was only the beginning.

I was being hurled into the future at such speed I'd lost control. Stop it — let me think, breathe, try to see, understand. But there was no pause. I was a diner trying to scan the menu while being brought six courses, seven desserts, and ordered to eat it all simultaneously.

Well, *I'd made it* — start with that.

It went against all logic — even more than I knew at the time. A U.S. Air Force signals operator later told me the bombing schedule for the next two weeks called for wiping out all rail-distribution centers in Tokyo. Our exact address. Someone up there was playing footsie with me. Considering the trials of the last four years, I would not call myself lucky, yet I felt the luckiest man alive. I thought of the ones who hadn't made it — well, not now. This wasn't the time for mourning. I thought of Newfie, twisted, tortured, closed off in a cave of fear, suspicion, depression . . . of Grant, whose heart was out of whack, pulse skyrocketing, blood pressure soaring with some strange undiagnosed malady. Where was Bob — free? alive?

The family waiting at home — what a reunion that would be. And Evelyn — was *she* waiting? What would they all expect? The same old harebrained clown? Would anyone guess at the staggering changes? No, it was all hidden. I would be an interloper, an alien from another planet wearing an Earth mask.

What was taking place here? I wondered. More than profound change, it was beginning life all over again. Everything around me was to be rediscovered, retasted. This was a New World and I was a New Man. A babe in arms and a sage in one, emerging from a devil's womb into this luminous pleasure palace.

Images of the day passed before me . . . the clothing, the food, the red-headed nurse, the hefty cooks, the space, the anxiety-free eyes, the perfection. It was as though I'd passed through a great soaring gateway into paradise — a kind of death, the death of misery, and this was a new Nirvana run by winged creatures of mercy, of power, all innocent of taint. They knew nothing, understood nothing of evil, of want, of filth, of hatred, of humiliation. Their wings glowed with fresh paint, scrubbed clean with disinfectant and deodorant. Truly immortal, with their envied sunlit interiors. Would I ever be a part of all that? Or was I bonded forever to that other? Condemned to live in both worlds. Well, maybe there was meaning to it all — some grand design whose outline still eluded me.

Was all this really happening? Like Newfie I kept hearing the question repeating itself like an ominous drumbeat, a rhythm of anxiety touching nerves with small electric charges. *It was too good . . . too perfect.* This ship was not on earth. It floated, as I did. This soft mattress was a magic carpet . . . this radio music a celestial chorus . . . . Just as I had needed to touch that first marine, I had to reach out to touch the blanket, slide my fingers along the clean sheets to reaffirm again and again their crisp, sturdy reality. A man, an angel-man, was singing beside my head, soothing, caressing, as sleepy thoughts drifted off into a golden future: *"Gonna take a sentimental journey . . . ."*

My uneasy fingers crept out to touch the soft blanket once again . . . .

Chapter Twenty-One

OCTOBER 1945

CROSSING CANADA, THIS TIME from west to east. The same Rockies, same prairies, unchanged, as though nothing had happened. Well, not to them, maybe. I tried to picture that other train ride: that eager, adventurous youth, brimming with optimism, always bubbling on the edge of laughter and unalloyed joy. Life was a good book, full of escapades, with a happy ending guaranteed for all. Now I was gazing back over the years with the eyes of an old man reviewing a long life of trial and tragedy. It *was* an entire lifetime. And this? This was another, a new life. And it certainly was new . . . everything.

I reviewed the lightning changes of the past few weeks. First the U.S. rest camp outside Manila, where I was shocked by the luxuries, the food, the way they had turned war into a fun thing. How in the world could we expect people to understand? I had wandered through it like an actor miscast in a surrealist play. Then the ship to San Francisco and on to Victoria. The newness of strolling through the streets *alone*, going nowhere, savoring the strange luxury of this startling solitude — as though I'd stolen into a palace garden, slipping past walls and guards to discover hidden beauty. Another wish coming true. Recalling how often, trudging to work surrounded by gloomy scarecrows, I'd gazed so longingly down side streets, dreaming of this very thing: clean clothes on my back, full belly, no guards, free as a breeze — to stop, gaze my fill at the people, peep into windows, blessed with the joyful awareness of being one of these people, entitled to the same rights, the same food, the same respect. No one could command me, despise me, drive me away from a garbage can with a hose. I could light a cigarette anywhere, anytime, smoke it and *toss away the butt*. I had a deck of big fat Luckys in my pocket — in limitless supply! Dollar bills in my wallet, and more coming. It left the brain woozy — a bit like trying to imagine the length of infinity.

The first nightclub . . . and that song: "Besame Mucho," which reached my marrow, rousing chords of sweetest melancholy, turning a sentimental love song into a cry of welcome pain. It took me back to the Agony Ward; the faces of the dying and the sound of their hopeless weeping re-echoed in the sultry voice of the singer. All new, all strange . . . .

And the bloodthirsty reporters on the boat, hungry for stories. Pressing me to describe a beating. Disappointed at my version of how Yamanaka beat me, bloodied me, drew his sword threatening to decapitate me. "Is that all?" "Well — I thought that was enough." Too mild. "No, no, don't you have anything with more kick to it? Something really gruesome." Vultures.

Then the five-day binge of wild drinking and partying and violent mood swings. Ecstasy, depression, anxiety, hilarity, unreality. And the therapy of the streets: just an orderly row of happy houses, solid, permanent, unscarred . . . windows, doors, shutters, painted and bright . . . a revelation. A proof that life could go on, without any cyclonic threat from the holocaust that had crippled half the world. The small corner stores sat placidly in the sun, shelves and counters full of old familiar goods and brand names, proprietors dusting the counters, reading the papers. This was peace . . . and this was our country. And this must be *us*. The other was a nightmare from which we were waking. It would recur, of course — even follow us to the end of our days — but it would remain among the shadows of night, where it belonged. All this breathed security, comfort. We were strolling down heaven-blessed esplanades bathed in golden light under leafy trees planted by angels.

The children were a strange and wonderful phenomenon. A child skipping down the street, bright curls bouncing in the sun, giggling and carefree, was a vision of startling poignancy and joy; the innocent cries and laughter were flute music in the garden of the gods.

There had been mail, many brand-new letters from family, eagerly waiting. Still nothing from Evelyn. Why? Would she be waiting? If I could have peered into a crystal ball I would have seen our meeting in New York, a strange day fraught with tensions, groping through the darkness of four years of estrangement: the sad account of how she'd fallen in love with a GI who was killed . . . how she couldn't write, not wanting to lie or cause pain. The abyss was too wide by now, unbridgeable, and I was to end up marrying someone else within the year.

In Victoria there had been joyous reunions, telegrams, phone calls. Many POWs were in a bad way: Grant seriously ill in hospital; Newfie in the loony bin; Tony having a lung removed; Bob, too, having a lung removed in a Montreal hospital, and facing a painful divorce. Blacky, like many others, was to die of heart disease in the coming years. There was no counseling, no advice, no awareness that we might act or feel any differently. It was sink or swim, you're on your own, boys. Like good Canadians we expected nothing, got nothing. We were paid off in a lump sum — four years' back pay shoved into the pocket of my battle dress. Then five days that landed me on the train home, stomach inflamed, fingers trembling, nerves shot.

Winnipeg was the next stop and the thought was chilling. Hank's mother. I couldn't face those haunted, accusing eyes . . . . *Trust me*, I'd told her: the unkept promise, the whole open emotional floodgate . . . no, not in my state. With my DTs I was ready to jump at my own shadow. My cousin, a wealthy mogul in Winnipeg, had prepared a lavish reception in my honor, with a slew of relatives and friends waiting to pounce. The whole prospect appalled me. My only desire was to crawl into a hole like a groundhog and close out the human race.

No . . . no stopover in Winnipeg.

"Next stop Montreal! Montréal!"

The conductor's voice went off in my head like a grenade. Sumidagawa, hospital ship, British warship, Manila, across the Pacific, train, boat, train across a continent, and now . . . last stop. The moment I'd waited for, re-enacted a thousand times, had arrived. I couldn't tell if it was the DTs from drink or a natural response, but my body shook like the ague. It was the hardest entrance I'd ever made.

I shouldered my kit bag for the last time, poised for an instant at the train steps, then dived into the boisterous, milling crowd, my head twirling in all directions. There they were!

The family were lined up, grinning, waving, tense with

excitement. Ma, Pa, sisters, brothers, nieces, in-laws: I fell into welcoming, loving, enveloping arms — hugging, kissing, laughing, babbling. The shock waves of rising emotion overloaded the air till it seemed to be imploding about us invisibly. If its energy could have been turned to light, it would have been blinding. It was all over. A happy ending, a time for tears, tears, tears galore . . . tears suppressed, squeezing through, tears in gushers from the depths, tears of pure joy through happy grins, tears of unformed sadness. What did the family feel? After years of wrestling with fears and hopes and guesses and possibilities, moving down dark corridors of despair, visualizing death or torture or illness, images of beheading . . . years of struggling with the guilt of an enjoyable life, having babies, eating well . . . .

I was dry-eyed myself as, I'm sure, were all other POWs, our hearts well secured against all painful emotional onslaughts. I gawked at the faces, half seeing . . . so like it had been in daydreams . . . so much so that I had a flash of doubt — no, the touch, the smell, the perfumes, the vibrant faces were not the stuff of dreams. My dad's big, rough, straw-textured mustache bestowing a Russian kiss on the lips brought back all the memories of early childhood. He seemed gentler, quieter, I noted, even shrunken. His keen eye, trained to catch imperfection in horses, was the only one to pick up the beri-beri unnaturally swelling my face. The others thought it full and healthy. He grinned diffidently, sliding into the background as my mom took center stage, claiming me. They both seemed so much smaller, or was it my inflated memory? Everything was changed and changing. Some were bigger, older, taller, broader, moving, moving — would nothing stand still?

Squeezed together in a car on the way home, everyone talking at once, I was trying to pick up news of the last four years in a few disjointed sentences. Bob, they said, was at Queen Mary Hospital — yes, the family had met him. Blacky was in Trois Rivières and well. Great reunions coming up: parties, celebrations, visitors. I caught glances of familiar streets, the mountain, Park Avenue, the curving outdoor staircases — and my heart expanded in hidden bursts of joy. Home. Security. The womb . . . .

I was brought out of my rosy glow by the sound of my mother inveighing against the Japanese — what? My peace-loving, nonviolent mother, who never quarreled with neighbors? Another change, this one enormous. The war years had brought a new star into the firmament: anger. Made a wide space for it to swell and thunder and cast its glow on every side. I could hear her thoughts: how *they* did this to my child, my baby whom I breast-fed, cooked for, nurtured, guarded, trembled over with love and joy and worry. And then *they* took him and starved him nearly to death. How dare they! My primordial lioness was roused to defend her young.

For years, I learned later, she had gone to sleep each night with my photo under her pillow, weeping and praying for my deliverance. And once this cumulative pain was turned to anger, it could become a beast, chained and feeding on itself. How simple and easy it all was, this trough into which all things Japanese could be dumped. Was there no limit to this war's destructive powers?

Home . . . I walked slowly from room to room with the family following silently. Pictures . . . carpets . . . beds . . . radiators . . . cut-glass bowl . . . icebox . . . kitchen table where I'd played so many card games with my father. In 3D I replayed them longingly. Now he followed meekly in the rear, quiet, broken. I understood him better now — the world would not stand still for him either. Little change here, thank God. Everything in place, breathing peace and contentment, the end of strife. I wanted to linger over every detail, but not with this well-meaning but obtrusive audience. We sat down around the dining-room table for tea and honeycake.

I listened to how each of them lived, their work, problems, schoolwork. They spoke of ration coupons; they had been restricted to so many ounces of meat, butter, sugar. The difficulties. I found myself seeing, hearing, feeling everything with a kind of hyper-realism — I had seen and lived it all before, always through a nostalgic haze, a blur of misery and hunger. Now the clarity of a thousand details sprang out at me as though enlarged, in perfect focus, illumined from within. I could grasp every spoken word with a godlike power. And the distance between us was frightening. They seemed so unaware, their problems so tinsel-textured. It seemed all just words. More song without melody.

I felt totally, frighteningly disconnected. These things — were they important? Was it me, or was everybody *blind?* I wanted to shout at them to open their eyes to the real: to feel the clean clothes on their backs, the food they chewed so unthinkingly, the warm air coming from the radiators, the icebox full of goodies, the glitter of the cut-glass, the fine design on the carpet, the luxurious space they could move in, the crazy freedom of having breakfast, lunch, dinner whenever they pleased, of taking a stroll when they chose, of living without fear, anxiety, beatings, hunger, of living with the certainty of waking up in a warm bed to face a free day . . . on and on, a thousand blessings that went uncounted, unseen. They should be down on their knees each day in gratitude. Maybe this vision was my reward. The world I saw was shining new, all a function of this magnificent birth. Would I too become blind and dull to this wealth? Never, I swore. "If I forget thee, Jerusalem . . . ."

The family sat about me, watching every move and gesture with avid curiosity, reading untold connotations into every word and expression. They may have read some pamphlet on the handling of returning prisoners, because I found the constrained, artificial tones and guarded answers a growing irritation. I was a prize goldfish in a a bowl.

"Pass the sugar," I said. They passed it silently and swiftly, exchanging significant glances. "Oh, for chrissake!" I snapped. "All I said was pass the bloody sugar. There is no hidden meaning — no psychological implications!"

Silence. More glances.

"It's just that . . . we feel sad," Sal said cautiously, "that you haven't had any for so many years."

I sighed. "I know. Forget it. I understand."

I also understood that the barrier between us was insurmountable and seemed to grow wider with each passing hour. I knew I didn't belong here. I was expecting the impossible, after all. They all meant well, loved me in their way, but our worlds could not connect. The more I strove to become part of this setting, the more it eluded me. Along with this awareness came an undefined anxiety that gnawed at me as though some furry tarantula had slipped into my brain and was creeping about with soft threatening steps. This was to be the hallmark of former POWs in the years ahead. I could enjoy everything, yet not really enjoy it, with this vague cloud of uneasiness, this sense of dislocation, darkening the brightness. What was wrong? I felt myself in a losing bout, wrestling with something that had no body. It was suffocating me silently, lovingly, and I nursed a mad desire to be back in 3D, where everything really *existed* — away from this glowing make-believe. I had to get away — to see Bob, now. They couldn't understand.

"Why today? You just got home!"

"I have to . . . . It's important. It's . . . hard to explain."

More significant glances, this time with good reason.

I made my way to the hospital, located his floor and ward and, with mounting tension, a little fearful of what I'd find, hurried past the beds full of sick and wounded. *There!* He was reading a magazine. He looked the same, only neater, trimmer, face pink and scrubbed and hollow.

I said quietly: "Howdy, bub."

He looked up and the long face opened wide in a familiar, welcoming grin, followed by a happy self-conscious chuckle. "Holy Jeezus!"

We shook hands. "You made it, lucky bastard!"

"You too."

"I knew you would."

"Yeah? It was too close for comfort. I was almost ready to pack it in at the end there."

He told me about the coal mine where he'd been sent after 3D: Sendai. Far worse than anything we'd experienced, a total destruction of soul, hope, self-esteem. We talked as I had not talked for months with all barriers down. Where all day today I had little to say and what I did say was guarded, strained to fit, to please, now there was no end to the storm of intimate thoughts, sensations, impressions that flew back and forth at high speed. His divorce, his parents, my parents, his lungs, it all poured out in a torrent. It swept us back to the naked honesty, the penetrating insights of 3D, where life was stark but real. The froth was blown away. He too had been watching everything, thinking, feeling the same joys, terrors, delights, anxieties, confusions.

We sang snatches of the new songs to each other: *"My momma done tol' me . . . ." ""Gonna take a sentimental journey . . . ."* We planned to party together, see the movies we dreamed of, buy *patates frites* with salt and vinegar from the street vendors . . . .

I found myself laughing with a new freedom, the tensions dissolving, the darkness fading away before me as we sat together on this new plateau, where a fresh dawn was breaking and the air was pure and cool and the horizon grew steadily brighter. Now the glow was all around me and pulsing with the realization that I had been offered the best of both worlds. I was a vessel in which a unique and wonderful wholeness *could* be fused, passing beyond all contradictions. A discovery that should never be lost. Camp 3D must hover at my side, continuous, to the end of my days. That was the meaning . . . of everything. I was happy.

I was home.

Epilogue

LATE AFTERNOON IN THE PALACE grounds. I sat back on the ground, leaning against a slanting rock beside an old Shinto shrine that dozed placidly in the sun. An old man paused before the shrine, waited, listened, then clapped his hands to summon the gods. I waited with him. He fell into a reverie . . . they must have come. They were communing with him now. He had left the fleeting wisp of reality I belonged to and was far away . . . free . . . listening.

When he was done he moved slowly away, face serene, immensely peaceful. His spirit and mine were joined.

I didn't want this day to end . . . . The sun was losing its intensity, tossing long shadows. On my left an old stone bridge curved gracefully over a wide tranquil pond crowded with silvery-edged lily pads and reflections of tall trees. Flowering bushes lined the banks like dainty maidens smiling down at their reflected beauty. A tree overhead stretched long gnarled arms over the water to frame an old royal pavilion on the far bank, tucked discreetly away among the trees. From its balcony over the water I could make out a group of ladies in ceremonial kimonos. Their voices came fluttering across the lily-pads blending with occasional bird song, dipping and vanishing into silence.

Bliss . . . voices . . . a frog croaked . . . peace, beauty, on every side, sending out a thousand soothing little tendrils that wound their way through my being. Ah, if only the whole world could feel this, all the biting, snarling, cursing, killing would vanish . . . . I was quite willing to spend the rest of my days right there. Why so happy? In this land that had stood for the very opposite?

I had made my peace with it all. Mission accomplished. But how could I ever forgive and forget? Didn't forgiveness imply tacit approval — a pat on the head, three Hail Marys and all's well?

Never that. And forgetting? Impossible. That would mean I'd learned nothing from it all — the antithesis of what I sought.

Nothing could be forgotten, even if I tried. It had all returned as I wandered through the Nippon Kokan Shipyards, seeking familiar signs . . . even though all landmarks were gone, burned out. This was the lunchroom here . . . where Yamanaka savaged me and offered to remove my head. The paint shop here, where I'd found a friend in Kondo-san . . . he was here in this land, along with thousands of other Kondo-sans, encircling me in the Kyoto crowds. And the Yamanakas?

The good and the bad were here . . . . No, it was not a question of forgetting. It was more a stepping back for a proper view, of my own experience and that of thousands of other POWs — and of the thousands of victims of Hiroshima and Nagasaki. Understanding, balancing it out. After all, to retain hate only meant continuing it. And where would it end? You can't continue to carry poison in the blood without infection.

Forget — no. But forgive — yes, if forgiving could encompass disapproval. And a knowing that "they knew not what they did." To *really* understand was to forgive, to grasp the nature of the illness, the historic path of a virus in the bloodstream of a nation. It was to understand too that no one had a corner on evil any longer. Open the gates of war anywhere, and hellish monsters roam the earth. The rape of Nanking was a matchstick beside the ovens of Belsen. Anyway, hate and war were luxuries we could no longer afford.

Now I could look down the centuries at a thousand years of Japanese history, Japan's long traditions of art, drama and poetry, its phenomenal energy, its elevation of honor, death, duty, to sacred heights. I could see its ability to erase World War II as a time of sorrow, a shameful blemish paid out in full, and go on to rebuild, as after every earthquake, with the talent to "endure the unendurable."

But the old drug of militarism, violence, evil — was all that still alive, but suppressed, simmering under the slick surface? Anything was possible. Yet this was a land where children wrote *haiku* poetry and adults went into the woods to listen to the sound of insects. This was a nation of Noh actors who could slide into the world of festive dreams and be intoxicated by it. To see them as a nation of poets, not consciously but viscerally poetic — that was the ticket.

And what about the Now — the dizzying, obsessive high-tech world? That was another tangent, like World War II or the Meiji Restoration — a temporary amnesia.

But wasn't I idealizing it all, shaping it into what I wanted — *needed* — to believe? I thought of the people I'd met over the past weeks, such as Nao: Naotaka Kuroda, sent by Nippon Kokan to help me find Kondo-san or anything else I sought. We failed, but formed a lasting friendship in the process. Nao felt responsible for the sufferings I'd undergone.

"Why should I blame you for that?" I had asked. "After all, you were only three years old."

"That is easy excuse," he had answered. "But I feel pain . . . *here*," pointing to his heart. I believed him.

I thought of the young Japanese officer, a poet friend of Shura's at Sham Shui Po, who, overwhelmed by shame at the atrocities, had committed suicide.

It came to me that there was a secret to be learned in this. This was a people who could think, live, die collectively. It was a sharing of glory, a shouldering of debt and destiny. What a grand continuity it offered, giving death itself more meaning, more attraction, making it a work of art and spirit and removing its sting. They had it made.

No wonder they'd shrugged off our deaths. How we'd struggled to survive! Our individual end was a catastrophe, while they couldn't understand what all the fuss was about. The *kamikaze* pilot knew he'd continue, as a blossom or as a country reborn — it was all one. How easily those soldiers tossed their lives away in battle — scattered blossoms. Crazy to us, as we seemed crazy to them — choosing life with dishonor.

Differences . . . could they be understood? Similarities . . . could *they* be understood? Anomalies . . . so many.

Where did I fit into all this? What could I do?

As I lay dreaming in these Elysian fields beside the shrine, I mentally clapped my hands, summoning the Shinto gods, and they came . . . hovering about me, filling my brain, counseling. "Harmony is all," their voices murmured. "Anger, bitterness, hatred, have no place in the smooth-running universe." And they drove away the mists, revealing the outlines of a grand design . . . .

As an artist I would paint a path toward peace, paint as I'd never painted before, stretching to the limits, soaring, exploring new forms, new harmonies. Visions of giant canvases marrying East and West unfolded before me: opulently costumed figures came drifting through giant floral patterns and unearthly mists . . . dreamlike processions floated down through history, solemn, festive . . . priests, maidens, resplendent horsemen, dazzling floats, fierce samurai in a storm of blossoms . . . temples, golden pavilions, Kabuki dancers in flowing robes of silver, purples, crimsons . . . Noh ghosts, masked and haunting . . . . They must all be called up and offered new life! I would work like a demon — for years, if need be. I would sail without a compass, guided only by the stars. Who knows? These tiny flute notes of reconciliation might stir a calming breeze somewhere among the discordant winds of our planet. It was worth a try.

This, then, was the call, the meaning of being here. It was, in a way, the paying out of a long-outstanding debt, a heavenly gift of the Shinto gods, duly accepted, with a grateful and deeply reverent bow.

The god-voices receded. They had spoken. Brewers of gushing harvests and thunderous rain, of soundless snows and moonlit whisperings, they didn't fool around. They knew all about the eternal verities. Just as that old man knew, serene in his secret. And now his reamed face, his quiet bliss was my own. Briefly, for those few moments, I was able to see it all through their ancient eyes — the wars, the plagues, the destruction — to them it was no more than a brief collision of meteors in the quiet galactic night, a swift flash, a quivering, then calm . . . and the inevitable return to the silent music of the spheres.